"The word *naked* can mean exposed—and not many businesses enjoy that thought. But times are changing fast. *The Naked Corporation* demonstrates convincingly that from now on, candor and transparency will be the essential foundations of trust; and that trust will be the key ingredient of success. Any corporation failing to heed this book's important message may find itself very exposed indeed."

—Sir Martin Sorrell, Group Chairman and CEO, WPP

"A rare thing these days—a business book with a profound and important new idea. *The Naked Corporation* explains how a new force is changing the corporation and competitiveness. There are relevant, sometimes jarring insights in every chapter. And what a great read."

—Indra Nooyi, President and CFO of PepsiCo, Inc.

"We need a corporate philosophy for the twenty-first century. Tapscott and Ticoll's book *The Naked Corporation* provides this—not only the rationale for a transparent corporation but also the principles of leadership in an open world."

—Klaus Schwab, Founder and President, World Economic Forum

"Tapscott and Ticoll are ahead of the wave. The era of transparency and all its implications are about to crash down on corporations everywhere. *The Naked Corporation* is the first survival guide."

—Paul Taaffe, Chief Executive Officer, Hill and Knowlton

"A well-researched and timely book. The authors show how trust—powered by broad corporate transparency—isn't just about ethics, it is about success."

—John Chambers, President and CEO, Cisco Systems

"The Internet has spawned a new era of openness and transparency that has turned the power relationship between corporations and stakeholders on its head. Tapscott and Ticoll offer compelling insights into how to manage change and succeed in an increasingly networked world."

—Debra Dunn, Senior Vice President, Corporate Affairs,
Hewlett-Packard Company

"Tomorrow's markets will be x-ray environments. *The Naked Corporation* brims with priceless advice for business leaders determined to survive and thrive in this see-through world order."
—John Elkington, Chair, SustainAbility

"Every organization needs new kinds of leadership to meet the urgent challenge of sustainable development. Tapscott and Ticoll powerfully demonstrate how transparency is essential to making this new leadership possible."
—Ernst Ligteringen, Chief Executive, Global Reporting Initiative

"Tapscott and Ticoll show, with abundant recent cogent examples, how concealment of truth is at the core of many corporate problems. Their solution is straightforward, clearly written, and compelling. You should read this book. More, you should buy it, as you will want to refer to it frequently."
—Robert A.G. Monks, Author of *The New Global Investors*,
Coauthor of *Power and Accountability* and *Watching the Watchers*

"*The Naked Corporation* is a must-read for corporate directors and sets the agenda for corporate governance in the twenty-first century."
—Beverly Topping, President and CEO, Institute of Corporate Directors

"This thoughtful, insightful, and eminently readable book promotes corporate transparency with vigor and verve. But it's really about the crying need for honesty and trust in a world betrayed by greed run amok."
—William Dimma, veteran of fifty corporate and forty not-for-profit boards,
author of *Excellence in the Boardroom: Best Practices in Corporate Directorship*

"Don Tapscott and David Ticoll hit the bull's-eye with *The Naked Corporation*. The demand for openness and candor has never been greater. *The Naked Corporation* is a leadership tool kit for turning the relentless demand for transparency from threat to advantage."
—A. G. Lafley, Chairman, President and Chief Executive, Procter & Gamble

VIKING
CANADA

DON TAPSCOTT

AND

DAVID TICOLL

THE NAKED CORPORATION

HOW THE AGE OF TRANSPARENCY WILL REVOLUTIONIZE BUSINESS

VIKING
CANADA

VIKING CANADA

Penguin Group (Canada), a division of Pearson Penguin Canada Inc., 10 Alcorn Avenue,
Toronto, Ontario M4V 3B2

Penguin Group (U.K.), 80 Strand, London WC2R 0RL, England
Penguin Group (U.S.), 375 Hudson Street, New York, New York 10014, U.S.A.
Penguin Group (Australia) Inc., 250 Camberwell Road, Camberwell, Victoria 3124, Australia
Penguin Group (Ireland), 25 St. Stephen's Green, Dublin 2, Ireland
Penguin Books India (P) Ltd, 11, Community Centre, Panchsheel Park,
New Delhi—110 017, India
Penguin Group (New Zealand), cnr Rosedale and Airborne Roads,
Albany, Auckland 1310, New Zealand
Penguin Books (South Africa) (Pty) Ltd, 24 Sturdee Avenue, Rosebank 2196, South Africa

Penguin Group, Registered Offices: 80 Strand, London WC2R 0RL, England

First published 2003

1   3   5   7   9   10   8   6   4   2

Manufactured in the United States of America.

Designed by Amy Hill

National Library of Canada Cataloguing in Publication

Tapscott, Don
The naked corporation : how the age of transparency will revolutionize
business / Don Tapscott and David Ticoll.

ISBN 0-670-04398-2

1. Corporations.   2. Corporate power.   3. Corporations—Investor relations.
4. Corporations—Public relations   I. Ticoll, David   II. Title.

HD2741.T36 2003   338.7'4   C2003-903676-6

American Library of Congress Cataloguing in Publication Data available

Visit the Penguin Group (Canada) website at www.penguin.ca

ACKNOWLEDGMENTS

Transparency is a new global business issue as we discovered in our research, consulting, and travels several years ago. The existing work on transparency is sparse, limited primarily to issues of financial reporting, corruption in emerging economies, and arms control(!). Yet in the networked economy, transparency cuts to the center of vast, newly controversial and urgent topics like leadership, trust, and sustainability. As we've grappled with these issues, many people have contributed invaluable help, insight, and creativity.

Bill Gillies ably headed our core research team and repeatedly provided the gift of hard-nosed realism to challenge our assumptions. Social science researcher Phil Courneyeur made a unique and special contribution. Jody Stevens and Antoinette Schatz of New Paradigm Learning Corporation kept us organized and productive; they put in many long hours over the course of this one-year project. Stephen Hamm, Jennifer Punn and Bruce Geddes worked diligently and enthusiastically; each contributed unique gems. We thank each of you personally for your insight, hard work, and collaboration.

This book was preceded by a series of multi-client research programs that we led from 1994 to 2002 at Digital 4Sight, a firm we founded with Alex Lowy.[1] Funded by corporations and governments, the research described how the Internet changes business and society.

We offer deep thanks to our many former clients and colleagues of Digital 4Sight.

Among the global practitioners who strongly influenced our work in progress were Chris Coulter, Debra Dunn, John Elkington, Ann Florini, Lise Kingo, Roger Martin, Robert Monks, David Vidal, David Wheeler, Anthony Williams, Simon Zadek, and Jeffrey Zalla.

We also thank the many others who contributed their time, insight and experiences to this project, including Chris Anderson, Bob Bertram, Kathy Bushkin, George Carpenter, Mildred Cho, Bruce Cleveland, Tony Comper, Jennifer Corriero, Bill Cox, John Dalla Costa, George Dallas, Robert Darretta, Derrick de Kerckhove, Stanley Fawcett, Roger Fine, Charlie Fine, Michael Furdyk, Jim Griffin, Keith Harrison, Robert Herz, Adrian Hosford, Jon Iwata, Steve Kerr, Kate Kozlowski, Joel Kurtzman, Alan Lafley, Ralph Larsen, Ken Larson, Lawrence Lessig, Mark Letner, Bud Mathaisel, Mike Mitchell, Bill Nielsen, Gordon Nixon, James R. Olson, Charlotte Otto, Robert Parker, Howard Paster, Eugene Polistuk, Mike Powers, James Reeves, Glenn Renwick, Ron Ricci, Michael Rice, Cynthia Richson, Mike Roach, Saskia Sassen, Mohan Sawhney, Eric Schmidt, Joshua Sharman, Damon Silvers, Tim Sinclair, Claude Smadja, Doug Steiner, Anke Schwittay, Tom Stewart, Paul Taaffe, Lester Thurow, Chris Tuppen, Bill Watkins, Sister Patricia Wolf, and Bob Young.

Bruce Nichols of the Free Press provided brilliant editorial guidance and support from outline development to final product and showed a deft hand with the virtual blue pencil. He has been a wonderful colleague in all respects. Joan Ramsay of *The Globe and Mail* was an invisible conscience who coached us to be direct and precise. Wes Neff, our literary agent at the Leigh Bureau, was a patient and insightful partner. Bill Leigh immediately grasped the potential of this project when it was an amorphous idea; his insight and encouragement helped us sharpen the vision.

In the spirit of transparency we would like to disclose that we have had consultant or business relationships with some of the organizations that we mention, quote, or discuss in this book. In the past three years we have had relationships with Cisco, CKI, the Conference Board, Hewlett-Packard, Hill & Knowlton, IBM, KPMG, Microsoft, and Motorola. Also, Don Tapscott is a corporate director of Celestica.

Our respective wives, Ana Lopes and Tracey Macey, provided valuable ideas and advice that repeatedly brought us down to earth. We owe them our highest gratitude.

Having said all this, we as authors take full responsibility for the content of this book, as well as for any errors or omissions.

We dedicate this book to our children, Alex and Niki Tapscott and Amy Ticoll. We hope that you and your generation find it helpful in the construction of a more transparent and sustainable world.

CONTENTS

An old force with new power is rising in business, one that has far-reaching implications for most everyone. Nascent for half a century, this force has quietly gained momentum through the last decade; it is now triggering profound changes across the corporate world. Firms that embrace this force and harness its power will thrive. Those which ignore or oppose it will suffer.

The force is *transparency*. This is far more than the obligation to disclose basic financial information. People and institutions that interact with firms are gaining unprecedented access to all sorts of information about corporate behavior, operations, and performance. Armed with new tools to find information about matters that affect their interests, stakeholders now scrutinize the firm as never before, inform others, and organize collective responses. The corporation is becoming naked.

Customers can evaluate the worth of products and services at levels not possible before. Employees share formerly secret information about corporate strategy, management, and challenges. To collaborate effectively, companies and their business partners have no choice but to share intimate knowledge with one another. Powerful institutional investors today own or manage most wealth, and they are developing x-ray vision. Finally, in a world of instant communications, whistleblowers, inquisitive media, and googling, citizens and communities routinely put firms under the microscope.

Corporations have no choice but to rethink their values and behaviors—for the better. If you're going to be naked, you'd better be buff!

This conclusion may seem at odds with current thinking about corporate values and behavior. At the end of 2003 the corporate world was still weathering a crisis of trust on a scale unseen since the Wall Street crash of 1929. Many say this latest crisis proves that companies are worse than ever, and irredeemably so. For these critics, the corporate corpus isn't buff, it's obese.

We believe the opposite is true. To build trusting relationships and succeed in a transparent economy, growing numbers of firms in all parts of the globe now behave more responsibly than ever. Disgraced firms represent the old model—a dying breed. Business integrity is on the rise, not just for legal or purely ethical reasons but because it makes economic sense. Firms that exhibit ethical values, openness, and candor have discovered that they can better compete and profit. Some figured this out recently, while others have understood it for generations. Today's winners increasingly undress for success.

Opacity is still alive and kicking; in some situations it remains desirable and necessary. Trade secrets and personal data, for example, are properly kept confidential. Sometimes openness is expensive. But more often, opacity only masks deeper problems. Armies of corporate lawyers fight openness as part of a good day's work. Old cultures—the insular model of yesterday's firm—die hard. Nevertheless, the technological, economic, and sociopolitical drivers of an open business world will prevail.

Corporations that are open perform better. Transparency is a new form of power, which pays off when harnessed. Rather than to be feared, transparency is becoming central to business success. Rather than to be unwillingly stripped, smart firms are choosing to be open. Over time, what we call "open enterprises"—firms that operate with candor, integrity, and engagement—are most likely to survive and thrive.

This is good news for all of us—customers, employees, partners, shareholders, and citizens—no matter what stakeholder hats we wear, because corporations have become so central to our lives and communities.

Most of us are shareholders, whether directly or through pension and mutual funds. Our retirements hinge on corporate success.

Because they own shares in the companies they work for, workers now think twice about going on strike. Societies have willingly made way for corporations and capitalists to innovate and create wealth around the world; yet we worry when firms become untamed global powerhouses, and we wonder why economic divides have worsened. We love brands and new products, but we are uneasy about the companies behind them. Firms mine vast amounts of information about us to build one-to-one relationships, but we fear the loss of our privacy. We seek out low prices, but despair when our jobs move offshore to low-cost geographies. We prize our communities and Main Street, yet flock to Wal-Mart.

Business has become the most controversial institution in society. Business leaders, who just yesterday were revered, are today mocked and reviled. There is widespread outrage regarding the eight- and nine-figure incomes of executives who preside over the destruction of shareholder wealth. The integrity of the accounting industry—the sector responsible for ensuring the financial honesty of corporations—has been undermined. For all demographic groups, public trust in CEOs is now only slightly higher than that of used car dealers. Young people are particularly uneasy about corporate behavior.[1]

Stakeholders have historically unprecedented opportunities to focus these anxieties and scrutinize the corporate world. They have new power to influence performance or even cripple companies almost overnight. What will they do with this new influence? And how should firms operate in the face of it?

We have been investigating the impacts of information technologies and new media on business and society since the early 1980s. Transparency is one key piece of this puzzle, yet there are virtually no books or articles about it. The few authors who have addressed transparency tend to treat it merely as the disclosure of financial information to shareholders or the prevention of bribery.

With this book we have attempted to develop a theory, body of knowledge, and set of leadership practices for transparency. We explain how and why transparency has moved to center stage, including its bumpy rise through the history of industrial capitalism. You will meet new concepts like forced transparency, active transparency, reverse transparency, stakeholder webs, transparency fatigue, values dissonance, the transparency divide, and what we call "the new business integrity." You will read how opaque firms that lacked integrity were devastated and, in some cases, reborn. You will also learn how open enterprises thrive and succeed through candor and ethical core values. Among our conclusions are:

- Transparency and corporate values enhance market value: there is a competitive business case for strategies that focus on stakeholders and sustainability. "Good" firms that optimize the needs of all stakeholders are more likely to be good for investors.

- Transparency has an organizational form which we call the stakeholder web": a network of stakeholders who scrutinize a firm, whether it knows it or not. Oblivious to their stakeholder webs, some firms have been devastated or destroyed.

- Employees of an open enterprise have greater trust in one another and their employer—resulting in lower costs, improved quality, better innovation, and loyalty.

- Transparency also brings a power shift to employees who share more information than ever before.

- Transparency is critical to business partnerships—lowering transaction costs between firms and enabling collaborative commerce. The invisible hand of the market is changing the way firms orchestrate capabilities to create differentiated products and services.

- Another power shift—from corporations to customers—has emerged from price wars and "accountability" wars. Corporate values are now central to many brands.

- Corporations that align their values with those of the communities they touch, and behave accordingly, can develop sustainable business models.

The best firms have clear leadership practices that others can adopt. They understand that investments in good governance and transparency deliver significant payoffs: engaged relationships, better quality and cost management, more innovation, and improved overall business performance. They build transparency and integrity into their business strategy, products and services, brand and reputation, technology plans, and corporate character.

We hope this book will help managers who are striving to build effective firms in the new business environment. We also hope the book helps employees, customers, partners, neighbors, and shareholders understand the changing role of the firm in society, how to hold corporations accountable for the benefit of everyone, and how to work and live while wearing many hats. For additional cases, information, readings, and discussion, join us at www.nakedcorporation.com.

PART I

The Transparency Imperative

CHAPTER 1

THE NAKED CORPORATION

The 2002 trust crisis was arguably the worst on Wall Street since the 1929 market crash and the Depression of the 1930s. Enron, World-Com, Arthur Andersen, Xerox, Tyco, Citibank, J. P. Morgan, Credit Suisse First Boston, Tenet Healthcare, Jack Welch, Martha Stewart—we could go on. The response—Sarbanes-Oxley, new rules from accounting standards boards, and an explosion in corporate governance reforms—is the greatest leap in corporate transparency since Franklin Delano Roosevelt's securities laws of 1932.

Meanwhile, business leaders rank near the bottom of surveys on public respect. Consumers are fickle. Loyalty between employers and employees is shaky to nonexistent. Police and protestors clash at international meetings. Litigation proliferates. Terrorism and war justify secrecy, breaches of privacy, and covert acts.

When there is a crisis in trust, transparency seems wanting. The openness of our society, its firms and other institutions, always fragile, is tested. Yet the fact is, growing, not declining, transparency was a prime cause of the 2002 crisis.

Leaders see transparency as a threat or an opportunity. Some fight it or hide from it. Others believe they will do better for shareholders when they openly align their business with the interests of stakeholders, sorting out trade-offs along the way. Increasingly, in the face of transparency and legitimate expectations, smart firms take the second path.

"Do well by doing good" sounds simple, maybe too simple. Isn't that what preachers have been telling us for thousands of years? Why is this any truer today than yesterday? One reason: Today's business environment depends on trust—and mandates transparency—like never before.

"WHAT IS FIDELITY HIDING?"

Chances are, if you live in the United States you are a Fidelity investor whether you know it or not. Fidelity is the world's largest mutual fund company and the nation's number one provider of 401(k) retirement savings plans. In January 2003 it held $1.4 trillion in customer assets, of which it directly managed $760 billion.

In September 2002, we decided to use the Internet to check out what Fidelity Investments was doing on your behalf about the corporate governance crisis. We expected to find evidence the company was out there fighting the good fight—demanding that corporate boards clean up their acts on behalf of the millions of individual investors that it represents. Our first stop was Fidelity itself, where we found nothing on the topic in its collection of press releases. If the company was doing anything about the mess, it wasn't publicizing that fact.

We searched elsewhere, and quickly discovered, of all things, a trade union (AFL-CIO) campaign that charged Fidelity with *betraying* shareholder interests. It demanded that the Securities and Exchange Commission (SEC) force the firm to disclose how it votes the shares that it controls. Fidelity's response, according to *The Wall Street Journal?* Disclosure wouldn't help its funds' returns and could harm the diplomacy it practiced with corporate executives with the goal of making companies more investor-friendly.[1]

The AFL-CIO noted that Fidelity, partly through its management of 401(k) and other pension accounts of union members, had been a major shareholder of Enron, WorldCom, and other cases of corporate burnout. Fidelity, with its big voting power at such companies' annual meetings, was "responsible in part for these companies' corporate governance—including decisions about executive compensation and conflicts of interest in corporate accounting oversight."[2] It accused Fidelity and its peers of "inherent conflicts of interest: mutual fund companies are in business to sell lucrative 401(k) retirement plans and other financial services to the same corporate decision-makers whose governance proposals they vote on." The AFL-CIO speculated that Fidelity had voted with management against corporate reform and shareholder interests at another half-dozen troubled companies. It wondered whether the company had supported resolutions to move headquarters to Bermuda (where corporate taxes are low) in order to escape U.S. taxes at Accenture, Ingersoll-Rand, Stanley Works (where Fidelity was the largest shareholder), and other firms.[3]

"What is Fidelity hiding?" asked the union. Its campaign included media releases, information sessions for its members, and a demonstration outside Fidelity's Boston headquarters. Its Web site asked visitors to sign a letter to the SEC:

> An investment advisor has a fiduciary duty to vote the shares of its clients in a manner that is consistent with the best interests of its clients. Disclosure of individual proxy voting decisions is the only way that I can insure that my mutual fund company is fulfilling its fiduciary duty to me. Requiring disclosure of individual proxy voting decisions by mutual funds will also promote accountability and transparency, two qualities sorely needed to restore investor confidence in our capital markets.

The appeal worked. In September 2002 the SEC amazed the AFL-CIO by saying that it would consider requiring mutual funds to publicly disclose how they vote in corporate proxy contests. Fidelity led the fund industry's fight against the measure, over several months coming up with a cascade of reasons why transparency was a bad idea.

- Disclosure could affect a company's stock price. (Better now than later, we say.)

- "We view how we vote as proprietary information."[4] (How is your vote on the choice of a director or a new share issue a proprietary secret?)

- The cost of disclosure would be too high. (Have you heard about the Internet?)

- Most shareholders don't care how fund managers vote. (The "ignorance is bliss" gambit.)

Then in January 2003, Edward Johnson III and John Brennan, the chairmen and CEOs of Fidelity and its largest competitor, the Vanguard Group, cosigned an article in *The Wall Street Journal* saying that "the proposal's unintended consequences could undermine the best interests of 95 million mutual fund shareholders in the U.S." Their main argument was that disclosure "would open mutual fund voting decisions to thinly veiled intimidation from activist groups whose agendas may have nothing to do with maximizing our clients' returns. A fund manager's focus belongs on investment management, not on becoming an arbiter of political and social disputes."[5]

Despite such opposition—and with the support of two important Republican House committee chairmen (Michael Oxley and Richard Baker)—the SEC announced in December that it would proceed with the rule, effective in 2004.

The CEOs of big private mutual funds refused to buckle under. Continuing to refer to the SEC decision as a "proposal," the industry took the unusual step of appealing to the U.S. government's Office of Management and Budget on the grounds of "paperwork burden."

Welcome to the world of the naked corporation.

This debate reveals many things about how the United States and the world are changing.

First, it points to how the Internet exposes Fidelity and every other company to public scrutiny like never before, day after day: forced transparency. Pick any big brand, enter a search term or two in Google, and chances are you'll find someone to tell you what's wrong with its picture.

- "Exxon" brings you to the Exxon Valdez Oil Spill Trustee Council site, featuring a jaunty, crayon-colored headline, "Kids: Are you doing a class report?" The up-to-date site reminds us that a U.S. government inquiry found the company responsible for the 1991 spill. It informs us that, though Exxon has paid $1 billion in penalties, the economic and environmental cost was a multiple of this number and that over ten years later most of the civil litigation remains unresolved.

- "McDonald's" delivers McSpotlight, a London (U.K.)-based site that grew out of the infamous McLibel case, when in 1997 the company won a Pyrrhic victory after a two-year libel trial against its Greenpeace critics. Today the site crows about the company's plans to close 175 restaurants, leavened with news about a partially built site in Grenoble that has just burned down. "The police suspect arson," it comments with barely disguised glee, along with the information that neighbors had earlier won a court order temporarily suspending construction.

Such drops in the ocean of information are on permanent display, easy to find or stumble on by accident. Transparency is being done to the firm, whether it likes it or not. No firm can safely protect any secret, particularly any that angers stakeholders. Increasingly, corporations are naked.

Second, rather than suffer forced transparency from a trade union–led campaign, Fidelity might have chosen a different route—active transparency.

Several mutual fund managers and other institutional investors (such as Domini Social Investments and the $135 billion California Public Employees' Retirement System [CalPERS]) began disclosing their proxy votes via the Web in 1999. But other union-based institutions, like the Teachers Insurance and Annuity Association–College Retirement Equities Fund (TIAA-CREF), responded to the SEC proposal by saying that shareholders are better represented when votes remain confidential. (After the SEC announced that it would proceed with the rule, TIAA-CREF dropped its objections.)

Third, pension holders in the millions are not just shareholder-type stakeholders. They have broader interests as employees, consumers, future retirees, and citizens. These diffuse interests give them at least as big a stake in the well-being of the entire economy, their communities, and the natural environment as in the profitability of any one company in their portfolio. Corporate governance reformer Robert Monks comments that today's shareholder is a many-hatted stakeholder because the distinction between the interests of shareholders and other stakeholders is becoming irrelevant:

Many shareholders are the beneficiaries of defined benefit pension plans, people who will work, say, eighteen more years and then retire. They want to retire into a clean, safe, civil world. So this is a world in which the interests of the environment, employment, and the community are essential to the functioning of the corporation. Once you identify who the owner is—not some arbitrager or computer trading program—but a guy with some eighteen more years to work before retirement—you begin to see convergence between stakeholders and shareholders.*

When the AFL-CIO complains that Fidelity may have voted for the departure of Accenture's head office to Bermuda for tax evasion, it presumes to represent the broad self-interest of pension holders as taxpayers, in other words, as citizens and community members. This point of view creates dilemmas for any firm—Fidelity or not—that seeks to vote in the interest of the shareholders that it represents. Values are also part of the issue. Is there a way to align multiple interests with enhanced shareholder return? How do you decide what to do when interests conflict with returns?

Finally, Fidelity and the AFL-CIO—and the apparently competing interests that they represent—are at the heart of structural changes in U.S. capitalism, changes which themselves are churning up the transparency wave. Retirement and pension funds own about one quarter of the value of all shares in the United States: they are the largest block of institutional shareholders. In other words, through pension funds ordinary employees own a big chunk of the shareholder economy. Also, 95 million Americans—half of the country's households—have invested personally in mutual funds, most with an eye to retirement.

The AFL-CIO proposal cuts to the quick of corporate governance in this environment: how does this new breed of pension fund shareholders ensure that the CEOs and executives of the firms they own act in their interests? Up to five layers of governance can exist between a pension shareholder and the mass of employees of a company in which he or she ultimately owns shares:

- A pension manager who is responsible for the entire pension pool of a company or government employee group

- One of several investment firms (like Fidelity) that the pension manager hires for its expertise in buying and selling shares

* All quotations without end notes were obtained through interviews by the authors.

- The board of directors of each invested company, which is the investment firm's primary official interface

- The CEO, who reports to the board of directors

- The company's management team that reports to the CEO

These entities, singly and in combination, regularly encounter lucrative opportunities to place their own interests ahead of shareholder interests. Many executives view their owners as a mere abstraction to be manipulated rather than as real people to whom they owe duties of trust.

The AFL-Fidelity conflict raises core issues that we address in this book:

- What is the challenge of transparency and how are firms responding?

- What kind of transparency will leading firms actively provide to their stakeholders?

- Will transparency cause firms to change their values and behavior?

- Can firms do well by doing good?

- How will we know if this is happening?

THE NAKED CORPORATION

There was a time when firms managed to keep most things to themselves. Many did not even publish annual reports until the 1930s when U.S. national legislation required them to do so.

Media and governments have always functioned as watchdogs on behalf of the firm's various constituencies. But increasingly, skeptical and self-empowered stakeholders are taking matters into their own hands. Whether they like it or not and whether they cooperate or not, firms face direct scrutiny and exposure from all manner of interests: employees, customers, shareholders, business partners, community members, and interest groups.

Some firms have always argued that they are only accountable to their shareholders. Others, like Johnson & Johnson with its 1940s-era corporate credo, have for generations said that shareholders benefit as a result of meeting the legitimate expectations and needs of customers, distributors, suppliers, employees, and the local and global communities in which it operates. We agree with the latter view, the school of thought that says that the firm, in exchange for the many privileges, benefits, and protections it obtains from all these entities, has reciprocal obligations to them and that its enduring success depends on achieving alignment among all these interests and the company's core mission. In doing so, a company has an obligation to minimize or pay for negative "externalities"—bad impacts on people or the environment that result from its activities. It also has an obligation to treat these entities with reciprocity and accountability, seeking their counsel on how they expect their interests to be taken into account and then meeting its commitments. In all these respects, the firm must identify and work with its legitimate stakeholders—the people and organizations who affect or are affected by the activities of the firm. The reason to do this is neither obligation nor ethics. Rather if the firm does these things right, it is more likely to prosper.

But today, in a world where trust is in deficit, the dialogue between firms and stakeholders is too often wanting. In response, stakeholders—all stakeholders, not just employees, business partners and competitors, and consumers and shareholders but ultimately society as a whole (sometimes through government)—have seized the tools at their disposal to shed the bright lights of transparency on the corporation like never before. This is a many-sided crisis.

Employees

Employees are the first to know. Thanks to email and instant messaging, every worker has an electronic printing press at his or her fingertips. It's uncanny how fast news and rumors spread across organizations. This process amplifies an atmosphere of growing mistrust and cynicism. Insecure employees can easily compare their pay packages to those of seemingly underperforming senior executives whose pay plans are publicly available on corporate proxy statements. Only 45 percent of workers had confidence in their senior management in early 2002, down from 50 percent two years earlier.[6]

Increasingly, employee-driven transparency is public. Roughneck

Web sites like Internalmemos.com routinely publish internal correspondence ranging from CEO missives to the resignation letters of individual employees. For color commentary, readers are referred to an affiliated site, Fuckedcompany.com. There, discussion ranges from the banal to the highly analytical—most of it with a cynical twist.

Fortune described Vault, Inc., as "the best place on the Web to prepare for a job search." At its core a matchmaker that competes with the likes of Monster.com, Vault attracts job seekers and potential job hoppers with up-to-date inside skinny on thousands of employers in a variety of industries. Visitors can purchase Vault's proprietary company reports, but for the real dirt they join its "electronic watercooler" (for which Vault has nabbed the trademark). Employees and job seekers congregate in its hundreds of company and issue-specific chat rooms to share news, analysis, and advice. As with most such sites, some of the information is questionable, and savvy employees are encouraged to have their "BS detectors" engaged. An alleged Johannesburg-based McKinsey employee says, "Any layoffs here too? Things here have been slower than slow so I wouldn't be surprised." A chatter counsels a Siebel Systems job prospect, "It's just a high tech sweat shop. . . . Do yourself a favor and pass on by."

Type "Wal-Mart" in Google and you'll quickly uncover a tangle of exposés. Foremost is a union drive by the United Food and Commercial Workers which provides a detailed critique of the company's pay policies, alleged mistreatment of injured workers, alleged sexual discrimination, and environmental and community impacts.

Employees, especially those in large corporations, also scrutinize their bosses' commitment to social responsibility. The Corporate Social Responsibility Monitor 2002 survey by Environics International reports that 80 percent of U.S. large-company employees say that social responsibility increases their motivation and loyalty, and 85 percent would participate in company-sponsored community programs. However, 58 percent say that their firm needs to focus much more on being socially responsible.

Wherever you look, employees are looking back at the firm. Every action by its leaders is scrutinized, analyzed, and judged, and employees use the Internet and other communications tools to reach shared conclusions that directly affect morale and productivity. No firm can afford to ignore this force.

Business Partners and Competitors

Most companies and market participants are awash with information about customers, suppliers, channels and competitors, industry practices, and market conditions. What once was considered top secret—such as product and technology trends, operational best practices, and company market performance—is now, more often than not, industry common knowledge if not in the public domain. Trade publications, conferences, benchmarking collaboratives, professional job-hopping, syndicated research, competitive intelligence consultants, job boards, patent records, mandated public reporting, online resources of all kinds, Wall Street analysts, and the better-equipped-than-ever mass media ensure that strategic information is readily available. The challenge is to capture, analyze, and draw the right conclusions from this mountain of available data.

Every industry depends on a common set of unique technologies: retail depends on logistics; pharmaceuticals depends increasingly on bioinformatics. And all industries depend on information and communications technologies. But these specialized technologies evolve in a transparent world. Much advanced research is in the public domain, and most products can be reverse engineered. In such an environment, how do companies sustain competitive advantage? Why would they desire *more* transparency? Answer: Innovation is, as economists say, "path dependent." A company that already has strength in, for example, next-generation breathable waterproof fabrics (e.g., GoreTex) enjoys a technological, manufacturing, brand, and infrastructure lead that only a handful of competitors can touch. Absent massive capital investment, a traditional cotton mill has no chance of joining the fray. Path dependence is painfully apparent in automotive, a technology-intensive industry beset with global excess capacity. After 25 years of reverse engineering Japanese design and production techniques, Detroit's Big 3 are still having trouble producing a reliable, energy-efficient, and value-priced competitive vehicle. All the competitive intelligence in the world won't change their organizational genetics.

In the networked global economy, firms increasingly function in networks—what we call business webs or b-webs.[7] Rather than attempt to do everything from design to component manufacturing, assembly, marketing, distribution, and customer service, firms are focusing on what they do best and relying on partners for the rest. Some automotive manufacturers have gone so far as to outsource the assembly of entire vehicles. In radical business models, like eBay and Amazon, the core company does very little. eBay essentially operates a Web-based auction site, where its 28 million active users handle all aspects of inventory, marketing, pricing, delivery, and trust creation for the goods that they sell and buy. Amazon runs a growing online retail mall, where consumers and freelancers write most of the product reviews and the products themselves are all sourced from third parties (no house brands here); the company itself focuses its software technology on physical fulfillment. In all these cases, clear, precise, trustworthy communication is the sine qua non of success.

Within a business web the most valuable information is often quite boring. Much of it has to do with knowing the specific demand signals that drive activity: How much will we sell tomorrow, and therefore how much should we produce today? Will Albertson's put Crest on sale next week? In this arena, transparency is uneven. Often, the answers are simply not known. When they are, transparency depends on sharing specific information at the time and place of need—which neither the Internet nor a market intelligence system can systematically drag out of an unwilling participant. Sometimes a buyer has the clout to demand information from suppliers. Other times, information is shared in an environment of mutual trust (though in the first two examples below, trust is often betrayed, but not often enough to kill the system).

- Sellers on eBay accept that buyers will publicly rate the quality of their goods and the attentiveness of their service.

- Genome researchers share insights and techniques, trusting that collaborators across academic and business boundaries will not sneak off and patent them.

- Procter & Gamble (P&G) receives specific, real-time performance results from every Wal-Mart store so that it can replenish shelves as needed. Wal-Mart lets P&G in on its store-by-store sales because it is confident that P&G won't give the information to K-Mart.

- Competitors Celestica and Solectron give capacity production forecasts and costs to competitors Dell and IBM, which in turn share market demand signals with Celestica and Solectron. Celestica builds products to IBM's forecasts because it trusts that IBM will not stick it with the bill if demand fails to materialize.

As it turns out, many business partnerships are not very good at sharing such information. Some of that has to do with lack of certainty: market demand can't be anticipated accurately enough. In other situations, the problems are more systemic. Buyers withhold information in order to maintain the upper hand with suppliers. Or buyers fail to use the information they get. Dell's supply chain is optimized for producing single personal computers tailored to single end-customer shipments. But a customer that wants 500 identical PCs every Monday over a three-week period might get better service from Hewlett-Packard (HP), which has more of a mass production supply chain model. Of course, Dell and HP will each accept business that is more appropriate for the other's supply system, risking the trust of customers and suppliers.[8]

Such conflicts are not sustainable. Celestica CEO Eugene Polistuk comments: "Before, companies guarded and filtered information. Now we're all naked. It's like the CNN of business—instant availability. No room for bull. Transparency and networking squeeze out all the zero value-added information, distortion, and ineffectual management." Neither authoritarianism nor cronyism can survive the market forces unleashed by transparency. Firms must manage to results with discipline and integrity.

Shareholders

We are all shareholders now: in 2002 half of U.S. households invested in stocks directly or through mutual funds. But we also may be employees, customers, and community-impacted neighbors of a firm whose shares we own. In addition, institutions such as mutual and pension funds—not individuals—own 64 percent of publicly traded shares. Few people can name the companies that their mutual funds have invested in. In fact, many pension funds put half or more of their money into index funds—for example, one that follows the entire Standard & Poor's (S&P) 500—rather than a stock-picker's selection.

Ironically, among all the stakeholder groups that look on the corporation, shareholders—the owners of the firm—seem most-poorly served and in the dark. The situation is paradoxical. On the one hand, the United States has been the world leader in corporate reporting for decades. The Securities and Exchange Commission requires massive depth and detail in quarterly and annual reports, as well as special filings for all sorts of "material" events. Yet it is clear that the crisis of 2002 was a crisis of disclosure and transparency.

Enron is a case in point. Its peak market capitalization was $90 billion. When Enron went bankrupt on December 2, 2001, it was after a string of unanticipated nonrecurring charges and restatements to its corporate balance sheet, mostly due to improper reports of dealings with partnerships run by—and to the personal benefit of—company executives. Nevertheless, the case is strong that, while Enron's management had intentionally misled the markets, enough information was available for canny investors to have seen trouble and dumped the stock. Market analysts were well aware that "bodies were buried in off-balance sheet entities that were cryptically described in Enron's pre-crisis disclosure documents."[9] Arthur Andersen's conflict of interest was public knowledge: it was doing $25 million in consulting and tax planning while also functioning as Enron's auditor. This practice had already caused Andersen grief with other clients like Waste Management. Market analysts and investment managers, in the heady dot-com bubble, chose to ignore all this publicly available information and treated Enron as a "faith" stock rather than as the lemon that it was. So much for the theory that markets efficiently take all available information into account when they price securities.

What applied to Enron applied to many others, whether AOL, Nortel, or Yahoo! The market engaged in an irrational gold rush, in many respects no different from the U.S. railway boom of the 1840s. But even in the midst of the madness of crowds, disclosure issues are real, and shareholders have lost their patience:

- Few companies publish financial reports that the average investor can readily understand, even less identify and interpret critical nuggets buried in footnotes. If anything, there is too much information, presented in a confusing manner. This is opacity in the guise of transparency. At the 2003 annual meeting of investment company Berkshire Hathaway, CEO Warren Buffett said: "If you can't understand a company's financial statement in two minutes it means that management doesn't want you to and that they are probably hiding something."

- Few investors—other than insiders and the supersophisticated—have time, focus, or capability to become fully informed. Even fewer have time to be active—assiduously reading company reports, raising issues, or attending annual meetings.

- Stockbrokers combine conflict of interest (they are typically rewarded for churning portfolios rather than increasing their value) with professional optimism.

- As we described earlier in this chapter, shareholders are many layers removed from the people who control the companies they own. Most mutual funds that represent them prefer to keep shareholders in the dark about their proxy votes and other activities.

- Hundreds of firms have cooked their books. According to the U.S. Office of Management and Budget, between January 1997 and March 2002, 689 companies—10 percent of all publicly traded firms—restated their results. With the Sarbanes-Oxley Act of August 2002, CEOs are required to certify the accuracy of their reporting. The jury is out on whether this will make a difference.

- On top of the crises of major corporations from Adelphia to Xerox, Wall Street itself proved to be deeply complicit. Star analysts had knowingly recommended lemon stocks of customer firms. Brokers had routinely given clients (many of whom ultimately became exposed as engaged in corporate frauds of their own) special access to lucrative initial public offerings.

Shareholders (most of whom are also employees) are in a deep crisis of trust, and for good reason.

Customers

Once upon a time in the 1950s, consumers were only too happy to buy just about any good or service that came their way. Abundance—what John Kenneth Galbraith called the affluent society—was a novel experience for Americans, and they embraced it with gusto. No more. Today, many industries and markets are battlegrounds where consumers and sellers wage battle in a fog of mutual mistrust. This problem is not universal: great brands like Coca-Cola, IBM, Disney, and BMW retain their sheen despite ups and downs. But it's nasty down in the trenches.

Martha Stewart's downfall is emblematic. The icon of the pastel-tinged family lifestyle, her message was trust at the highest level. "What I'm really giving," she has said, "is a reality that looks like a fantasy." Ersatz maybe, but her fantasy was how to articulate an aesthetic of caring into daily life. If not Martha, who?

Increasingly consumers depend on transparency to protect themselves and prepare for marketplace combat. In a 2001 survey by Environics International, 88 percent of Americans said they gather information about products before a major purchase.[10] American consumers have high expectations of companies reporting on both their financial and social performance honestly: 85 percent and 78 percent respectively, hold companies completely responsible for this degree of transparency.[11]

- Consumers prepare for the car-buying process with military precision. The Internet provides, mostly for free, government crash test results, product reviews from a variety of perspectives, personal advice and consultation, and several versions of dealer pricing. One site offers dealer price comparisons by zip code.[12]

- The travel industry's economics are beset by transparency. Internet air and hotel bookings continue to increase: analysts predict that in good times and bad, online bookings will push prices down.[13]

- Not only did Wall Street lose the confidence of consumers, but banking is also under pressure. E-Loan, a dot-com survivor, returned to television advertising and turned profitable in 2002. It ended the year with $13 billion of consumer loans on its books. Its site lives and breathes the transparency of its lending process.

- Type "insurance rates" in a search engine and find all sorts of resources, from the Progressive Insurance Company to pure information sites like Insurance.org, that provide advice and comparative deals for your particular situation.

- The recording industry has been in crisis since MP3 took off in 1998. Because music is pure information, transparency in this case challenges a century-old business model.

- Millions of Americans think the health care system misleads them. Tenet is but one example of a major provider that lost public trust under suspicion of overcharging Medicare and conducting unnecessary operations. Physicians and pharmaceutical companies seem to be in an unholy alliance, doing battle with a new mini-industry in Canada that sells low-cost branded drugs and generics to U.S. patients via the Internet. Pharmaceutical companies malign the integrity of Canadian exporters; Glaxo Smith Klein even threatened to cut off their supplies. But elderly patients on fixed incomes know that this idea works.

In the past, consumers were isolated. A few joined quaint consumer groups; others talked to neighbors about products they might buy, or read the main source of objective advice, *Consumer Reports*. Today, they self-organize. They get other readers' book reviews on Amazon from their home, workplace, or coffee shop—even from a screen in a competing bookstore. To learn what others think about a car, movie, music CD, computer, camera, stereo, garden tool, home furnishing, office product, vacation destination, restaurant, wine, or perfume, they can consult numerous sites from Epinions.com on.

Access to information has created power struggles in many markets. Sellers see customers commoditizing them, going to Wal-Mart and Internet merchants to challenge their prices and profit margins, and ready to launch a class action suit for the least provocation. Consumers see sellers ripping them off, providing bad service, and invading their privacy. Notable exceptions exist, but nastiness rules in many industries, especially big-ticket ones like automobiles, travel (hotel, air), financial services (brokerages, banks, insurance), health care, pharmaceuticals, and telecom.

Meanwhile, values-oriented activist consumers have agendas that go beyond personal benefit. They probe deep into a company's supply chain to expose environmental and human rights practices, then demand and force change. In 1996 they publicized the fact that Wal-Mart's Kathie Lee Gifford celebrity collection of clothing was being stitched by Honduran children who often worked 24-hour days for wages as low as 31 cents an hour. Gifford broke into tears on national television when confronted by the evidence. The consumer reaction soon led not only Wal-Mart but also eventually Nike, Gap, Disney, and others to revise labor practices in their supply chains.[14]

Communities

In the mid-1990s, U.S. big-box retailer Home Depot would never have believed that a coalition of rain forest activists would force it to phase out old-growth lumber from its product lines. Nike wouldn't have guessed that the factories used to produce its goods in distant countries would become vilified as sweatshops, spurring it to establish a code of conduct for global labor standards and a nonprofit partnership to help improve the lives and communities of offshore workers. Monsanto didn't foresee that it would grossly underestimate public fears about the safety of genetically engineered products, only to find itself committing to goals of dialogue and transparency around new products and technologies. These companies didn't understand the new power of citizens to look deeply into their operations and suffered as a result.

In a transparent world with unprecedented access to information, employees, shareholders, business partners, and even, to a degree, consumers want evidence that firms are trustworthy and behaving according to their values. These groups still must pry out the truth about a firm's actions and impacts. Events frequently occur behind closed doors; stakeholders are bound by confidentiality or ignorance. *Some* people know where the bodies lie, and that information will stay hidden for shorter and shorter periods as the world becomes more connected.

Environics International has found that many people form impressions of individual companies based on social factors such as labor practices, business ethics, and environmental sustainability—sometimes ahead of product quality and value. In their most recent U.S.

survey, significant majorities held companies responsible for how they treat employees, environmental protection, human rights, and having the same high standards everywhere they operate.

Some stakeholders—community activists, nongovernmental organizations (NGOs), and the like—have little or no direct power over the firm. Their main tool is transparency: the ability to learn, inform others, and organize on the basis of what they know. When community stakeholders use information to gain the support of others who do have economic power—like the firm's customers, shareholders, or employees—their power multiplies.

The complex and diverse community sphere includes several categories of stakeholders:

- Communities themselves—of geography (local to global), of identity (race, age, gender, nationality, etc.), and of interest (shared beliefs or concerns).

- Independent organizations—clubs, religious groups, business associations, lobby groups, political parties, community groups, and NGOs. Their philosophies and goals traverse the political spectrum from the National Rifle Association to Greenpeace.

- Media, whose contribution to transparency is central when they do a good job. Unfortunately, this is not always the case even where the press is free.

Firms ignore at their peril the scrutiny and reactions of this complex array. Events like the Chernobyl nuclear meltdown, the Bhopal gas leak (Union Carbide), the Brent Spar oil spill (Shell), and the Exxon Valdez oil spill taught firms that they can neither conceal nor evade the external impacts of their actions.

Civil society is now organized in networks of NGOs which scrutinize and respond to the activities of firms around the world. NGOs span a range of activism from social and community service delivery to advocacy, including lobbying and civil disobedience. Some, like Transparency International, align with business and government agencies; others, like the Independent Media Center, attack established institutions. Many also work in partnership with firms and govern-

ments to define and implement solutions that are socially, environmentally, and economically sustainable. Increasingly, NGOs operate
globally, and nearly all use the Internet to learn about corporate
behavior, inform others, and organize. Dozens of firms, like Shell,
British Petroleum, Squibb, Chiquita, Ford, Hewlett-Packard, and General Motors, now work closely with selected NGOs to achieve mutual
transparency and alignment of interests and programs.

All this occurs in the context of a heightened global consensus on
the core issues of social development and the environment, which came
into focus around the 2002 UN summit on sustainable development:

> The shadows of environmental degradation, poverty, and lack of eco-
> nomic opportunity lie across the regions of the world that are fertile
> ground for ethnic conflicts, hatred, and violence. The private sector has
> a more important role than ever before to develop products and prac-
> tices and to support policies that protect and restore the environment,
> that eradicate poverty, and that create a fair and transparent society.
> The challenge of the future is to choose a course that satisfies the
> market requirements for growth, maintains the natural balance that
> sustains our economies, and meets the needs and rights of global com-
> munities awakening to new dreams of health, prosperity, and peace.[15]

Any local activist can—and does—invoke this emerging consensus
as the yardstick of a firm's actions and values.

Because of transparency, market forces are increasingly brought to
bear on the corporation. Firms compete for human capital in open
labor markets; mobility has never been greater. Firms compete for customers, never better informed, better connected, and more powerful.
They compete for suppliers, distributors, and business partners as the
business web becomes an open and ever-shifting playing field. They
compete for shareholders and institutional investors, who draw on
powerful tools and resources for x-ray vision. And they compete in a
global society for the hearts and minds of citizens and regulators who
are increasingly plugged in, interconnected, and hunting for bear.

But what exactly do we mean by *transparency*? It is something
more than merely being information-rich?

TRANSPARENCY DEFINED

Transparency is information about an organization that is available to people or other organizations. But this statement begs a number of questions. Which other people or organizations get the information? For what purpose do they get it? What information do they get? In what form?

In practice, transparency can mean many things. Since the cold war, countries have sought transparency to verify compliance with arms control rules. Ronald Reagan delighted in dunning USSR premier Mikhail Gorbachev with the Russian proverb "Trust, but verify." In a very different context, a software design is said to be transparent if it is easy to see what a program does at a particular moment and what it will do next. In business, we hear about the need for transparency in corporate governance, executive compensation, and financial reporting.

Transparency does not mean telling all about an institution or process. *Shareholders* of Kellogg Company need to separate signal from noise: they don't care, for example, how often the company puts out the garbage (but some may want to know about its recycling program). They need specific information to help them decide whether to add, keep, or sell Kellogg shares. They need transparency into such matters as sales, costs, executive compensation, and merger and acquisition plans. Kellogg *customers* make very different decisions; they want information about taste and nutrition. *Regulators* like the Food and Drug Administration (FDA) need to know whether Kellogg's plants are sanitary and its products meet safety rules; they really do care about the garbage (we hope!). Any of these may increasingly want to know about Kellogg's management ethics, sourcing, and environmental practices.

Transparency, then, we define as the *accessibility of information to stakeholders of institutions, regarding matters that affect their interests.*

Transparency can be active or forced. Active transparency occurs when companies consciously decide to be transparent in order to achieve business goals. Formal reports, such as press releases, annual reports, and sustainability reports, are a vital link in the chain of active transparency. But they are not the whole story. Active transparency is part of everyday life. It occurs when a manager speaks to an employee and when an employee speaks to a colleague, customer, supplier, government, or community person. It is evidenced on Web sites, in advertising, at company events, and in media interviews—and in the actions, products, and services that a company produces every single day. Whenever the company and its people do anything, they communicate the company's priorities and values, for better or for worse. Open enterprises have the ability to ensure that active transparency in all its dimensions consistently reinforces their priorities and values.

Forced transparency happens when transparency is done to corporations by stakeholders or the media.

Kellogg has felt the impact of misalignment between the level of stakeholder activism and the firm's approach to transparency (Figure 1.1). For several years, Greenpeace and other environmental, health-conscious groups claimed that Kellogg and one of its subsidiaries, Morningstar Farms, were distributing genetically modified foods. In 2000, Kellogg had announced that no genetically modified foods were being sold by Morningstar Farms. Yet Kellogg failed to engage with the environmental groups or to initiate any active process for rigorously addressing their concerns, and Greenpeace didn't believe the 2000 announcement. In the face of stakeholder activism, Kellogg became opaque. It occupied the Danger Zone.

On March 8, 2001, Greenpeace announced that an independent lab had found StarLink corn, a genetically modified variety not

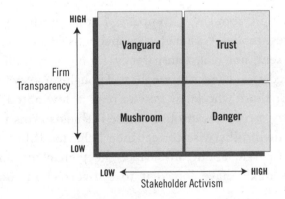

Figure 1.1 Transparency Alignment

approved for human consumption, in a Kellogg Morningstar corn dog. Greenpeace called on the FDA to order a recall and investigation. Its spokesperson said, "Americans have asked Kellogg's over and over to stop this genetic experiment on our food, yet Kellogg's refuses to listen and tries to mislead consumers. No one should trust the Kellogg's or Morningstar names again." Kellogg waited a few days (seeming to vacillate and further hurting its cause), conducted a test of its own, admitted the presence of StarLink, and recalled the corn dog from retailers on March 13. Kellogg would have escaped this embarrassment if it had taken the German poet Friedrich Schiller's advice, "It is wise to disclose what cannot be concealed."

When a firm is so focused on transparency and "sustainable" policies that it loses sight of the things that its stakeholders care about, it may enter the Vanguard Zone of our diagram, which brings its own costs. This happened with Iceland, a U.K. retail food chain that went bankrupt after converting its produce section to 100 percent organic foods.[16] To rephrase the Panasonic commercial tagline, with transparency it's best to be 'just slightly ahead' of your stakeholders. Patagonia, an outdoor sports clothing and equipment manufacturer, illustrates how to succeed in the Vanguard Zone. It was the first in its industry to move to organic cotton clothing, leading customers, and eventually competitors like Nike, to buy into the idea. In the process, Patagonia strengthened the differentiation of its brand and maintained its sales growth during the 2001–02 economic downturn.

Arguably, Enron was in the Mushroom Zone—shareholders were kept in the dark and covered with manure. Through a flood of deceptive information about the company, Enron proffered glamour, a "cool" business model, Washington connections, and a rocketing share price—apparent, not real, transparency. Employees, trading partners, investors, media, and analysts bought it. Though some evidence of risk was there for those who knew how to read it, few noted it. A Mushroom strategy can be disastrous because it shields firms from market forces that might otherwise correct their behavior. If Enron had been actively transparent about off-balance-sheet financing, for example, stakeholders might have forced it to self-correct in time to avoid implosion.

What is the right balance? Consider British Telecom. It actively consults, using a variety of structured mechanisms, with a broad range of stakeholders from suppliers to communities to shareholders in the United Kingdom and abroad. It seeks transparency in its daily operations and is considered a world leader in the quality of its corporate reporting. An inhabitant of the Trust Zone, the company claims that its social responsibility strategy contributes 25 percent of the image and reputation component of its customer satisfaction measures and provides a competitive advantage in the marketplace.

Transparency cuts both ways. In a sense, the firm is a stakeholder of its stakeholders. We use the term *reverse transparency* to denote the ability of corporations to look into the actions of stakeholders. Reverse transparency too can be active or passive. When ethical mutual funds like Domini Investments and pension funds like CalPERS (stakeholders) publish their proxy voting policies, investee firms (companies) gain visibility into what they might do in an upcoming board election. Typically, firms find out more today than ever before about their employees and, to varying degrees, their customers. As they increasingly face expectations from activist shareholders, NGOs, and community groups, firms seek transparency into these organizations. Sometimes this is a cloak-and-dagger operation, other times a public relations function. At their best, open enterprises find ways to authentically consult and collaborate with *everyone*.

Transparency is by no means universal. Forces for opacity are fighting hard. But transparency is clearly on the rise.

DRIVERS OF TRANSPARENCY

In the twenty-first century, transparency and trust have become critical to the operation of organizations and economies, for economic, technological, social, and sociopolitical reasons.

- *The success of market economies and globalization.* As market capitalism moves to a global scale, the competitive success of firms and nations depends on genuine performance; the crises of 1998 in East Asia and 2002 in the United States exposed the consequences of cronyism, corruption, and false reporting in both the private and public sectors.

- *The rise of knowledge work and business webs.* Firms' means of production exist in the crania of their employees and the resource of their business partners. Knowledge worker productivity depends on openness and candor regarding business and production matters, as well as trust, integrity, and values-based leadership.

- *The spread of communications technology.* The Internet, in particular, is ever more pervasive, granular, immediate, and impossible to control. It is the quintessential medium of transparency, archival completeness, creativity, innovation, business productivity, and self-organization—a technological challenge to traditional hierarchies.

- *Demographics and the rise of the Net Generation.* Someone once said that technology is anything that was invented before we were born. Today's children and young adults perceive the Internet as part of everyday life, just like their parents saw television and their grandparents saw radio. In parallel, many have a stronger sense of civil values than did members of earlier generations.

- *The rising global civil foundation.* Crises, fanaticism, and uneven development from one country to the next cannot mask the fact that the world's ever more educated generations continually raise the standards for the quality of human interaction. Whether through law, precedent, or norms of interaction, it's becoming more and more difficult to get away with bad behavior.

None of these drivers is likely to disappear any time soon.

Economics: Business Webs and Knowledge Work

Economic growth depends on trust. In the World Values Survey, people in 37 rich to poor market economies were asked whether they believed that "most people can be trusted" or "you can't be too careful in dealing with people." Trust levels (those who said most people can be trusted) varied from 5.5 percent in Peru to 61.2 percent in Norway.[17] Researchers found a direct correlation between trust and national economic growth. In fact, high-trust poor countries grew faster than both rich countries and low-trust poor countries.

In the industrial economy, what powered the engines of production—the fuel—was physical energy: coal, electricity, gasoline, and chemical reactions. Machines also needed grease to work smoothly rather than grind apart. Today's economy depends on knowledge, human intelligence, agility, and relationships inside and outside the firm. The fuel is information, and the lubricant is trust. The revolution in information and communications technologies is at the heart of these changes. The Internet and other technologies enable thinking, communication, and collaboration like never before.

Today's organizations require the ability to learn faster than their competitors and to compete one b-web against another. Technologies, products, even entire strategies can be copied. Competitive advantage is ephemeral as firms constantly seek new ways to create value. Survival and success hinge on the knowledge and creativity of product strategists, developers, and marketers. And they also hinge on sustained, trusting relationships with many different stakeholders across the b-web and beyond.

Brains require motivation to perform. You can turn up the speed on an assembly line, but you can't set a quota on bright ideas or the fruits of engagement. Money is not the only motivation for today's employee or market partner. Motivation also depends on intrinsic value and fulfillment; continuity of relationships; dignity and respect; meeting commitments; and mutual trust.

The need for transparency and trust in a knowledge economy seems self-evident. When knowledge is the basis of productive activity, the firm must make it readily available. This pushes the door ajar: by definition, productivity depends on having the right knowledge at the right place and time in a useful form. The knowledge must be true, accurate, and up to date. We see this focus on knowledge enablement and deployment in everything from use of the Internet as a collaborative tool to just-in-time production and real-time accounting systems to enterprise risk management. In a world of interdependent business webs, such systems extend beyond the enterprise to its suppliers, distribution channels, and customers.

Employees who are self-motivated will perform best, not just when they have the knowledge that they need but also when they have a sense of dignity and self-worth—mutual trust with their employers that is based on ethical values, practiced every day. Again, the only basis for such trust is transparency, as human resources professionals say, open, honest, and direct communication.

Simply put, organizations that wish to sustain high performance in the knowledge economy have no choice but to create an environment of trust, founded in transparency.

Technology: Media and the Internet

The pervasiveness of the broadcast media alone creates a culture of transparency; people expect that they can know anything instantaneously. We are bathed in broadcast news and information, from global to local interest, from personal to economic to political. TV screens are in every restaurant and airport gate, elevator, and even corporate office—a hundred channels and growing, with technologies like TiVo ready to time-shift at our pleasure. In case we missed the TV clip or print article, we can go to the Internet to catch up on the newspaper, TV channel, or financial information service of our choice.

Too much of it is one dimensional, merchandising the crisis of the week with the received editorial perspective (especially when national wars dominate headlines) and with little meaningful differentiation in point of view from one channel or commentator to the next. But alternative points of view do seep through—easy to find for those who care to look.

The Internet raises transparency to a whole new level. Broadcast media are one-way, centrally (and corporately) controlled, single message. The multidirectional Internet is the opposite of all these. Anyone can use it to originate messages from any location, any time. You can find any point of view you want if you care to look. And no one controls its content—except for all its users. The Internet, as the saying goes, "routes itself around obstacles": it's virtually impossible to block it. The Net has boundless versatility! Simple person-to-person communications, fancy and complex informational Web sites, the instant personal soapboxes known as Weblogs, real-time activity coordination (business, personal, political), financial transactions, information capture, long-term archiving—the list goes on. All these are new and powerful tools for transparency.

By the Internet we mean more than just the World Wide Web: it extends from Weblogs and email to mobile phones and hand held computers and, just out of the gate, cameras in our mobile phones; wireless communicators for specialties like health care, education, security, and gaming; and communicating chips embedded in everything from running shoes to soup cans to door handles, production lines, and prosthetics. Using commercial remote-sensing satellites, anyone with a few hundred dollars can buy detailed images of any spot on the planet. Surveillance cameras are everywhere; you can't take a half-hour walk in downtown New York or London without having your picture taken 200 times. Individuals have them too; cameras that communicate with the mobile Internet are becoming commonplace.

The Internet empowers individuals and grassroots groups to learn, inform others, and organize like no other medium. The search engine Google (see "The Greatest Show of Planet Earth" sidebar, page 30) and others like it are among the greatest forces for transparency in the world today. Type just about any search term, and you are bound to find what you need to know, as well as any dissensions or debates that pertain to the topic.

The Seattle protest (November 29–December 3, 1999) against the World Trade Organization (WTO) set a benchmark for use of the Internet to change the dynamics of transparency and dissent. It was a first in many respects: the breadth of its use of the Internet; its coalition that ranged from trade unionists to environmentalists, anti-corporate-globalists, and Third World indigenous people; the extent to which it galvanized a new generation of youth; and how the official delegations in hotels and conference rooms felt obliged to deal with the people in the streets. It was also the first time since the 1960s that an international diplomatic meeting had raised such a ruckus on U.S. soil.

The Internet was at the center of the protest. Protesters made extensive use of email and discussion boards, virtual sit-ins, Web-based information and counterinformation, and audio and video broadcasting.[18] Under the code N30 (November 30) organizers rallied a series of actions via the Internet. The site "A global day of action" published a call to arms in ten languages and provided a directory of local contacts all over the world.

Seattle also gave birth to the now-permanent Independent Media

The Greatest Show of Planet Earth

The lobby of the Googleplex in Silicon Valley is a humble place. There's a piano that a number of employees play from time to time, the usual awards cabinet, a collection of lava lamps, and a video game system. Amid the bustle is a sample of real-time Google queries scrolling on the wall behind the receptionist. People gawk at them like Nasdaq electronic tickers during the bull market.

The depth, breadth, and variety of Google searches is astounding. At any point in time people might be using the search engine to research a book on transparency, check out tonight's date, get the scoop on Exxon's environmental record, locate a view of Mars through the Hubble telescope, choose a holiday recipe, or seek help for a child's medical problem—not to mention multimedia delights for all appetites, healthy and decadent. We have been astounded at how easy it is to type in a couple of leading keywords and just about any company name to discover dirt that we didn't know.

With 800 employees and a network of over 10,000 servers around the world, Google has become a universal engine of transparency—the greatest show on Earth. On a typical day it fields over 200 million queries in 88 languages, tracking over 3 billion Web pages.

Center (IMC), established by various independent and alternative media organizations and activists. The center disintermediate mainstream journalists who quickly came to rely on it. The IMC Web site became a key source of up-to-the-minute reports, photos, audio, and video. IMC produced five video documentaries, uplinked to satellite, and distributed to public access stations across the United States. It claims to have logged more than 2 million hits during the protest.

This is not to say that all communication brings clarity. If anything, the protesters were opaque. Ordinary citizens were not plugged in—they had trouble understanding what the protesters wanted—and indeed a variety of agendas were at play. Yet Seattle was proof positive of the power of the Internet as a mechanism that enables stakeholders to find out what is going on, inform others, and self-organize to advance their interests.

Demographics: The Power of the Net Generation

Another powerful force for transparency is the so-called baby boom echo, or as we have dubbed them, the Net Generation.[19] Between the ages of 6 and 26, these are the children of the boomers. This generation is bigger than the boom itself—80 million strong in the United States alone—and through sheer demographic muscle they will dominate the twenty-first century. But this is also the first generation to come of age in the digital age. They are growing up bathed in bits. The vast majority of North American adolescents know how to use a computer and almost 90 percent of teenagers in the United States use the Net. They watch less TV than their parents, as time online takes time away from television.

This generation has an outlook on life different from their parents. It is always tricky making generalizations about an entire generation, as they are divided by gender, class, race, geography, psychographic characteristics, and other important factors. Nevertheless, some themes characterize a majority of this demographic group. Rather than be passive recipients of television (24 hours per week for their boomer parents), they spend more time online—searching, reading, scrutinizing, authenticating, collaborating, and organizing (everything from MP3 files to social parties and political protests). The Internet makes life an ongoing, massive multimedia research project, and the kids love it. They typically can't imagine a life where citizens don't have tools to constantly think critically, exchange views, challenge, authenticate, verify, or debunk. They have unprecedented access to information and they are more knowledgeable than any previous generation. And with so much false or misleading information in the digital world, they develop good authentication techniques at an early age.

While they have greater self-confidence than did their parents at the same age, they worry about the future. It's not their own abilities that they are insecure about, it's the adult world and how it may lack opportunity. They also mistrust governments and elites.

This generation tends to value individual rights—the right to be left alone, the right to privacy, and the right to have and express their own views. As they enter adolescence and later, they tend to oppose censorship by governments and by parents. They also want to be treated fairly; there is a strong ethos among many, that for example, "I should share in the wealth I create." Many have a strong sense of the common good and of collective social and civic responsibility.

This generation wants options. Availability of choice is a deeply held value. The marketer's mantra should be "Give them options to buy their loyalty." Having grown up in a free and interactive world, artificial constraints are foreign. Even with a product as mundane as light bulbs, Net Generation consumers want information and choice regarding environmental/energy use, tone, wattage, and brand. They resent it if this information is not readily accessible. This attitude derives from surfing in a world of seemingly limitless choice.

They want to change their minds. Video games and the Net are environments in which mistakes can be immediately corrected and situations re-created. When your video game hero runs out of life because of a motor skill mistake, you just flip the reset button. A link to the wrong Web site is easily corrected with the click of the back button. Not only do they expect mistakes to be easily corrected, they want to be able to change their minds. In the words of singer/song-writer Shania Twain, "Change my mind a thousand times." Marketers should echo what she goes on to sing, "Hey, I like it that way."

As this generation enters the workforce and marketplace in developed countries, they will be a powerful force for transparency. The evidence is strong that they will scrutinize firms and other institutions like never before. They will demand choice, authenticity, and value. Once they find out something important, they have at their fingertips the most powerful tool ever for informing others and organizing.

Sociopolitical Changes:
The Rising Global Civil Foundation

Around the world, the "civil foundation," as Roger Martin has called it, is on the rise. People living and working in their communities keep adopting ever-higher standards of expectations, norms, customs, and laws that regulate—whether formally or informally—the behavior of corporations toward stakeholders.[20] Slave labor may be OK on the Ivory Coast, but don't let your company be found using it.

In the United States and Canada, the civil foundation is much higher today than even 25 years ago. Rules now cover a huge variety of activities and practices such as discrimination, smoking on the job, and sexual harassment. Many parts of the civil foundation—such as shareholder disclosure, environmental care, intellectual property rights, and consumer protection—include rules and norms that force companies to be more transparent. In many European countries (the United Kingdom, Scandinavia, France, and Germany), standards are even higher. In most rich capitalist countries, the civil foundation provides a sturdy platform for those who wish to raise standards even further.

A high civil foundation signifies a society's high integrity and values, and therefore implies that business success depends more on actual performance and genuine trust than on backroom dealings. Trust, as we have already said, is a good predictor of national economic success, so countries with a high civil foundation are most likely to enjoy higher per capita GNP growth.

Increasingly, people on all continents peer into Western businesses skeptically, hoping for fair and equitable treatment to the standard of the rising global civil foundation. The saga of basmati rice is a case in point. This national treasure had been a community resource in several regions of India for hundreds of years. The breed was not static: it evolved in the hands of farmers through personal trading, hybridization, and natural and human selection. It took off in global markets, and soon global agribusiness took note. Basmati, along with a wide variety of other indigenous agricultural products, was the target of patenting rules being lobbied to the World Trade Organization at the instigation of U.S. firms in the early 1990s. If these rules were passed, foreign corporations would control the core intellectual property of an Indian national resource. Indian farmers took notice.

On October 2, 1993, half a million Indian farmers joined a daylong procession in Bangalore to protest the proposed rules. Accusing Cargill, the world's largest agribusiness, of biopiracy, a group of protestors ransacked one of its facilities. The demonstrators pledged to protect "sovereignty over our seeds" with a program to support the free exchange of seeds among farmers, along with the protection and development of community intellectual property rights.

In 1995 the WTO went ahead and adopted rules that called on countries to patent their native seeds. Such measures could then provide a basis for commercial exploitation by multinationals who would sell the patented seeds back to local farmers and genetically engineer new strains on top of the original patents. Essentially, it was a legal framework to facilitate handing over indigenous intellectual property shared in community "commons" to corporations.

In the midst of this battle, RiceTec, a small Texas company, filed 20 U.S. patent claims that covered natural basmati rice, the name "basmati" itself, and three unique strains that it had developed. One was (and still is) retailed as Texmati. Under these patents RiceTec would "own" India's indigenous strains of basmati rice. Indian exporters could then theoretically have been forced to pay RiceTec for the right to sell their produce in the United States, as well as license fees to use the name "basmati." This resulted in a huge international furor, a massive outcry in the Indian media (barely a peep in the United States, however), and broad support from a variety of (mostly European and Indian) NGOs, the Indian government (which presented a counter-case to the U.S. patent office), and even India's archrival, the government of Pakistan (where basmati is also an important crop).

The U.S. Patent Office made its ruling in August 2001. A RiceTec spokesperson described it as "a Solomon type result." The company withdrew some of its broad claims and the Patent Office threw out the rest. It did, however, grant RiceTec patents for Texmati and two other hybrids. It also ruled the name "basmati" a generic term rather than one that, like champagne, is reserved to a place of origin. In other words, U.S. growers or seed manufacturers could use the name basmati if they wished. The resulting uproar in India, as all along, was heavily debated in Parliament and the national press. The government claimed victory, but others weren't so sure.

This is one example of how the rise of global trade and institutions like the WTO create new kinds of pressures. Transparency cuts many ways. It provides information and ideas to cloners like RiceTec who seek new kinds of monopolies. Their strategy: use global legal processes to privatize—render opaque—what for centuries has been in a transparent indigenous commons. But transparency also enables these communities to defend their interests. The new arrangements remain to be worked out, and at time of writing the uncertainties of this global battle loom larger than ever.

Fusion of Economics, Technology, and Sociopolitical Changes

The economic, technological, and sociopolitical are converging in emerging economies. In many countries these changes will happen quickly. While the digital divide between haves and have-nots will not be filled completely, the growth of information and communications technologies in emerging economies will change the balance of power. Some indications of where this is going are:

- By 2001 the pace of Internet expansion in the United States had slowed down to 15 percent, while it was 36 percent in Latin America and 46 percent in Asia and Africa. In the same year, the number of Internet users in Asia surpassed those in Europe and North America for the first time.

- In 2001 China had as many Internet users (34 million) as all of Africa and Latin America combined, and more than the United Kingdom, Australia, and New Zealand together. It had one-quarter as many Internet users as the United States.

- Mobile telephones have outpaced fixed-line telephones in developing countries; expect the same with the mobile Internet. China has the largest number of mobile telephone subscribers in the world (170 million mid-2002) and is projected to have over 400 million by the middle of the decade. Latin America is forecast to have 50 million mobile Internet users by 2005.

- Short message service (SMS) allows people to send and receive text messages via their mobile phones. In Singapore, China, and the Philippines, half of all telephone users utilize SMS more than once a day. In January 2001, thousands of Filipinos, unhappy with the corrupt government of President Joseph Estrada, took to the streets and forced him to resign. SMS played a key role in stimulating and organizing the protests. First it was used to send political jokes; then users spread the word on demonstration sites.

- Much Internet commerce in developing countries will be mobile, including micropayments, financial services, information services, and business services like logistics and customer relationship management.

- In 2000, developing countries originated 36 percent of the world's exports of information technology (IT) products, mainly due to the outsourcing of manufacturing by global corporations. The value of IT exports from developing countries now exceeds the total value of their agriculture, textile, and clothing exports. China, Korea, and several other countries are now building homegrown IT product companies, which increasingly compete in global markets. Several countries, such as India, Pakistan, the Philippines, and Malaysia, are global exporters of software and services.

- Major information and communications technologies firms, including Hewlett-Packard, IBM, Microsoft, and Motorola, have invested tens—even hundreds—of millions of dollars to build their own capabilities in countries like China and India. They all want to participate as sellers in these markets as the opportunities mature.

As emerging economy firms and citizens become integrated into the global economy, they will perforce learn to live with pressure for transparency in their business practices. They will also increasingly expect—and gain the ability to demand—visibility into Western firms' business practices, and monitor any Western governments' preferential support for these business practices. Both emerging economy and Western firms will be under increasing pressure to practice what they preach about open trade and level playing fields, as well as to behave responsibly toward people and the environment. Technology and economic participation will strengthen the visibility, market clout, and moral power of such demands.

The tale about basmati rice illustrates that transparency and trust have their limits—and their opponents. We take a close look at these issues in Chapter 2.

CHAPTER 2

TRANSPARENCY VERSUS OPACITY: THE BATTLE

Transparency may in general be a good thing, but it's not always the right thing nor may it always be practical. And it has its enemies. Transparency can be controversial, poorly executed, or placed at risk. All in all, while the world is becoming more open, there are many obstacles to complete transparency, some valid and some not.

OBSTACLES TO TRANSPARENCY

Limits of Knowledge

We can only take action on what we know. Critical information, like Enron's role in manipulating the California energy markets, may not become known in a timely manner. Information, events, and complexity tend to increase geometrically. Science and technology have limits. Indeed, the more we know, the more we realize what we don't know. As H. L. Mencken once said, "Penetrating so many secrets, we cease to believe in the unknowable. But there it sits licking its chops."

Environmental impacts are often only discovered after they become irreversible. A 2002 study by the World Bank, the World Resources Institute, and the United Nations said that several ecosystems are fraying under the impact of human activity and that in the future, ecosystems will be less able than in the past to deliver the goods and services on which human life depends. The study concludes, "It's hard, of course, to know what will be truly sustainable" because "our knowledge of ecosystems has increased dramatically, but it simply has not kept pace with our ability to alter them." In another study, the World Economic Forum reached a similar conclusion: "Businessmen always say, 'What matters gets measured.' . . . Yet look at environmental policy, and the data are lousy."

The good news is that, thanks to technology, we chip away at the mountain. Says Daniel Esty of Yale University, "I see a revolution in environmental data collection coming because of computing power, satellite mapping, remote sensing and other such information technologies."[1] One example is the long-running battle between U.S. midwestern states, which are heavy coal users, and northeastern states, which suffer from acid rain. Technology helped prove New York's claim that its acid rain problem was not just the result of home-grown pollution.

The Business Value of Secrets

Much of a company's information is rightly confidential, whether for competitive or for privacy reasons. Innovations, market entry plans, proprietary business methods, pending mergers and acquisitions, and a host of other matters must be kept secret for varying periods of time.

Parties to a transaction also benefit from information asymmetries. Your car dealer may have more information about the problems with your car than you do. You may know more about your health than your life insurance company. Parties will attempt to gain advantage through a monopoly over information if they can.

Firms have ethical obligations of confidentiality as well. They must protect employee records, customer information, and the like. Transparency means visibility into the operations of institutions, not the personal information of individuals. Experience shows that good privacy policies pay off.[2]

Firms sometimes have good business reasons to be opaque and play in the Danger Zone. But the Danger Zone can be risky, as the Kellogg's corn dog fiasco illustrates.

These are shifting sands. What yesterday was considered proprietary (executive compensation, for example) is today on the public record. Some firms, following strategy guru Michael Porter's long-proven advice, preannounce plans to outflank the competition, while others play close to the chest. Even in areas formerly considered competitive and proprietary, transparency is changing the rules. The open source model of fostering innovation, such as with the Linux computer operating system, relies on cocreation and aggressive transparency on matters that some firms still consider proprietary. Open source has scored major successes: Linux, for example, has migrated from the fringe to the mainstream.

The Cost of Openness

Active transparency costs money for new organizational functions, tracking and reporting, interaction with stakeholders, and outside auditing. For a small or low-margin business, such expenses can be practically a showstopper. Borland Software, a California company with $300 million in sales, says that the 2002 Sarbanes-Oxley rules for corporate disclosure result in new bills of $3 million a year, about 10 percent of its earnings. This is due to the added costs of accounting scrutiny, legal help including two newly hired in-house attorneys dedicated to compliance, and $1 million in added director and officer insurance costs.[3]

Companies like BP, Ford, and Hewlett-Packard spend millions on social responsibility staff, annual sustainability reports, external verification, consultants, and the like. The business case exists, but each company needs to make it.

Even when the spirit is willing and the money is there, few firms have a culture of transparency and most need to invest time and money to build the required processes and infrastructures.

Pseudo-Transparency and Deceit

Active transparency strives to be inclusive: to address the aspirations and needs of all stakeholders.[4] And it aspires to be trustworthy: verifiably material and true. In the past, some firms have benefited from opacity and dishonesty. Today, more companies than we care to imagine still maintain old practices. Others, understanding the growing demand for candor, present themselves as open though they change little in their values and management style.

Faking it—what we call pseudo-transparency—is likely to result in information overload, confusion, bad communication, or whitewashing. SustainAbility, a U.K. firm, publishes—in partnership with the UN Environment Program—a global survey on the quality of corporate reporting related to financial, environmental, and social practices.

Its 2002 report points out that few companies around the world provide this scope of transparency reporting, and of those that do, a mere handful have adopted rigorous reporting methodologies. Many companies excluded from SustainAbility's top 50 engage in what some call "greenwash"—self-promotion in the guise of transparency.

SustainAbility points favorably to "the invasion of the suits," as companies increasingly draw on the services of blue-chip accounting firms and consultants to audit and validate not only financial but also environmental and social reports.

By the way, only 5 of SustainAbility's 50 top-rated reporting companies are headquartered in the United States: Bristol-Myers Squibb, Baxter International, Chiquita Brands International, General Motors, and Procter & Gamble. Three (Suncor Energy, BC Hydro, and Alcan) are Canadian.

Transparency Literacy

A lack of experience with transparency can lead to missteps on the frontier of openness. It will take time for businesses to become literate about transparency, to understand its dynamics and boundaries, and to develop the competency and skill required to manage in an open economy. Corporate transparency requires its own form of literacy. As the online bookselling leader, Amazon often sails in uncharted waters. In September 1999 the company introduced "purchase circles," which disclosed the book preferences of its corporate customers. Amazon revealed that customers from Microsoft were snapping up *The Microsoft File: The Secret Case Against Bill Gates* by Wendy Goldman Rohm. Amazon's review said the book "paints a harsh and unforgiving picture that's not at all flattering to Gates or the rest of Microsoft's top brass." Meanwhile, a book on Linux was a hot seller at Intel.

Amazon.com spokesman Paul Capelli called purchase circles a "discovery tool." "We know that people don't make purchases in a vacuum," he said. "You buy things based on what others around you are buying or what they have to say. You look to family, friends, or neighbors. What purchase circles do is allow insight into groups of people that may have significance for you."[5]

Some customers, however, thought Amazon's innovation was voyeuristic. Buyers were uncomfortable with the idea that their book purchases might reflect poorly on their employers or betray a corporate agenda, and the disclosure made them feel as if someone were looking over their shoulders. After asking employees for their reaction to the Amazon program, IBM CEO and chairman Louis Gerstner received five thousand email responses within hours. More than 90 percent objected to having their book-buying habits as a group disclosed online. After IBM complained, Amazon removed its purchase circle listings. Gerstner wrote to Amazon CEO Jeff Bezos saying, "I'm certainly not going to tell you how to run your business, but I do urge you to view this as an enormously important issue."[6]

The negative reaction forced the company to modify the service. Today customers can ask that their information not be used in generating purchase circle lists, and companies can tell Amazon to de-list them. Some privacy advocates insist such policies are still wanting, since the burden is on the consumer or company to opt out. Amazon says the feature is popular and now offers purchase circles based on geography, educational institution, industries, and government departments.

This amazing story shows that businesses must become transparency literate to better understand what transparency means and how to harness its power.

Structural Obstacles

While the world becomes more open, structural supports for opacity continue to rise. United States litigiousness dissuades companies from revealing more than they need to; the main blockers of transparency within firms are often their own lawyers.

A May 2002 California Supreme Court 4–3 decision against Nike led many to conclude that social and environmental reporting would become more risky in the future. The court ruled that when Nike had denied reports that workers were mistreated in the Asian factories that manufactured its shoes, the company's statements constituted "commercial speech," and were therefore not covered by the First Amendment.

At issue were statements about the factory conditions in press releases and correspondence sent out by Nike in 1997, including a letter to the editor, that said the sneaker company was doing a good job with overseas labor but could do better. "Because in the statements at issue here Nike was acting as a commercial speaker, because its intended audience was primarily the buyers of its products and because the statements consisted of factual representations about its own business operations, we conclude that the statements were commercial speech for purposes of applying state laws designed to prevent false advertising and other forms of commercial deception," wrote Justice Joyce Kennard for the majority. The action had been brought against Nike by environmental activist Marc Kasky. Nike appealed to the U.S. Supreme Court, which in June 2003 sent it back to the state courts. In the meantime, the effect of the ruling has been that companies could be sued and penalized if their social or environmental reporting broke truth-in-advertising regulations. As a result, Nike has said it will not issue such reports until the case is resolved.

Bigger potential threats loom. War and national security may be used to justify restrictions on free speech and information access. Also, as Lawrence Lessig argues, there is a real danger that the Internet of tomorrow will be less open and free than the Internet of today.[7]

Transparency Fatigue and Paralysis

As the world becomes more open, information proliferates and individuals face increasing numbers of ever more complex choices, possibly to the point of paralysis. Ignorance may not be bliss, but it's less work. Now that I know the effects of carbon combustion on global warming, should I dump my SUV? Should I accept a job with Exxon despite its environmental policies? Should I leave my broker that has been fined for conflict of interest between research and investment banking? This is more than information overload. It is choice overload.

Similarly, some business executives are showing fatigue from scrutiny, perhaps leading to "transparency paralysis" as seminaked corporate executives fear making moves that might further expose them to controversy. Exhibit A? With the extended cratering of the stock market, companies are cheap. Billions of dollars sit in corporate treasuries; there are dozens of overexposed sitting ducks and all sorts of industries in crises of overcapacity—airlines, automotive, financial services, you name it. One would expect lots of merger and acquisition activity. But all there has been is a handful of big deals. Few are buying these bargains.

Gordon Nixon, CEO of RBC—a financial services firm with assets approaching $300 billion—says that transparency is causing business executives to act like politicians and consider how a decision will be perceived rather than its economic merits. Some executives may retreat to fortress thinking. Others, paralyzed by fear of scrutiny, may hesitate to make the bold moves they need to succeed. Hewlett-Packard CEO Carly Fiorina showed courage when she led her company to acquire Compaq in May 2002. The evidence so far suggests it was a good move. But the flak she received from shareholders and commentators has not gone unnoticed by others. Maybe, for example, we'd see more foreign direct investment if companies weren't worried about the supersensitive, politicized business environment.

The New Power for Obfuscation

The Internet's transparency is a double-edged sword. It is a tool for information access, verification, and discovery. But it can also be used to deceive. A 2003 Federal Trade Commission study found that two-thirds of all spam contains inaccurate information. Just about anyone can put up a Web site claiming virtually anything. Parody Web sites and campaigns illustrate this duality. Are they vehicles for transparency, opacity, or both?

December 3, 2002 was the eighteenth anniversary of the chemical disaster in Bhopal, India, where an accident in a Union Carbide plant caused poisoned gas emissions that killed 4,000 residents in their sleep and injured several hundred thousand others. On that day journalists around the world received via email a press release appearing to be from Dow Chemical, which inherited the Bhopal issue after it acquired Union Carbide. In the press release, Dow apologized for the death and suffering caused by the industrial accident and explained that its hands were tied on the matter of financial compensation to the victims. The company's first allegiance, it said, was to shareholders and the paramount need to ensure a healthy bottom line. "We understand the anger and hurt. But Dow does not and cannot acknowledge responsibility. If we did, not only would we be required to expend many billions of dollars on cleanup and compensation—much worse, the public could then point to Dow as a precedent in other big cases. 'They took responsibility; why can't you?' Amoco, BP, Shell, and

Exxon all have ongoing problems that would just get much worse. We are unable to set this precedent for ourselves and the industry, much as we would like to see the issue resolved in a humane and satisfying way." For information, the release referred the readers to www.Dow-Chemical.com.

The overbearing attitude of the widely circulated press release sparked thousands of complaints. But the complainers had been duped; Dow had no connection to either the press release or the site. Both were hoaxes, the production of the Yes Men, a group of Internet activists who had earlier gained notoriety for bogus sites satirizing the World Trade Organization and the General Agreement on Tariffs and Trade. The press release and site attracted enormous negative publicity for Dow. Dow's lawyers quickly forced the original hoax site to shut down, but another spoof site, dowethics.com, picked up its content. It offers this tongue-in-cheek corporate boast: "Did you know . . . Dow is responsible for the birth of the modern environmental movement. Rachel Carson's 1962 book *Silent Spring,* about the side effects of a Dow product, DDT, led to a groundswell of concern and the birth of many of today's environmental action groups. Another example of Dow's commitment to Living. Improved daily."

The site goes on to parody various PR initiatives of the company, such as www.bhopal.com, an authentic Dow-sponsored site that presents the company's position on Bhopal.

Corporate parody sites are a spin-off of the boom in political parody sites. Virtually every politician with a recognizable name has been skewered by mock sites. A parody site so angered George W. Bush during the presidential election campaign that his officials petitioned the FCC to shut it down. When told the Constitution's freedom of speech provisions protected parody sites, Bush uttered his famous remark "There ought to be a limit to freedom." The Bush campaign's reaction immediately caused the parody site's audience to soar. In May 1999, the site received 6 million hits, while the candidate's official site received 30,000.

Parody sites can confuse people, as the Dow story illustrates. With off-the-shelf software and a few spare hours critics can savagely ridicule any company. Appreciative audiences easily forward the bogus press release or site address to friends around the world. The same viral marketing that made Napster an overnight success can now pummel an unsuspecting company with sarcasm. As George W. Bush discovered to his chagrin, trying to crush a parody site simply boosts its notoriety and drives up traffic. The only real defense is to behave in a manner that doesn't invite ridicule.

THE GEOPOLITICAL CONTEXT

We have already mentioned companies that aggressively resist being open.

- Fidelity and other big mutual funds want to keep their proxy votes secret. They say it's because of cost and the need to keep politics out of business decisions. Many suspect it's because Fidelity has a conflict of interest as provider of services (like the management of employees' 401(k) retirement accounts) to companies whose shares it owns.

- RiceTec sought patents on the name and genetic coding of basmati rice, with the goal of privatizing—rendering opaque—the common intellectual property of India's farmers.

- Kellogg failed to disclose the genetically modified contents of its corn dog and paid the price when Greenpeace revealed the information.

But the battles around openness are being fought on a much broader front.

In 2002–03, political leadership, terrorism, war, and compliant media combined in the United States to pose challenges to disclosure, transparency, and indeed freedom of expression. Some have charged that the government is using national security to strengthen opacity. Information restrictions are necessary in areas related to national security. But a broader atmosphere of secrecy provides an example that like-minded business leaders can point to. Meanwhile, the government enacts some measures that protect opaque business practices that arguably *threaten* security or are irrelevant to it.

The Homeland Security Act of 2002 gives the Department of

Homeland Security broad powers to receive information from corporations about weaknesses in the country's "critical infrastructure." This information becomes automatically exempt from the Freedom of Information Act. Companies also gain immunity from civil liability if the information reveals wrongdoing, and immunity from antitrust suits for sharing the information with the government and each other.[8]

United States Senator Patrick Leahy, a Vermont Democrat, believes these exemptions will be counterproductive. He said they would "encourage government complicity with private firms to keep secret information about critical infrastructure vulnerabilities, reduce the incentive to fix the problems and end up hurting rather than helping our national security. In the end, more secrecy may undermine rather than foster security."

Leahy also described impacts that have no bearing on national security. For example, if a company submits information that its factory leaches arsenic in ground water, "that information no longer could be used in a civil or criminal proceeding brought by local authorities or by the neighbors who were harmed by drinking the water."

Meanwhile, public support for the underpinnings of transparency has weakened. Since 1999 the Freedom Forum has surveyed Americans on the following question:

> The First Amendment became part of the US Constitution more than 200 years ago. This is what it says: "Congress shall make no law respecting an establishment of religion or prohibiting the free exercise thereof; or abridging the freedom of speech, or of the press; or the right of the people peaceably to assemble, and to petition the Government for a redress of grievances." [Do you agree or disagree with the statement] The First Amendment goes too far in the rights it guarantees?

In 1999, only 28 percent of respondents replied that the First Amendment goes too far, and in 2000, this number dropped to 22 percent. But it jumped to 39 percent in 2001 and to 49 percent in 2002. Furthermore, according to the survey, the least popular First Amendment right is freedom of the press: 42 percent of respondents said the press has too much freedom to do what it wants, 40 percent said that newspapers should not be allowed to freely criticize the military, and so on.

Globalization has unleashed new, often invisible forces that frame the issues differently but the results are similar. World Economic Forum senior adviser Claude Smadja comments:

> The decisions that affect my life—whether my job will be eliminated, will I have a mortgage with higher interest rates, what returns I'll get as an investor—are being made by vague institutions and organizations. The taste of beer I drink is decided by European Union bureaucrats in Brussels. There is increased opacity. In the old world, if the corporation did well my job was secure and I could anticipate a raise. Now if my corporation does well my job may be more at risk. My company can decide to rationalize production or move our plant to a cheaper geography. Or, this guy John Smith shows up here occasionally. He's a consultant of some kind; I don't know who he is but I know he has huge control over my life. Today a bunch of young fund managers in a room in London, New York or elsewhere decide that my national currency is a bad risk, interest rates go up, and it's harder for me to pay for my house. I don't know what I'm eating: ten years ago I didn't need to ask myself if my corn is genetically modified.

Such shifts are unfortunate, because the costs of opacity are immeasurable. Let's dig deeper.

THE COSTS OF OPACITY

On July 18, 1997, the world awoke to an alarming wave of selling that was devastating currencies and stocks in financial markets across Asia, Latin America, and Europe. Massive waves of capital fled into safe havens as investors lost faith in previously booming developing economies. A series of bankruptcies began. As the meltdown continued over the following months, Malaysian prime minister Mahathir Mohamad charged George Soros and other international investors with sucking the wind out of his country's economy. The Asian financial crisis lasted three years, spilling over to Wall Street and Western economies. A similar crisis hit Russia in 1998.

These crises brought transparency to the fore. Several factors caused the problems, in particular an Asian financial bubble that presaged the Internet economy of the late 1990s. Many claimed that lack of transparency was one of the causes. Western politicians, economists, and media identified emerging economy corruption, nepotism, and favoritism—along with poor corporate governance—as drivers of the meltdown. Lack of disclosure by companies, commercial banks, and even central banks had fanned the crisis. The International Monetary Fund (IMF) in particular declared that, henceforth, transparency must be the "golden rule for a globalized economy" and that it would take charge of strengthening the supervision of financial and banking systems in developing countries.

Under strong pressure, many emerging economy leaders opened their economic systems to new levels of international scrutiny. In retrospect, some analysts—notably Joseph Stiglitz—have argued that the transparency issue raised by the IMF was itself a smokescreen designed to mask the failures of its own aggressive policies of economic liberalization. The corruption charges also masked the extent to which Malaysian prime minister Mahathir Mohamad was right in his claim—at the time dismissed as bombast—that the crisis resulted more from international speculative money flows than from the fiscal policies of emerging economies. Countries most hurt by the crisis, like Thailand, Russia, and Indonesia, were those that had most thoroughly bought into the IMF's prescriptions.[9] Meanwhile, equally opaque but much more protectionist countries like China and Poland, which relied on the state to manage more careful and incremental market liberalization, weathered the storm much better.

The costs were big. Millions lost jobs across Asia. In many countries interest rates—the cost of capital for business expansion and consumer purchases—mushroomed to 50 percent and more for over two years. Share prices collapsed, further crippling the ability of businesses to raise capital. The international financial community forked over $110 billion in bailouts to Indonesia, South Korea, and Thailand alone.[10] Foreign business investments in emerging markets plummeted from $280 billion in 1997 to $150 billion in 1998, then languished around $180 billion for several years. Interest rates that emerging-economy governments had to pay on their bonds became and remained much higher. The average premium over U.S. government bonds shot up from 5 percent precrisis to over 13 percent, then slowly faded to 7.5 percent by mid-2001. Today, many Asian economies are recovering. South Korea is a star. But investors remain far more selective about putting their money into emerging economies and exact a much higher price when they do.

This crisis spawned a new mini-industry, the transparency industry. In 1997 the Organization for Economic Cooperation and Development (OECD) passed an antibribery convention. Transparency International (TI), formed in 1993, became a focal point for exposing and fighting political corruption in emerging economies. Corruption, in the old-fashioned sense of envelopes stuffed with cash, is something that happens in secret, hence Transparency International's name and focus.

The TI *Global Corruption Report 2001* includes articles and research from over a dozen agencies and organizations, including the IMF, the United Nations, the U.S. government, academics, and consulting firms. While transparency was the catchphrase, the focus was corruption, particularly government corruption. Despite politically correct mentions of rich-country issues (like U.S. campaign finance), the target was government bribery in poor countries. Corporate transparency and governance received short shrift. Typically, Western firms were depicted mainly as victims (sometimes as willing accomplices), forced to cope with (or choosing to pander to) shakedowns by sleazy local politicians and officials. A TI survey reported that 74 percent of all publications on corruption between 1990 and 1999 focused on politics and public administration, only 1 percent on business ethics.[11] Transparency, a real issue, was merchandised as a salutory matchup between the bad effects of corruption on developing economies and the desires of multinational corporations to reduce transaction costs.

Despite the shaky motives of some of those (like the IMF) who surfaced the issue, the costs of corruption in emerging economies were and remain all too real. Transparency International and its partners have shed the light of transparency on many specific examples of endemic corruption, illuminated its costs, and convinced growing numbers of leaders to tackle the problem. In so doing, they built the elements of a cost impact case that now can be applied to the 2002 rich-country corporate governance crisis.

- Transparency International's 2001 corruption perception index ranked more than 120 countries on the use of public power for private benefit, on the basis of a composite of expert sources. The least corrupt top 24 on the list were rich market economies. Finland, with a score of 9.9 out of 10, came first. The United States, ranked sixteenth, scored badly relative to its peers, an embarrassing 7.6. It ranked below Singapore, Canada, Australia, the United Kingdom, and Hong Kong but above Germany, Japan, and France.

- TI also surveyed business leaders in 14 major emerging market economies such as Brazil, India, and Russia to learn which countries that invest in emerging economies are least likely to house companies that pay bribes. Again, the United States showed up in the middle of the pack, outdone by Sweden, Australia, Canada, the United Kingdom, and others (i.e., these states were less apt to host bribe payers than the United States); the United States rated better than Singapore, Japan, Italy, and China. Other surveys rated U.S. companies among the most likely to have antibribery codes of conduct. But in the absence of transparent and verifiable reporting—and given the perceptions of emerging market leaders—U.S. firms' virtuous codes of conduct may not predict virtuous behavior.

- In another survey, respondents ranked the U.S. government as by far the most likely to engage in questionable practices like diplomatic and political pressure, commercial pressure, dumping, financial pressure, tied aid, official gifts, tied defense, and arms deals.

- Corruption, according to TI's research, detracts from economic, social, and environmental performance. It diminishes science and technology; it is often employed by those who cause direct harm to air quality and water quality—among other measures. In other words, corruption corrodes the foundations of sustainable competition.

A parallel PricewaterhouseCoopers (PwC) study looked at the costs of opacity, "the lack of clear, accurate, formal, easily discernible, and widely accepted practices" in the business environment. Its expert survey of 35 (mostly emerging) economies rated corruption and four other areas of concern: the legal and judicial environment including shareholder rights, economic policy, accounting and corporate governance, and regulatory uncertainty/arbitrariness.

Believe it or not, respondents rated Singapore as least opaque (i.e., most transparent) on these business criteria; its weak record on civil rights was not factored in. The United States, Chile, and the United Kingdom followed closely. Then PwC quantified the impact of opacity as if it were a tax on foreign investment or an incremental cost of doing business, with Singapore as the zero baseline. The United States's opacity tax was measured as 5 percent, Hong Kong's 12 percent, Mexico's 15 percent, Japan's 25 percent, and China's 46 percent. PwC also assigned an opacity risk premium to each country, equivalent to the amount of interest above the U.S. level that opacity would add to the cost of government bonds. Hong Kong's risk premium came out at 2.3 percent, Mexico's 3.1 percent, Japan's 6.3 percent, and China's 13.2 percent.

By early 2001, the international policy community, spearheaded by many U.S. experts, was teaching several lessons from the Asian financial crisis. First, opacity combined with corruption and self-dealing can cause deep and sustained economic crises. Second, opacity hurts businesses and raises their transaction costs. Investors lose trust, withdraw from capital markets, and increase the price they exact from companies for loans and investments. Third, opacity costs taxpayers—businesses and consumers—as governments are forced to intervene with bailouts and social safety nets, while their cost of borrowing increases due to the opacity risk premium.

All the research we've cited was pre-Enron. In the PwC survey, U.S. respondents were highly optimistic about the quality and impact of accounting standards in their own business environment. From the beginnings of the Asian crisis through early 2001, U.S. commentators, often supported by leaders of global institutions like the IMF and World Bank, preached that the U.S. system of corporate disclosure was the model for the rest of the world to emulate.

Enron and the shock and scandals that followed silenced the preachers as they realized that their claimed causes of the Asian financial crisis applied to the United States: the chickens had come home to roost. Opacity combined with corruption and self-dealing had led to a deep economic crisis. The crisis may not turn out to be as sustained as it was in Asia because of the fundamental strengths of the U.S. economy (though current fiscal and disclosure policies further undermine this strength). But the costs of the 2002 meltdown will remain with us for a long time. The crisis has hurt many businesses. Investors withdrew from capital markets and set higher performance hurdles as a precondition for their return. Although the cost of borrowing declined rather than increased, this was because the fallout from the transparency crisis (combined with a trade deficit, industrial overcapacity, and productivity growth) delayed a recovery from recession. As a result, the Federal Reserve continued to push rates down. But even though interest rates were low, risk money remained hard to get.

Specific costs of the U.S. transparency crisis were clear and diverse. Enron's fraudulent, semiconcealed off–balance sheet activities and subsequent bankruptcy destroyed $90 billion of market capitalization, 21,000 jobs, and a major accounting firm (Arthur Andersen) and helped dash the retirement plans of millions of Americans. WorldCom could have avoided its fiasco if it had come clean about the losses on its balance sheet instead of disguising them as expenses. It falsified over $7 billion in costs and went into bankruptcy with debts of $41 billion. These and other failed companies created billions of dollars in bad debts for banks and other lending institutions. The federal government opened more than 100 corporate crime investigations and charged over 150 people with fraud. The trustworthiness of Wall Street's biggest names—Goldman Sachs, Citibank, Merrill Lynch, Morgan Stanley, and Credit Suisse First Boston—was cast into doubt. Brokerage firms eventually faced fines of $1.4 billion and laid off thousands of employees as millions of individuals dropped out of the stock market.

The damage swelled into a market panic reminiscent of the days of the Robber Barons. From March 19, 2002, to July 19, 2002—the peak of the transparency crisis—Standard & Poor's 500 index lost 28 percent of its value, dropping from 1170 to 848, long after the technology stock bubble had burst. In an August 2002 analysis, the Brookings Institution estimated that for as long as the transparency crisis prevents the stock market from recovering to March 2002 levels, it will cost the U.S. economy a significant—and ever-growing—portion of its gross domestic product due to reduced consumer buying and business spending.[12] Specifically, it forecasted a reduction in gross domestic product between 0.20 and 0.48 percent over a one-year period (equivalent to $21 billion to $50 billion), compounding to 0.50 to 1.19 percent over three years and 1.05 to 2.50 percent over ten years.

The Brookings forecast assumed no corrective action. But the cost of the crisis was all too obvious to government and business leaders. Steps were taken to improve both the appearance and realities of corporate transparency beginning in early August, starting with congressional hearings and legislation. In hopes that the worst was over, by late fall, the markets started to improve. A springtime rally pushed the S&P up to the 1000 range by early July 2003; this was still well below its precrisis peak. Investors remained skittish.

STAKEHOLDER WEBS: COUNTERVAILS TO OPACITY

Whether it knows it or not, every company has a stakeholder web (s-web), maybe several. A stakeholder web is a network of stakeholders that scrutinizes and attempts to influence a corporation's behavior. Recently many have studied these networks and given them different names including transparency networks, corporate responsibility clusters, network armies, and smart mobs. But as business critic Amy Cortese says, "Whatever you choose to call them, these forces are products of the Internet Age, united not by geography but by common cause and technology that lets them communicate freely and instantly."[13]

A key characteristic of many s-webs is self-organization. Self-organizing systems, such as the open source movement that produced Linux, are fundamentally different from—often subversive of—traditional hierarchical organizations. They display "intentional emergence," whereby strong patterns emerge from complex, initially random systems, through the application of a few simple rules. Emergence has captured the imagination of scientists, researchers, and analysts in many disciplines including biology, mathematics, and economics. Unlike most naturally occurring emergent systems, humans apply intentionality in many of their emergent systems. They make deliberate choices, on the basis of their ideas, goals, and desires. Nonetheless the cumulative effect is self-organized rather than orchestrated.

Stakeholder webs actively investigate, evaluate, and seek to change the behaviors of institutions (such as corporations) to achieve better alignment with the values and interests of their participants.

Seven Characteristics of Stakeholder Webs

1. The Embodiment of Transparency

Transparency is not an amorphous, disembodied force. Its tangible expression, the s-web, realizes the ability of stakeholders to find out information, inform others, and self-organize. S-web participants connect via interactive media like the Internet, email, the telephone, instant messaging, fax, and face-to-face communications. They also use traditional print, radio, and television mass media. The new transparency increases the power and influence of s-webs.

S-web structures and behaviors—made possible by the Internet—very much resemble it. A s-web works very differently from a typical top-down company or business web. Its modus operandi is peer collaboration rather than hierarchical control. Like the Internet's, an s-web's structure is highly distributed. A s-web is highly adaptive: it can spring into action quickly and fade just as fast. Instead of spending energy trying to tear down obstacles, it routes itself around them. Ironically, there is often considerable opacity within a s-web, as various participants may not be fully aware of who the other members are.

Nestlé's stakeholders (Figure 2.1) focused initially on the company's reported efforts to encourage mothers in developing countries to abandon breast feeding in favor of using its packaged infant formula. More recently the chocolate industry was rocked by revelations that its supply chain was tainted by child slavery, in turn changing the composition and activity within Nestlé s-web. The effects rippled from NGOs to nearly all the company's stakeholders. Some customers were turned off by the stigma of eating chocolate made by slaves, employees were demoralized by bad press, supply chain partners were forced to raise standards and participate in new monitoring systems, and investors worried that the scandal might affect the firm's stock price and long-term prospects.

2. Varying Participant Motives and Roles

S-web players can be motivated for a variety of reasons. Religious groups use moral principles to examine and change corporate behav-

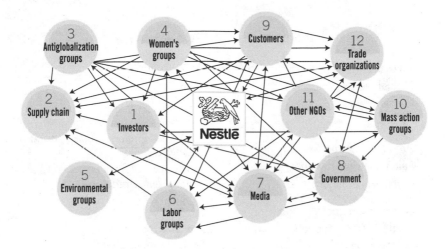

Figure 2.1 Nestlé's Stakeholder Web

ior. Some players, such as employees who organize to change a company's pension policy or shareholders who try to force a company to adopt good governance, are motivated by self-interest. Some have an ideological motivation, ranging from a desire for better corporate citizenship to a desire to weaken corporations and end corporate power. Some may turn out to be agents of competitors. Government regulators are mandated to uphold the law.

Participants also play different roles. Some s-web participants act as leaders, coordinating the rules and activities of others. The AFL-CIO is central to the s-web that scrutinizes Coca-Cola, coordinating investigations, exposés, and activities aimed at changing labor practices in the company's bottling plants. Some play the role of *content provider*, researching and communicating critical information to other members. Greenpeace provided intelligence to the Rainforest Action Network about Home Depot's old-growth-forest logging. Some play other roles—linking to the corporation, amplifying and relaying communications to other network participants, conducting litigation, proposing shareholder resolutions, and so on.

Malcolm Gladwell describes three kinds of people (the same model could also be applied to organizations) who play special roles in mobilizing human networks: Connectors, Mavens, and Salesmen.[14] Connectors know lots of other well-connected, influential people; they also

Participants in Nestle's A-web

Investors
Mutual Funds
Pension Funds
Others

Antiglobalization Groups
Fair Trade Foundation
Globalexchange.org

Women's Groups
Women's Reproduction Health
    Initiative
Mothering Magazine

Media
BBC
Knight Ridder
New York Times

Government
Ivorian Government
British Government
Government of Burkina Faso
U.S. Department of Labor
U.S. Department of Defense
U.S. Agency for International
    Development
U.S. Government Cocoa Task
    Force
UNICEF

Mass Action Groups
Stopchildlabor.org
Elimination of Child Poverty
    (IPEC)
Hundreds of individual web
    sites providing petitions,
    letters, addresses

Supply Chain
Cargill
Archer Daniels Midland
Cocoa Farmers
Society of Commercial Agricultural
    Product of Daloa

Environment Groups
Greenpeace

Labor Groups
Global March against Child Labor
International Labor Organization
Anti-Slavery International
Free the Slaves

Customers
Mothers
Teachers
Children
Individuals who set up information
    Web sites
Godiva Chocolates
Ghirardelli Chocolate

Other NGOs
Save the Children
Center for Unhindered Living

Trade Organizations
Chocolate Manufacturers
    Association
World Cocoa Foundation
National Confectioners Association
European Cocoa Commission

have a special gift for bringing the world together. Mavens are obsessive experts in a narrow field; they love to share their knowledge, and other people trust their advice. Gladwell suggests that Paul Revere, who mobilized a stakeholder web that sparked the American Revolution, was both a Connector (he knew lots of important people) and a Maven (he had the inside scoop on the British army's plans—and shared it with the important people who trusted him). The third type of mobilizer is the Salesman, a person with an infectious—sometimes subliminal—ability to persuade. Given the right situation and an effective mix of such special people, an s-web becomes an unstoppable force.

3. *Changing Dynamics*

S-webs can be relatively inactive—quiet, benign, reflective, small, stable, and slow moving. Or they can be intensely active—huge, volatile, and powerful. Several dynamics are at work:

- An s-web can move from one state to another—inactive to active, small to large, hostile to cooperative—almost instantaneously.

- Network effects come into play. A bigger network is exponentially more valuable to participants and impactful on its target.

- In s-webs, transparency works a bit like osmosis. Says researcher Anthony Williams, in networks like these, "Information flows freely from areas of high concentration to areas of low concentration where it disseminates rapidly across space and time."

- Rumors travel fast, but validation can be swift as well. Sophisticated s-webs have good nonsense detectors, because misinformation, especially when initiated by members, can hurt the network.

- Local networks can become global fast, as digital information does not respect boundaries.

- The s-web has a marvelous quality—persistence—based on its ability to archive. Information that was placed in it years ago can still be available today, ready for reuse. Similarly, linkages among s-web participants may lie dormant for a time, ready to be reactivated when needed.

4. Variable Corporate Engagement

Firms have various levels of *engagement* with their s-webs. A company may not even be aware that it is operating under the scrutiny of an s-web. Some s-webs we analyzed had no interaction at all with the target firm.

Other firms systematically engage their s-webs: to learn, influence them, or harness their power to help build a better business. Engagement pays off. Hewlett-Packard uses consumer input to identify product problems. Johnson & Johnson engages employees to ensure that its Credo guides their behavior. Shell turned parts of a hostile a-web into a network that supports its sustainability agenda.

When activity in the s-web is high while engagement is low, companies can be drawn into a trust crisis (Figure 2.2). Unengaged activity has a centrifugal effect, where the s-web migrates away from the firm and can become alienated from the firm, its values, and its activities. Conversely, lack of engagement robs a corporation of the opportunity to evolve and strengthen its values to be consistent with those of its stakeholders. For both parties, lack of engagement undermines the quest for commonly shared values, in turn generating mistrust.

5. Big Trouble: Trust Crisis

Gladwell's concept of the tipping point is an apt description of what happens when a small event suddenly turns a stakeholder web, with the force of an epidemic, from an amorphous collection of stakeholders into an uncontrollable trust crisis.[15]

New information or events can suddenly precipitate a trust crisis.[16] When Baxter International became implicated in the deaths of patients of its renal care products (for kidney treatments), the company was swept into a trust state, where everything became subservient to dealing with the trust crisis.

Most big companies have faced at least one trust crisis precipitated by a trust event. They muddled (Exxon Valdez) or managed (Johnson & Johnson Tylenol) through with varying degrees of damage or new strength. The generalized trust crisis of 2002 was precipitated by several companies that disappeared almost overnight. Trust destroyed, society revoked their license to operate.

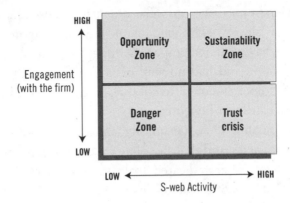

Figure 2.2 Corporate Engagement and Stakeholder Web Activity

6. *A Company's Response to a Trust Crisis: Effect on Its Future and Its Viability*

Firms have shown two diametrically opposed methods of dealing with a trust crisis. One is to use conventional public relations tactics to quell it. The other is to engage the s-web in active discussions and processes to resolve issues.

The traditional approach uses advertising, PR campaigns, spin, mis-information, criticizing the critics, spoofing (posing as an s-web mem-ber and providing phony information), pitting one group against the other, and other dirty tricks. Such approaches usually have the oppo-site to the desired effect. They tend to inflame activity in the s-web—an attack is fodder for increased communications—as participants inform others, rebut or reply to the attack, and reorganize themselves. The s-web is an organism whose antibodies gain strength by combat-ing intruders.

Engagement is a far more effective philosophy and approach. A corporate spirit of open communications, listening, consideration of participants' interests, admission of wrongdoing if appropriate, consul-tation, commitment to change, abiding by commitments, accountabil-ity, and transparency—all have the effect of reducing crisis activity and restoring trust.

Nestlé is again a case in point. A 1999 BBC documentary revealed that several cocoa plantations in the Ivory Coast used slave labor to produce the raw materials sold to chocolate retailers like Nestlé, Cadbury, and Hershey. Observers were quick to accuse the industry of complicity in slavery. The chocolate industry vigorously denied responsibility, saying that companies bought raw materials on commodity exchanges and had no way of knowing how cocoa was produced. A deadlock seemed inevitable, and many individuals and organizations called for boycotts.

But after further dialogue among antislavery NGOs, concerned government agencies, and the chocolate industry, a consensus emerged that slavery had to be eradicated from the supply chain. Everybody understood that boycotts would cause great harm, not just to the reputations and profits of manufacturers and retailers but also to the many African farmers who depend on income from cocoa production. In a July 2002 agreement the industry agreed to fund research into the extent of the problem and to take steps in cooperation with the government of the Ivory Coast to eliminate slavery. Also, an independent board consisting of a broad array of stakeholders was set up to monitor progress. A potentially explosive issue was resolved without boycotts or lawsuits, relying instead on dialogue and cooperation. And with NGOs and governments as partners, the chocolate industry can legitimately claim that its supply chains are free of slave labor.

7. A Powerful Force for Corporate Transformation

S-webs existed in pre-Internet days. But their speed of communications and therefore effectiveness was glacial. The Net supercharges an s-web, enabling it to quickly become a powerful, often global force for change.

Because engagement is the only effective way to deal with crisis, s-webs change the behavior of corporations. The firm engages, information begins to flow back and forth, both parties learn, and behavior changes. Engagement creates new feedback loops which constrain or help correct unacceptable behaviors, while encouraging new values and behaviors that conform to the expectations of the network. Anthony Williams says, "When information disclosed to the public reveals inconsistencies between the conduct of corporations and acceptable standards of behavior, network participants put new forms of accountability into motion." As we shall see, s-webs, by motivating corporations to be accountable, reward them for being trustworthy.

We live in an era in which stakeholder webs supersede government's ability to influence some behaviors of the private sector and market. Ever since the South African boycotts hastened the end of apartheid, activists have been perfecting this new kind of market campaign. Now the Internet enables stakeholders to construct far flung networks to influence corporate behavior by attacking corporate brands and mobilizing public opinion. Any company with a reputation and brand to protect is vulnerable. Even firms that are isolated from consumers can be made to acquiesce, usually by targeting the firm's partners at the retail end of the supply chain.

When we explain the notion of s-webs to business executives, some react with concern, even fear. Memo to business leaders: S-webs are good for you. They will help you be trustworthy. Engage with them, learn and build trust. Trust is the sine qua non for viability and performance in the new business environment, and s-webs are a new force for corporate success and shareholder value.

In summary, there are real limits to transparency, and forces mobilized in favor of opacity. The experience of emerging economies and of the United States clearly shows that opacity breeds corruption, market failures, and poor underlying business conditions. Stakeholder webs are an unstoppable force for a new *glasnost* in business and capitalist society. The train has left the station. Nevertheless, as we've seen, battles around openness rage on.

CHAPTER 3

THE OPEN ENTERPRISE

WHAT IS "GOOD"?

For smart firms, transparency is a corporate value, reflecting the corporate culture in general. Yet transparency brings other corporate values, as market forces require firms to rethink what they stand for and how they behave toward their various stakeholders. Transparency and corporate values have a chicken-and-egg relationship.

If words were drops of water, the literature on values and ethics would be an ocean. For millennia philosophers and clerics have struggled with the question "What is 'good'?" This book is about how transparency changes corporate values and becomes a corporate value itself—an ethical compass for navigating the stormy seas of the future. But how do we define "good" behavior?

No entrepreneur has made a bigger imprint on the U.S. retail landscape than Sam Walton, founder of the merchandising juggernaut Wal-Mart Stores, Inc. What started in 1962 as a small store in the rural backwaters of Bentonville, Arkansas, has grown to be the world's largest retailer. With 2002 sales of $245 billion, Wal-Mart's U.S. operation includes more than 2,870 discount stores, Supercenters, and Neighborhood Markets and more than 520 Sam's Clubs. Internationally, the company operates about 1,275 units. Wal-Mart employs over 1.3 million associates worldwide. It makes a big economic contribution. But is Wal-Mart a "good" company?

The company has certainly delivered value to shareholders; it is one of the most valuable firms in the world. It has also brought low-cost consumer goods to communities across the United States. Many admire Wal-Mart's success and good works. In 2001 its employees raised and contributed $196 million to support communities and local nonprofit organizations. In 2002 Wal-Mart received the Ron Brown Award, the highest presidential award for employee relations and community initiatives. In 2003, the firm was number one on *Fortune*'s "Most Admired Company in the United States" list.

Wal-Mart's extraordinary success has been the subject of many studies, but an essay in the *Journal of Retailing* perhaps captures it best:

> Wal-Mart has grown in the U.S. market because it connects itself symbolically to the dominant ideologies of American life. Through the imagery of frugality, family, religion, neighborhood, community and patriotism, Wal-Mart locates itself centrally on Main Street of a nostalgic hometown. These symbolic connections not only positively dispose shoppers to Wal-Mart but also "decouple" . . . Wal-Mart from unfavorable outcomes of its success. These consequences include local retailers being forced out of business, small town "STOP Wal-Mart" campaigns, accusations of predatory pricing and allegations about products being sourced from overseas sweatshop suppliers.[1]

As one newspaper noted, Sam Walton was "the folksy tycoon with a killer instinct."[2] The company has assiduously promoted a small-town aw-shucks veneer despite steamroller merchandising tactics that crush one competitor after another. Rather than sprinkle stores across the country more or less at random, the company methodically saturates each region with stores before moving on to the next, much like an army on the move. "We would go as far as we could from a warehouse and put in a store. Then we would fill in the map of that territory, state by state, county seat by county seat, until we had saturated the market according to area," explained Sam Walton.[3] Then, on to the next.

Rural poverty was caused, at least in part, by the fact that consumer goods were dramatically more expensive in rural America than in urban America. Sam Walton recognized this as a business opportunity. Says Red Hat cofounder Bob Young, "Arguably the most successful program to alleviate rural poverty since the Second World War has not been some government welfare program or a government agricultural subsidy program. The most successful program has been the free market at work in the form of Wal-Mart's rapid expansion serving the rural customer's demand for better service and lower prices. Wal-Mart believed so strongly in this opportunity that for the first forty years of its rapid expansion, Wal-Mart served small and mid-size rural markets exclusively."[4]

Depending on your perspective and self-interests, the arrival of Wal-Mart in your community can be invigorating or devastating. Wal-Mart creates lots of jobs in its stores; it has close to 1 million employees in the United States alone. Critics insist, however, that any community Wal-Mart moves into suffers a net loss of jobs because of the bankruptcies that ensue among local shopkeepers. They say Wal-Mart has gutted the main streets of towns across the United States. As for those who end up working for the company, it strives to keep as many as possible on a part-time basis to avoid paying benefits. The company is stridently antiunion and has crushed organizing campaigns wherever they've occurred. Yet for consumers, the retail giant provides rock-bottom prices; often Wal-Mart's retail price is lower than what small merchants pay wholesale. And if you're a supplier, a Wal-Mart deal can potentially guarantee a market for life, assuming you can survive the grueling price reductions and operational integration the company demands.

Wal-Mart illustrates the challenge of defining what is "good," or ethical, in business today. How should we evaluate the company's behavior and the values that underlie this business?

Laws and jurisprudence don't help us much. Wal-Mart claims to be a law-abiding corporate citizen (though some accuse it of forcing employees to work overtime without pay). Assuming Wal-Mart's claim is true, abiding by the letter of the law is a necessary but insufficient condition for a company to be "good."

Religions have long-established concepts of good and evil. Some thinkers propose religious morality as a basis for business morality. John Dalla Costa explains how a cross-cultural comparison of the world's religions yields a surprisingly common set of moral standards suitable for governing commerce, law, and society. Religious norms, he says, enable societies to function and develop. The Ten Commandments, for example, set a number of basic rules for human interaction. In addition to such commandments as Thou shalt not lie or kill, common religious norms include the Golden Rule (Treat thy neighbor as thyself).

However, even though Sam Walton was a religious man, it's impossible to evaluate the company according to such lofty principles.

Wal-Mart must behave in a way consistent with the values of the communities within which it operates, as a community boycott could be devastating. If its relationships with business partners become predatory, Wal-Mart will have greater difficulty building networked businesses. If the company treads in the gray areas of the law, it will attract the attention of governments, maybe causing new legislation to control unacceptable behavior. If working and environmental conditions in its suppliers' manufacturing facilities in the developing world do not meet the rising international civil foundation, it could face a Nike-style trust crisis. If Wal-Mart terminates its philanthropic initiatives, it may lose media and public support, in turn causing it grief with other stakeholders. Wal-Mart's behavior increasingly needs to correspond to the value systems of stakeholders if it is to have continued success. Collectively these value systems constitute the ethical foundation of society.

Various stakeholder markets define what is good, and markets are becoming more demanding—holding companies to higher standards. Consider how corporate values and the definition of acceptable behavior have evolved. A decade or two ago, executives routinely took their families out for dinner and submitted the bill as a business expense. They would accept courtside tickets from suppliers to take their family to a basketball game. "If I did that today I'd be shot," says Ron Ricci, vice president of positioning for Cisco Systems. "And if I did it and kept it a secret, I'd be found out too. There are systems in place here to ensure transparency and honesty. People assume you need to be open and truthful."

RETHINKING CORPORATE RESPONSIBILITY

Because of the crisis of trust, the hundred-year-old debate on corporate responsibility has never been more intense. More than ever, the debate is characterized by emotion, vagueness, and confusion.

There are three dominant perspectives regarding the firm's relationship to society: the debt-to-society view, the shareholder-value view, and the do-well-by-doing-good view. We believe a new perspective is needed.

The debt-to-society view holds that firms should be good because they owe it to society. Corporations receive charters and special protections, in particular the benefits of limited liability, from society. In exchange, they have responsibilities to make contributions beyond the letter of the law.

Some who hold this perspective regard corporate initiatives in the area of social responsibility as motivated by self-interest—tainted at best and sinister at worst. They decry "the strategic thrust of corporate philanthropy"[5] and the "hidden motives behind corporate citizenship initiatives."[6] Extreme activists in this camp view "business ethics" as an oxymoron, right up there with "scented deodorant," "jumbo shrimp," and a new one—"accounting principles." This view holds that corporations, driven by the profit motive, are pretty much incapable of self-initiated ethical behavior: capitalism is greed. Capitalists cannot be counted on to behave well. They need to be regulated, protested against, and forced to act in the interests of society.

One leading exponent of this point of view is the International Forum on Globalization. In what it claims to be the "definitive document from the anti-corporate globalization movement," the Forum suggests that the concept of voluntary "corporate responsibility" (which we essentially defend in this book) is naive at best: "Institutions that habitually lie to their shareholders and treat obeying the law as a cost-benefit calculation may also lie about their compliance to voluntary corporate codes, with the complicity of their auditors."[7] The Forum is skeptical of government enforced standards of corporate conduct, because "they do not change the nature of the corporation itself, and they leave governments saddled with the burden of attempting to enforce the law on institutions that are able to spend millions of dollars on lawyers, lobbyists, and politicians to weaken the rules and thwart enforcement action."[8]

The Forum supports various restrictions on big companies (like revoking corporate charters and criminalizing all political contributions). But it wants more: a fundamental restructuring "away from the domination of global corporations and toward more democratic and socially and ecologically sustainable enterprises." This entails reversing the trend of "globe-spanning corporate concentration" toward

smaller businesses capable of functioning as human-scale communities of interest in which people know each other, are dedicated to a com-

mon purpose, and share rewards more equitably. . . . They must be
owned by people who have a direct involvement in the operation—
workers, community representatives, suppliers—rather than by distant
investors who buy and sell without personal engagement other than
profit, growth, and balance sheet figures. All businesses must be transparent and accountable to all stakeholders in the community.[9]

Notwithstanding the self-admitted "giant issues" of this prescription for a return to almost pre–Industrial Age local economics ("Who
would provide the food? Who would finance research into new medicines? Who would finance retirements?"),[10] the debt-to-society view
has some merit.

It is true that corporations are "creatures of the state . . . presumed
to be incorporated for the benefit of the public."[11] Society provides
them benefits like limited liability and the right to make a profit.
Many people legitimately question what firms give back relative to
what they receive and demand of society. Former U.S. Secretary of
Labor Robert Reich asks why corporations should have been allowed
to spend $100 million on lobbying, give 350 free trips to members of
Congress, and spend $50 million on advertising, all to defeat President
Bill Clinton's 1993–94 effort to provide health insurance to the 40
million Americans who lack it. "Where's the public benefit here? Just
what does the corporation owe society anyway?"[12]

Whether or not one agrees with any particular complaint against
corporations, the core insight of the debt-to-society view is that, at the
end of the day, society retains the right to regulate the firm, and this is
how it should be. The firm—like any citizen or other entity—is subject
to society's laws. Yet laws cannot make men or firms "good." They can
only define a low common denominator of acceptable behavior.

The shareholder-value view holds that since the job of the enterprise
is to create value for shareholders, it's inappropriate for companies to
take on the presumed costs associated with being "good." Firms,
according to this view, contribute to society by creating useful products and services, creating jobs, paying taxes, and generating wealth for
shareholders. This obviates the need for ethical considerations outside
the requirements of the law.

The purpose of the corporation, according to this view, is to make
money, not give it away. As railroad king William Vanderbilt said in

1882, "The public be damned. I'm working for my stockholders." He said, "I don't take any stock in this working for anybody's good but our own. . . . Railroads are not run on sentiment, but on business principles, and to pay." Or as Robert C. Goizueta, former CEO of Coca-Cola, stated, "Businesses are created to meet economic needs." When they "try to become all things to all people, they fail. . . . We have one job: to generate a fair return for our owners. . . . We must remain focused on our core duty: creating value over time."[13]

Economist Milton Friedman, the clearest and most widely quoted proponent of this view, is a lightning rod for vitriol from the debt-to-society camp:

> What does it mean to say that the corporate executive has a "social responsibility" in his capacity as a businessman? If this statement is not pure rhetoric, it must mean that he is to act in some way that is not in the best interests of his shareholders. For example that he is to refrain from increasing the price of a product in order to contribute to the social objective of preventing inflation, even though the price increase will be in the best interests of the corporation. Or that he is to make expenditures on reducing pollution beyond the amount that it is in the best interests of the corporation or that is required by law in order to contribute to the social objective of improving the environment. . . . In each of these cases the corporate executive would be spending someone else's money for the general social interest.[14]

The logical conclusion of the shareholder-value view is that if it's legal to dump pollutants and carcinogens into a river and it will improve the bottom line, then it's the right thing to do. If child slavery is legal in the Ivory Coast, then it is fine for a chocolate manufacturer to buy cocoa beans picked by child slaves, even if it is a global firm with headquarters in a country that outlaws child labor and slavery. If it's legal to advertise smoking in China, then do it. Where it's legal to cause harm, then, as the International Forum on Globalization says, all such decisions are cost-benefit calculations.

The do-well-by-doing-good perspective seeks to sidestep the moral debate and argue the business case for corporate citizenship. "Good" behavior is good for the bottom line. This is often—and increasingly—true, but not always. The Body Shop evidenced strong values and socially responsible behavior, but for other reasons faced problems in the marketplace. Companies must address all the basics and align their values-based strategies with their overall business strategies.

The idea that companies do well by doing good is receiving a lot of attention these days. But the past also provides evidence for the opposite view—that what some describe as irresponsible behavior produces a healthy return. Many companies have done well, sometimes for a long time, by being "bad"—having brutal labor practices (Sunbeam under Al Dunlop), engaging in monopolistic practices (IBM, AT&T, and Microsoft), neglecting environmental concerns (Exxon), exploiting developing countries (Nestlé), overpaying executives (you name it!), or selling products that routinely and predictably kill their own customers (the tobacco industry).

These are also examples of how inappropriate behavior can get companies into trouble. But what of the practices that haven't been banned or shamed out of existence? Consider the many activities that arguably are harmful but for which there are few sanctions: auto companies selling gas-guzzling SUVs, corporate tax planning that shifts head offices offshore, food companies that fail to divulge information such as the presence of genetically modified products, oil companies that pay politicians to fight environmental accords, and pharmaceutical companies that bribe doctors with free samples and vacations.

These activities are all legal. While many abhor such practices, the stakeholder consensus that such behaviors must be stopped has not reached the tipping point. Customers still buy big SUVs, offshore tax havens have just recently become an issue, corporate political contributions remain part of the American way, and drug companies continue to enjoy their commercial freedoms.

Conversely, good citizenship can harm a firm. Consider a power company that burns coal to generate electricity. Pollutants from the process create what economists call a negative externality—a cost, in this case to society, that may not be borne by the company (and therefore not reflected in its prices). A company that chooses to voluntarily absorb the costs of such negative externalities can place itself at a competitive disadvantage.

Another obstacle: Different stakeholders have competing interests. Shareholders, customers, and employees could all be harmed if a power company were the only one in its industry to raise its prices to pay the incremental costs of global warming that result from its coal-burning hydro plants. Yet, wearing their hats as citizens, these same people face the costs of environmental degradation such as increased health problems. Various stakeholder groups may have different perspectives on what is "good." Because win-win outcomes are not always possible, firms need to sort out the trade-offs.

In such situations, governments may choose to step in to impose rules and a level playing field. If all power companies must raise rates to convert away from coal or to pay for reforestation, then it simply becomes part of doing business. Taxes on automobile air conditioners and gas-guzzlers are weak examples of such actions.

But government action doesn't always level the playing field: it may also create winners and losers. Consider the debate over the Kyoto Accord. Pollution from factories and cars creates a negative externality—global warming. Government agreements like the Kyoto Accord require companies to internalize some of these costs by investing in emission reduction. Oil companies may suffer because of reduced use of carbon fuels. The rationale is that the burden of such costs should be placed at the point of origin in order to protect the welfare of society. It costs society less to reduce the use of carbon fuels than to deal with the consequences of global warming. Cleaning up after the fact is difficult, maybe impossible, so the burden is placed on corporations.

The world will benefit in the long term from Kyoto, but some companies, including their employees and shareholders, will lose. While a cash-rich company like Shell may be able to afford a 20-year transition plan to sustainable fuels, some small oil companies will go out of business. There are many such companies across the oil industry. For them, survival takes precedence over good behavior.

In fact, not many business leaders think of "good" behavior as a strategic imperative. When 700 U.S. executives were asked what drives their social involvement or citizenship initiatives, few mentioned business strategy (12 percent), customer attraction and retention (3 percent), or meeting public expectations (1 percent.) The vast majority said they are driven by noncompetitive—and therefore optional—factors like improving society, company traditions, or their personal values.[15]

Employees, customers, shareholders, and others see you when you're sleeping and they know when you're awake; they know if you've been bad or good, so you better be good. Of course firms can be harmed by engaging in activities or practices that are inconsistent with the values of relevant stakeholders as the cases of Nestlé, Tyco, and WorldCom show. But in the past, punishment rather than being swift was often glacial. Today, a competitor or protagonist can seize on every action a firm makes. Warts are tough to hide. Says George Carpenter, Procter & Gamble's director of sustainable development, "The hard data on 'doing well by doing good' may not be there yet, but it is clear that companies can do very badly by being bad."

"Avoid doing bad" is increasingly "not good enough." Evidence is mounting that a company can distinguish itself in the marketplace through ethical values and behavior, building trust with all stakeholders and achieving competitive advantage as a result.

Toward a New Perspective

Extreme holders of the first two views—debt-to-society and shareholder value—may seem diametrically opposed, but they actually defend the same logic: If a corporation behaves ethically, it can only be for altruistic or ethical reasons. Such choices invariably entail costs, so when companies invest in responsible behavior, there is always a net loss for shareholders.

Both views have the same conception of the impact of corporate social responsibility on the bottom line: it's a sacrifice. The only difference is in their conclusions. The debt-to-society folks say it should be forced on corporations by the state; the shareholder-value camp says it is intolerable. Both fail to understand that in a transparent world, firms must increasingly address trade-offs among the interests of many different stakeholders. Stakeholders other than shareholders are gaining power, and that means that firms must take them into account if they are to do well. Market forces are requiring companies to change their values and their behavior toward all stakeholders. Evidence is mounting that there is a relationship between corporate values and profits—a positive one.

As for doing well by doing good, often this perspective, while a step forward, tends to trivialize the emerging relationship between corporate values and corporate success. It implies that if companies invest in philanthropy, corporate citizenship, or corporate social initiatives that there will be payoffs. For example, philanthropy is viewed as a marketing investment or a way to create meaning for employees. While these points may be true—and philanthropy is certainly a good thing—something more important is happening. Being a good company doesn't just deliver benefits. Increasingly it is a requirement for success.

A new architecture for the firm is emerging, which requires a rock-solid foundation of ethical corporate values—values, not in the old, motherhood sense of the term, as inscribed in the dusty corporate values statement, rather values embedded in the corporate DNA. They must be values that are deeply held within corporate culture; that shape products, services, core business operations, brand image, reputation, relationships, and everyday personal interactions; and that drive everything a firm does and how it operates. Why? When the corporation is naked, shared values are the precondition for establishing trust and sustainable business performance—a force, as we shall see, that is the sine qua non of the new business environment and the networked corporation.

This is not to say that markets are sufficient to achieve social justice in society—a view held by so-called market fundamentalists.[16] The private sector is not competent to address social goals such as the redistribution of wealth. Nor does it have the right to do so. Companies may engage in philanthropy, but society has not given them the right to collectively address broader issues of social justice. They may behave well toward various stakeholders as a matter of economic necessity, but clearly markets are insufficient. Capitalist societies use the power of the state for setting and achieving social goals. Firms are not agents of democracy, and therefore they lack the representative governance and accountability mechanisms that governments have to set social priorities. Citizens may elect governments to enact their preferred social priorities, but they don't elect boards of directors.

The Open Enterprise

A new perspective is needed that goes beyond the three discussed so far. Firms need to build trusting relationships to thrive, and transparency is changing trust.

A new model of the firm is emerging: the open enterprise.[17] Open enterprises are actively transparent, while carefully managing their critical competitive information and security. They understand that transparency is a corporate value that must be connected to principles of honesty, accountability, and consideration to sustain trust. They embrace networked business models and understand that relationships—reciprocal engagements with customers, employees, partners, shareholders, and the public—are critical to success. Their goal is to create value for all stakeholder groups, applying collaborative processes to resolve the trade-offs among competing interests of stakeholders.

As we shall explain, open enterprises will enjoy better financial performance than traditional firms, which, lacking trust and sustainable business strategies, fall by the wayside. Capital market transparency and accountability will give them better share performance. They will tend to create better value for customers—critical in a transparent world where the best, rather than incumbents, are more likely to prevail. Open enterprises engage partners in high-transparency business webs to create products and services with lower costs and market differentiation. They treat knowledge workers as investors of intellectual capital and build loyalty through openness. They understand the liabilities of increased public scrutiny and the importance of societal trust, absorbing the costs of externalities within the framework of a sound business strategy. Regardless of where on Earth they do business, they operate with the highest standard of integrity and transparency, building trust, global stability, and social justice. Our research indicates these are the new instruments of wealth creation for a transparent, networked world.

The open enterprise is illustrated in Figure 3.1. In a transparent world, values enable the creation of trust. Trust strengthens relationships with all stakeholders, in turn enabling networked business models and the creation of value—competitive products and services for customers, motivated and effective employees, stable and supportive societies, and good returns for shareholders. We call this relationship between corporate values and stakeholder value the values-value ladder. Each step is a requirement for the next. Failure to execute at each level in a transparent world can be fatal. We step up the ladder in the balance of this chapter.

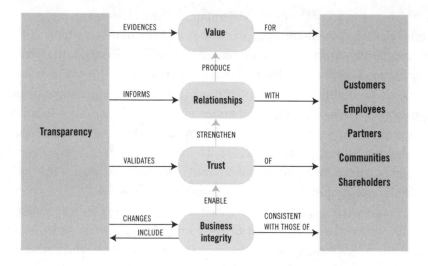

Figure 3.1 The Values-Value Ladder

STEP 1: CORPORATE VALUES

We focus on four values that form the basis of trust. Honesty, account-ability, consideration, and transparency—together constitute what we call the New Business Integrity and the foundation of the open enter-prise. Let's examine each of these.

Honesty

Honesty is not just an ethical issue; it has become an economic one. To establish trusting relationships with employees, partners, customers, shareholders, and the public, firms need to be open, fairly disclosing information. They must be truthful, accurate, and complete in com-munications. They must not mislead or be perceived to mislead. In everything from motivating employees, negotiating with partners, publishing product information, disclosing financial information, or explaining the environmental impacts of a new factory, companies are expected to tell the truth.[18]

As we described in Chapter 1, in the networked world, people and organizations have unprecedented access to information and the abil-ity to verify, authenticate, and evaluate what companies say. Today, legions of skeptical analysts, bold regulators, empowered interest groups, doubting Web surfers, and hardened journalists scrutinize any corporate statement or assertion. Want to know the compensation of a CEO? Check the company's 10Q or 10K filings or just type the CEO's name into Google. Want to know about the accuracy of an ad on eBay? Check the eBay feedback forum to see what 4,000 other people say about the seller. Looking for dirt on a company or want to receive regular "rumor alerts" about a competitor? Try fuckedcompany.com. Shell can claim it's green till the cows come home; but if it isn't, those who care will find out.

Accountability

To establish trust, firms must make clear commitments to distinct stakeholders and abide by them—do what they say they will do. And they must demonstrate with clear communication, preferably with the verification stamp of the stakeholders themselves or independent outside experts, that they have met their commitments.

In the past, accountability was often an undesirable state of affairs invoking liabilities, testing, and scrutiny. Better to keep your head low, stay under the radar, and avoid making promises. In the transparent world, where every stakeholder has radar, accountability becomes a requirement for trust. In fact, for those who embrace it as a value, it is a powerful force for business success.

People learn from history. Past experience establishes regularity and reliability. The networked economy has a new kind of memory. Network computing creates a global brain whose capacity to remember expands exponentially. As information, transactions, and communications turn into bits, firms and their stakeholders generate vast databases of business history. There is a searchable record of all kinds of information that was previously relegated to "the ashcan of history." Detailed information about who said what, what was promised, what was done, and what was transacted is available at the speed of light. No more shoving things under the table. The table is glass.

Most large firms subscribe to Nexis; that means your potential partners can quickly pull up a complete clipping file of every article published about you. Former or disgruntled employees can start a Web site to collect grievances. Your internal memos may be published at internalmemos.com. Negative publicity might be gathered at Corp-Watch.org. Your record is inescapable.

Abiding by commitments is clearly insufficient to establish trust; during the 1990s boom many companies consistently produced quarterly results identical to analysts' expectations. But many used "financial engineering" and other fancy footwork to achieve such consistency. Revelations about this destroyed trust, and stock prices cratered when shareholders held companies accountable. This instance underscores the importance of honesty in maintaining trust and also points to the third element of trust.

Consideration of Others' Interests

From our experience, a critical pillar of trust is the belief that a company shows regard for the interests, desires, or feelings of others.

One term to describe this is *benevolence*. Sometimes benevolence has a master-slave connotation, as we may think that only someone in a position of power or superiority can be benevolent. But any party can operate with benevolence, or goodwill, toward another. Of course, when a company shows goodwill through philanthropic endeavors, it can enhance trusting relationships. But goodwill is relevant to all stakeholders. Firms increase employee loyalty when employees believe that their company will be loyal to them—that they will not be discarded once the going gets a bit rough, or at least that the company will truly consider their interests and downsize only as a last resort, and then only with a fair and equitable severance.

Despite the availability of price-cutting Internet marketplaces, many firms choose to stick with existing suppliers to protect their suppliers' viability and the integrity of the supply chain. In doing so, they build trusting relationships and effective networked businesses. On the other side, in countless cases companies do the right thing for customers though it hurts short-term earnings.

When extraction companies like Rio Tinto and Shell refuse to pay bribes in countries where bribery is the norm, they sometimes lose opportunities to less scrupulous competitors. However, they have determined that bribery is harmful to the societies in which it is practiced, and decided that they have an obligation to behave with consideration for the long-term interests of the citizens of these countries. This is sometimes a difficult decision, but one that can pay off over the long run.

Baxter advised customers to discontinue use of its dialysis machines and stopped sales of them when it learned that they *might* be linked to patient deaths; it did not wait for further investigation. Of course avoiding litigation was part of its motivation, but the speed and completeness of the decision—causing it a significant loss in revenue—suggests a deeper business integrity was in operation.

Transparency

Clearly, trust depends on transparency. Sometimes, trust is given implicitly: A baby trusts her mother. But even a baby's genes guide her to seek evidence of maternal behavior. Trust depends on transparency, and transparency depends on trust. Indeed, as people learn to collaborate well over time, transparency and trust reinforce each other, generating a virtuous cycle.

We began this book with the question "What is Fidelity hiding?" The question "What are they hiding?" encapsulates the relationship between transparency and trust. It implies that if company executives hold secrets, they do so for a nefarious reason and therefore are undeserving of trust. Stakeholders know that the fewer secrets companies keep, the more likely they will be trusted. You are less likely to trust a firm that withholds information pertinent to your interests.

Firms cannot be transparent unless they are trustworthy, as openness will harm them. Firms that are trustworthy should be transparent because openness helps stakeholders validate their integrity. In an increasingly transparent world, active openness is becoming central to building trust between stakeholders and the firm. To coin a phrase, corporations should *undress* for success.

STEP 2: TRUST

How do open enterprises create trust and what role do values play?

Trust is hard to define because it is so fundamental, but you can usually tell when it's warranted. We seek it for robust workplaces and regret its frailty in our communities—local and global. In our increasingly transparent, networked business world, companies need it like never before just to stay alive. When trust falls, firms fail.

Three centuries before Christ, Aristotle's *Rhetoric* argued that *ethos*, the trust in a speaker by a listener, depended on the perception of three characteristics: correctness of opinions, character (reliability, competence, and honesty), and goodwill (benevolent intentions toward the listener).[19]

Over two millennia later the great philosopher's words provide a sound basis for our thinking. *Trust is the expectation that others will be honest, accountable, considerate, and open.*

Historically, when people or organizations have trusted a corporation, they have expected it will tell them the truth, abide by its commitments, and do the right thing—behave fairly with goodwill and take their interests into account. Today, transparency profoundly affects these three values. It is also a value itself; in the new business environment, transparency is critical to building trust. In many ways, transparency is the most important corporate value because it forces firms to embrace the other values required by various stakeholder markets. Indeed, as U.S. Supreme Court Justice Louis Brandeis said, "Sunlight is the best disinfectant." Transparency forces trustworthy behavior: If you're open, you are less likely to have something to hide.

We have already discussed how transparency is an important new value that creates trust. Transparency also affects the process whereby trust is generated. Trust is established through four practices—presence of shared norms and values, reciprocity, validation, and transference. The transparent environment changes each of these, accelerating the speed at which trust can be strengthened or weakened, consolidated or destroyed.

(a) Shared Norms and Values: Shared norms among parties support trust. Norms can range from interpersonal practices to formal laws set out by authorities, as in the case of rules governing expense accounts or regulations regarding the reporting of financial results. Norms often reflect deeply held values, as in the essential Western belief that people should be left alone if they aren't hurting anyone.

In a transparent world the *values* that underpin norms become ever more important. The business world is much more complex than even a generation ago. Transactions have grown exponentially. Communication has exploded and fragmented, as dozens of emails replace a meeting or enable previously impossible collaboration on a global basis. We communicate with a broader range of individuals. Markets are global, bringing a clash of local cultures to the table. Firms assemble and dis-assemble ad hoc partnerships overnight, where elaborate contracts are unfeasible. In this environment, it is not possible to anticipate the per-mutations and combinations of choices people need to make through formal rules alone. Rather, the most effective organizations and part-nerships are those based on commonly shared values. Trust drops transaction, interaction, and partnering costs. Autonomous individuals and groups are able to conduct business on a platform of shared values.

In the transparent world, values are also evidenced more easily. Consider the tale of coltan, a specialized mineral used in electronics equipment. Proceeds from coltan mining are alleged to finance civil wars and brutal regimes in Rwanda and Uganda. To mine coltan, rebels have overrun the Congo's national parks, clearing out large chunks of the area's lush forests and killing endangered elephants and gorillas for food. Yesterday no mobile telephone manufacturer would dream of trumpeting its coltan policy, or the values that underpin it, in its sales literature.

A recent dialogue on a consumer action Web site went as follows: "My wife and I have two kids in school and day care, we regularly waste time (and money and gasoline) that could have been saved if we owned cell phones, and we want to buy cell phones. We know we should be boycotting companies that use Congolese coltan but which brands are they? Are there companies which have renounced using Congolese coltan?" A reader quickly responded by citing a story on the U.S. National Public Radio Web site. He explained that every tele-phone uses coltan, so the trick is finding one that doesn't use African coltan. "I think your best bet would be a Motorola."

Most brochures tout battery life, pricing, instant messaging, Inter-net access, or MP3 capabilities. But this consumer doesn't care about all that. He wants to know if his purchase is fueling a civil war. And he can find out.

(b) Reciprocity: Trusting relationships engender reciprocal obliga-tions. This can occur in a specific situation, say, the sale of an item on eBay. The trust each party has for the other is enhanced through the transaction. Or every positive performance review an employee receives contributes to the sense of reciprocal obligation to perform a job well for the company. Reciprocity can take time to develop, where there may be a relationship that at any given time may be unrequited but over time is repaid and balanced. Again, this contributes to the development of long-term obligations between people.

Transparency is requiring firms to behave in a reciprocal rather than an authoritarian manner. Procter & Gamble senior management may hand down a game plan to its employees. Alternatively, it may engage employees in a collaborative process to determine work plans and commitments. In doing so, it creates reciprocal obligations. Modern management theory is rich with evidence that the latter approach works best in terms of employee motivation, comprehension of work plans, development, and the quality of work products.[20] Shell could have sought to impose its decision to build a plant in Angola on the population. It decided to adopt a different approach where it engaged the local government and communities, generating more confidence that they would benefit from the project.

(c) **Validation:** Visibility into the operations and behavior of firms enables individuals to authenticate and validate corporate statements and claims and even to evaluate the values of products and services. Honesty, reliability, and consideration must be verifiable and, increasingly, verified. That's why auditors exist—and why their integrity is so important.

Validation can be provided by *an independent authority*, for a specific topic. You may trust the American Medical Association to certify qualifications of a doctor to practice medicine. Should you trust the safety claims of automaker Kia? Check out www.crashtest.com or a dozen other independent evaluators on the Net.

Validation can also be achieved through *investigation*. Patients having laser eye surgery are vulnerable. Today they can choose whom to trust and reduce their vulnerability by doing an online investigation of suppliers in their area—checking for failure rates and patient satisfaction. Many local magazines publish annual "Best Doctors in Town" articles. Or you can try Bestdoctors.com to see if your doctor has any state medical board disciplinary actions in her record or to find a physician whose patients recommend her.

You're considering moving to a new neighborhood and you want to know if the local school is a good one. Check out the massive online database of all U.S. schools provided by Standard & Poor's Performance Evaluation Services. Slice and dice the data, asking for all the schools in the geographical area that have certain characteristics. "We're in the transparency business," says Performance Evaluation Services president Bill Cox.

(d) Transference: The networked economy accelerates the process whereby trust or mistrust transfers from one party to another. If you trust a doctor and your friend trusts you, your friend may place her medical care in the hands of your doctor. Trust can also be transferred indirectly to a diffuse population. Relatively large networks like eBay, a religious group, or a political party, Greenpeace, or the National Rifle Association may contain generalized trust—social capital—without close personal contact among all members.

Mistrust can spread through a stakeholder group like a prairie fire, however. For some inexplicable reason bad news seems to travel faster and generalize further than good news.[21] The evidence to support this observation is growing. Intel learned how mistrust could be transferred in a transparent business environment back in 1994. A rumor spread on the Net like a form of reverse "viral marketing," alleging that the Pentium chip was having trouble doing floating-point calculations. Trust in the Pentium brand evaporated and Pentium joke databases began to proliferate. (What's the difference between a nine-year-old and a Pentium chip? A nine-year-old can do long division.) Intel, which had not yet figured out the rules of a transparent world, responded with advertising and press releases. This merely inflamed and accelerated the transference of mistrust already under way. Intel didn't know at the time that maintaining customer trust is very different when knowledgeable stakeholders can sift through information and perform their own validation. Facts are quickly checked: loss of credibility can be instantaneous, second chances are rare and hard to effect, grandstand plays had better be perfect, playing one audience against another is easy to detect, and misinformation or rumors need to be tackled head on.[22]

Ultimately Intel had to stop production of the chip and write down $470 million. Yet with attentive relationship building, the Pentium brand stormed back and most people forgot the incident. Trust, as expressed in the Pentium brand image, was here today, gone tomorrow, and back again—not the next day but after months of painstaking work. Nike is another example. After suffering considerably for its labor standards in the 1980s and early 1990s, Nike has become a leader in advancing the interests of workers in poor countries. This includes policies that require their contractors to prohibit child labor and pay employees at least the minimum wage or the prevailing industry wage, whichever is higher. But old mistrusts die hard and Nike has had a terrible time shaking the image.

Blind trust is disappearing. Visibility means that validation of trust is a click away, as is the power to transfer or destroy trust. To establish and maintain trust, businesses today need to engage with various classes of stakeholders to find commonly held norms, generate reciprocal obligations, provide good value, and behave appropriately.

STEP 3: RELATIONSHIPS

The next step up the values-value ladder is business relationships. As individuals and organizations gain increased access to information and visibility into the operations of firms, new kinds of relationships become possible and even necessary. Within the corporation new kinds of relationships are possible among employees and between employees and the firm. Knowledge work demands unstructured collaboration. In the past, all important relationships were internal to the organization. Companies talked about "relationships" or "partnerships" with customers and suppliers, but these terms were typically euphemisms for a game of winner-take-all poker. Supply chains, more often than not, were adversarial. Similarly, companies sold products and services to customers—described as creating customer relationships. But car companies, for example, didn't have a relationship with their customers in any significant sense of the term. Automakers did market research to understand customers. They did mass advertising to establish brands. They sold and serviced vehicles. But few customers would describe this as a relationship.

The only important relationships existed inside the firm. There were reporting relationships, dotted-line relationships, and project teams whose members collaborated with one another. Such relationships were often carefully defined; you were part of the human resource with roles, responsibilities, reward systems, and the like. Great practitioners, such as Alfred Sloan who took GM to prominence, developed entire theories of management based on this paradigm.

But now the transparent business environment renders the vertically integrated corporation obsolete. A superior form of wealth creation has arisen—the business web. Because the Internet slashes the cost of sharing knowledge, collaborating, and meshing business processes among corporations, companies can now focus on their core competencies and partner or outsource to do the rest. In industry after industry, b-webs are proving more supple, innovative, cost-efficient, and profitable than their traditional, vertically integrated competitors.

During the early enthusiasm for B2B software companies, many pundits assumed that partner promiscuity based on lowest price was the new model—that all business flows to the lowest bidder. Cheaper widgets a mouse-click away would win the day. But price isn't everything. It often makes more sense to work closely with selected suppliers. Dell Computer, for example, could split its business for components among many suppliers in order to keep them all on their toes. Instead, it gives its business to a small group of suppliers in which it has the most confidence, and they work closely to produce the best components and the best computers. Through the Net, Dell gives real-time scorecards to all its suppliers that provide both feedback on their performance and customer data. For a components manufacturer, this relationship is extremely valuable; even if the sales to Dell earn low margins, the information allows the manufacturer to alter its product mix and manage inventories strategically.

Moreover, customers become part of the business web as they interact with services and even cocreate value with companies. For the first time, companies can forge two-way, interactive, personalized relationships with all customers on a mass scale. While the virtue of deep relationships was always self-evident in theory, in reality it wasn't practical. But now the ubiquitous, cheap, and interactive Net coupled with enormous low-cost databases enables producers to develop a meaningful direct relationship with each customer. Sellers and buyers have ongoing dialogue, establishing trust through reciprocity.

This concept seems to have been lost to the music industry, which has embraced the pick-a-fight style of customer relations. The industry has fought many of the major technological innovations that made music more accessible and engaged customers in the distribution of music—from cassette tape machines to MP3. Companies that earned consumers' gratitude for bringing them the Beatles and Simon and Garfunkel are now widely loathed as the enemy.

Transparency is enabling new kinds relationships with shareholders as well. The days when the industrial relations department simply issued press releases, answered the telephone, and mastered the spin in annual reports are disappearing.

Partnerships and other relationships become the foundation of wealth creation. The stronger they are, the more likely firms can create value and succeed.

STEP 4: VALUE

The final step in the ladder is value. The new integrity as we define it—honesty, accountability, consideration of stakeholders' interests, and transparency—is more than just a matter of values. Increasingly, the new integrity is becoming a foundation of value creation, competitive strategy, indeed, of competitive advantage.

A term commonly used to sum up what it means for a business to be "good"—to show genuine, long-term consideration for all its stakeholders—is *sustainability*. A widely accepted definition of sustainability is "meeting the needs of the present generation without compromising the ability of future generations to meet their needs." This is not just about healthy ecosystems or contented communities. Sustainability is also about engineering great businesses that will be there for the long haul, to the benefit of their customers, employees, business partners, and shareholders.

Here's a quick overview. A successful strategy has three basic parts, two of which are familiar. To consistently outperform its competition, a company can either grow faster (which we call "sustainable growth") or manage costs better ("sustainable efficiency"). The third part has to do with a company's very ability to exist; we call it "sustainable foundations" (Figure 3.2). We put the word *sustainable* at the front of these three terms not merely to make a rhetorical point. Sustainable firm

Sustainable Foundations	Peace, order, and good governance	
	License to operate	
	Access to capital	
Sustainable Growth	Best in class capabilities	Employees
		Partners
	Value innovation	
	Brand reputation and customer loyalty	
Sustainable Efficiency	Risk reduction	
	Process improvements	Lower transaction costs
		Process efficiencies
	Quality management	Eco-efficiency
		Codes and standards
	Minimizing regulation and litigation	

Figure 3.2 Business Integrity and the Creation of Value

economics are very much in demand, as company directors, officers, and institutional shareholders increasingly focus on long-term performance rather than quick hit—often misleading—quarterly results.

A parenthetical note: As with any general approach to building a business strategy, not all competitive drivers apply equally to all companies or to all situations. Sometimes only one or two drivers will apply, sometimes all. Every good strategy is unique and specific.

Sustainable Foundations

Any company's existence depends on three foundation stones. Companies may take these for granted when doing everyday planning; many even ignore these issues when strategizing for the long term. They do so at their peril.

1. Peace, Order, and Good Governance

The first driver is the overall social, political, and legal environment, including peace, political stability, free markets, property rights, rule of law, absence of bribery, and so on. Clearly, we are in a period when peace, order, and good governance are at great risk; and few companies perform sustainably well in the midst of war, terrorism, corruption, and political chaos.

Many of these problems are exacerbated by the great inequalities, hardships, and grievances—real and perceived—that separate richer and poorer countries. When the actions of dominant governments (like the United States) and global agencies (like the IMF) are blamed for local economic downturns (e.g., Argentina) or worse (e.g., war), Western corporations take a hit. Corporations face the reality that the very agencies that have represented their interests and promoted their worldview may indirectly spark boycotts or economic implosions. Competitive advantage comes from knowing when and how the winds of peace, order, and good governance are changing, and acting accordingly: being first out of a country when it's risky and first in when it's safe. It also comes from being there to enhance good governance so that when the opportunities arise, knowledge and relationships already exist. In such a manner, BP reentered the Russian oil industry on a large scale in February 2003.

2. License to Operate

Companies now face forces that, for all practical purposes, challenge their very right to exist—or at least their right to do business in a particular market. This is a trust factor that affects both individual businesses and groups of businesses—for example, several companies from a specific country or in a particular industry.

McDonald's has faced this in both the United States and Europe for years, and by early 2003 such challenges became a competitive disadvantage. In 2003 the company reported its first ever quarterly loss. McDonald's is a consummate marketing company. It has excelled in linking philanthropy and community involvement to its brand. But this challenge cannot be turned around by marketing and good deeds alone. Critics question the company's core product (fatty food from allegedly mistreated cows) and challenge its existence as an embodiment of the homogenizing forces of globalization.

More broadly, globalization faces a crisis of legitimacy. Engagement with local stakeholders—genuine localization—is one way to address this problem.

Global corporations that lay down deep local roots by hiring locally from the executive level on—and embrace local partnerships with suppliers and communities of stakeholders—are in the best position to gain a sustainable license to operate.

3. *Access to Capital*

In 2002, irresponsible behavior by executives and corporate boards devastated the capital markets and destroyed shareholder confidence. Regaining trust will require sustained improvements in corporate governance, behavior, transparency, and accountability. Healthy investor relationships are a two-way street where firms engage directly with shareholders, especially large institutions like mutual and pension funds that tend to invest for the long term. Open enterprises avoid spin in shareholder briefings, press releases, and annual reports, and increasingly deliver easy-to-follow factual information. Instead of the often misleading and one-dimensional quarterly financial guidance, open enterprises provide a more meaningful sort of guidance: clear explanations of past performance, current challenges, strategies, and plans.

One result of the 2002 governance crisis was that institutional investors—particularly pension, labor, and social funds—gained leverage. As we describe in Chapter 8, they will also increasingly place broader social and environmental issues on the shareholder agenda; companies that address such issues will be advantaged in gaining and maintaining access to shareholder capital.

Sustainable Growth

Three top-line competitive drivers stand out:

- Best-in-class capabilities, including leadership, employees and business partners

- Strategic innovation

- Brand reputation and customer loyalty

For any veteran business planner, these concepts are old hat. Yet all three are changing thanks to the new integrity and focus on sustainability.

Honesty, consideration of stakeholders' interests, accountability, and transparency—these are vital to attracting, retaining, and ensuring consistent performance from the key resources that firms require in an increasingly interdependent world. As companies focus ever more narrowly on what they do best, they need suppliers, distributors, and employees who take shared responsibility for delivering value to the end customer, for taking initiative in maximizing efficiencies, and for being flexible when market conditions change for better or for worse. Such *best-in-class capabilities* are hard to find, but when found, they become critical to a company's success.

Among firms, trust drops transaction costs and enables the free flow of information required for business web performance. Where transactions provide opportunities for misrepresentation, noncompliance, or fraud, mutual trust reduces the contracting costs associated with formal agreements. This social capital provides an effective enforcement mechanism that is far cheaper than elaborate contracts, extensive tracking systems, and litigation. Free flow of information in a trusting atmosphere also dramatically improves the productivity and performance of interenterprise collaborative business processes.

As we describe in Chapter 4, employees are easier to recruit, more productive, and more likely to stick around in companies that are actively transparent and accountable to their staff. The investment bank UBS Warburg describes how its support of the regeneration of London's East End tangibly enhances its recruitment, retention, and development of top employees. On the flip side, a veteran Nike employee had this to say about the impact of the sweatshop charges that this company has faced: "It comes up at every dinner party, and when it doesn't it's like the elephant in the corner of the living room. It goes from you have the coolest job to hmm, I'm not so sure."

Within firms, trust strengthens capability. Employees have unprecedented access to information about their company because new models of work demand it. Work systems in traditional firms were hierarchical, and relationships were based on control and authority. Today's smart companies design collaborative systems where teamwork harnesses the power of human capital more effectively. Companies replace the bonds of traditional hierarchy with bonds of trust, embodied in shared values, clear rules of engagement, and quality business processes. Trust builds motivation, security, and loyalty. It reduces inhibitions and defenses—essential for creative thinking and collaboration. Without trusting relationships, no company can ever hope to achieve high performance.

Capability is of little value, however, if a firm and its partners are pointed in the wrong direction. This is where *strategic innovation* comes in. In their 2002 book *Walking the Talk*, the chairmen of Anova Holding (Stephan Schmidheiny), DuPont (Charles Holliday, Jr.), and Shell (Philip Watts) describe how strategic innovation arises from the new integrity:

> The relatively straightforward concept of eco-efficiency has already encouraged some companies to make radical shifts from maximizing sales to selling no *thing* at all—and being cleaner and more profitable in the process. Instead of selling things, they sell services, or they lease things, or both. Companies that once sold auto paint to car companies now sell the service of painting cars. So, where once they improved the bottom line by maximizing cans of paint sold, they now improve the bottom line by minimizing the use of paint per car.[23]

As for *brand reputation and customer loyalty*, British Telecom (BT) asked a good question: Does a shopper really stop and think about corporate responsibility before making any one of thousands of buying decisions per year? Its market research indicates that a large and growing number of consumers claim they consider corporate social responsibility (CSR) in their buying decisions. Yet, BT notes, "It's only in a relatively small number of these cases (e.g., buying organic produce) that the consumer actually makes a conscious consideration of the supplier's environmental, social and ethical performance. But our model shows that a company's reputation has a significant influence over customer satisfaction ratings and, given that CSR is a component part of reputation, this would suggest that there could be an important subconscious CSR element to purchasing decisions. . . . If BT were to cease all its CSR activities (i.e. cease treating employees with respect, ignore environmental issues, no longer emphasize the need to act with integrity, ceasing non-profitable services and canceling all community activities) then our customer satisfaction rating would drop by 10%."[24] A difference of this magnitude is often the difference between market leadership and also-ran status.

No single initiative will necessarily change customer perceptions of a company. Yet the aggregate matters enormously. Companies can be liked, they can be perceived neutrally, or they can be actively disliked. A company may not realize it is sliding from one category to another until it is too late for a quick fix.

Sustainable Cost Control

The typical management discussion about competitive cost control is about cycle times, business processes, supply chains, and so on. As we shall discuss momentarily, sustainability strategies—related to eco-efficiency and other dimensions—can make a big contribution to such traditional areas of performance.

But we begin with a more stirring cost driver: *risk*. Increasingly, corporate officers and directors—sometimes with the encouragement of institutional investors—recognize that they must pay more attention to risk. They must identify and control a broad portfolio of risks. How? They can try to reduce or eliminate risks. Or they can set aside contingency funds or buy insurance policies to offset them. Some risks, once identified, can be eliminated in cost-neutral or profitable ways. Others impose costs—sometimes big costs. Corporations face a wide and growing variety of potential threats from new integrity issues, such as customer abandonment, legal fees, and scandal costs, or even executive crime or civil unrest (in some countries).

Hill & Knowlton CEO Paul Taaffe argues that the risk of a trust crisis entails far greater costs than firms recognize. "The cost is not just limited to share price hits. There's often a deep emotional cost. For example, after the Brent Spar [North Sea oil rig fiasco], Shell had trouble recruiting on campus. It previously was one of the top employers of choice by graduates." Brent Spar was an environmental issue, but it played out as a risk to Shell's reputation. True environmental risks may not be stakeholder driven, and therefore risk may be overlooked. Managers who treat environmental damage as only a reputation issue or an externality to be dumped on society ignore at their peril how Mother Nature bites back. Such self-delusion is a dangerous form of opacity.

Concerns about the real costs of global warming and climate, for example, are moving from the NGO barricades to corporate boardrooms. One statement of the issues is sponsored by two of the world's largest reinsurance companies (Swiss Re and Munich Re) and companies such as Abbey National, Allianz Insurance, Credit Suisse Group (CSFB), ING, Merrill Lynch, Rabobank, and UBS.

Their report argues that evidence of change is all around us. In 2003, hurricanes and tropical storms were projected to increase by about 25 percent over 2002. The warmest years on record were 2002 and 1998. If trends persist, weather-related natural disasters will soon create $150 billion in annual losses (versus $10 billion during the 1990s); two-thirds will not be insured.[25]

Sample impacts by industry are:

- Drought-induced crop damage is raising food costs. In 2003, bakeries in the United States faced the highest flour prices in over 70 years. Australian farm output fell by 12.5 percent during the three months to September 2002 and prices rose 1.4 percent.

- Weather-dependent tourist destinations like ski resorts, beach resorts, and the Great Barrier Reef face the risk of declining popularity.

- In late 2002, electricity prices increased in parts of the U.S. West as water shortages cut hydropower generation.

- Fires threaten the forestry sector. In 2002 over 70,000 fires burned down 7.1 million acres in North America, nearly double the ten-year average.

- In 2002, hurricanes in the Gulf of Mexico caused $700 million in damages and curtailed oil and gas production. One three-day shutdown alone led to industrial losses of some $2 billion.

The report argues that, in addition to the damage that climate change can do to their companies, directors and officers in carbon-intensive industries face the risk of negligence lawsuits from shareholders, employees, or communities.

Mitigating environmental risks can add another dimension to sustainable cost control.

- BP claims net present value savings higher than $650 million over three years from reducing fuel and gas venting and flaring.

- European semiconductor manufacturer STMicroelectronics reports a two-year payback on its energy conservation programs, with energy cost savings of over $1 billion between 1994 and 2010.

- IBM conservatively estimates a two-to-one return on its environmental investments in the five years since it began tracking its program; in 2001 the net benefit was $140 million.

Several components of the business case for sustainable cost control relate to three kinds of *process improvements*. Transparency and accountability enhance trust, and therefore reduce *transaction costs*. Also, extensive information sharing both within and among companies in a business web leads to dramatic *process efficiencies:* quicker response times and lower inventories. Procter & Gamble and Gillette predict that the next technological revolution in information sharing, based on the radio frequency ID tag (a wireless communicating electronic version of a bar code), could lead to inventory reductions of 10 percent or more, which would result in massive cost savings.

A third process factor has to do with *quality management*, which is essentially about reducing costs by minimizing defects and waste. Toyota, the world leader in quality management, has applied its quality protocols to energy and resource conservation—simultaneously improving its environmental conservation processes and reducing the consumption of materials, energy, and effort. Result: Toyota is one of the most efficient and profitable companies in the car business.

Another part of quality management is the use of *codes and standards* to prescribe how work should be done, to measure and report on outcomes, and to set targets for improvement. Historically, such codes, like ISO 9000, focused narrowly on product and service quality. Codes of practice are now a big part of the new integrity. They include corporate values statements, codes of social and environmental conduct, and increasingly sophisticated accountability toolkits for tracking and reporting on environmental and social performance. Typically introduced initially to drive "good" behavior, such codes and standards quickly take on double duty as new dimensions of a company's overall quality management arsenal.

A last dimension of cost control—the icing on the cake—is *mini-*

mizing regulation and litigation. When companies voluntarily take on the new integrity and a sustainability agenda—and prove it through engagement, accountability, and transparency—their governments are less likely to impose onerous and bureaucratic rules, policing, audits, and penalties. In the United Kingdom, for example, a high percentage of firms voluntarily produce corporate responsibility reports, so perhaps the government will not impose them through legislation, as the French and Japanese governments have done. And, as we have already suggested, fiduciaries will be less exposed to stakeholder lawsuits if they address the risks imposed by climate change.

Chances are that you are some combination of shareholder, customer, partner, employee, and citizen. In the following five chapters we look deep into how transparency changes the ways corporations behave toward you, in each of the hats you wear.

PART II

When Stakeholders Can See

CHAPTER 4

WHISTLEBLOWERS AND OTHER EMPLOYEES

Transparency for employees has come a long way especially compared with the days after World War II. Conflict between management and labor soared. The 12-month period after V-J Day saw 4,630 work stoppages involving 5 million strikers and 120 million days of lost work.[1] One of the more memorable management-labor confrontations—the largest in U.S. history—was the 1945 strike by 320,000 members of the United Auto Workers (UAW) against the nation's biggest company, General Motors. UAW leader Walter Reuther insisted that GM could afford to increase wages without increasing prices and demanded it be more transparent about its finances. He challenged GM to "open the books" and prove him wrong. This audacious behavior from a mainstream union incensed GM management.

GM vice president Harry W. Anderson told UAW negotiators that under no circumstances would the corporation reveal its records. He exclaimed, "We don't even open our books to our stockholders!"[2]

THE KNOWLEDGE WORKER

Today's open enterprises provide employees access to a vast amount of information about the firm and its management. They build trust with employees through openness and ethical values. Transparency and values begin at home. The surest indicator of how a firm treats customers, shareholders, partners, and other stakeholders is how it treats employees.

Wearing your employee hat, you now have unprecedented access to information about your employer. Some of this you don't need to know, such as the love life, salary, or work behavior of someone else's boss. A plethora of irrelevant, albeit juicy, information previously inaccessible is now readily available at the speed of light due to email and other technological innovations.

Lots of useful information is available, too. You can evaluate your job security by investigating your company's financial position, the current performance of your group, or your own performance, and most firms make this information available. You can strengthen your bargaining power in salary negotiations by knowing more about what your peers, both within and outside the company, are making. You can decide if your company is a good place to invest your intellectual capital by evaluating corporate values and senior management behavior.

It is in your company's interest to be open with you about many things. The idea of transparency in the workplace is relatively new. Social scientists, organizational learning aficionados, and human resource management experts have mused for decades about how new work models require openness and freely flowing information.

The modern corporation requires internal transparency because it is essential for effective knowledge work. Employees must share and use new knowledge, must be empowered to take responsibility for it, and must be self-motivated. Most firms need highly visible values, strategy, business processes, and operations for workers to collaborate and work effectively.

TRANSPARENCY AND KNOWLEDGE WORK

In the old corporation, information flowed vertically. People were separated into two groups—the governors and the governed. The supreme commander was at one end of the spectrum, and the permanently governed at the other. Information flowed imperfectly at best from top to bottom.

In the old industrial economy, the vast majority of those who worked for large vertically integrated companies contributed brawn, not brain. Management invested in big factories with production processes and sophisticated machinery that required little decision making or operator skill. Employees were extensions of the machine. Immigrant workers in Ford factories spoke fifty different languages and had little education. They were expected to follow orders and not to take much initiative—if any. Theirs was not to question why. Management was based on mistrust, command, and control, and its decision processes were totally opaque to employees.

Things weren't much better in the white-collar world. The goal was to climb the ladder and acquire more direct reports. For those outside management, the incentive was salary. The work goals were established higher up. This was the world of the "organization man."

By contrast, modern companies are fluid and supple. Many workers change their processes often and must continuously learn and adapt as they work. Consider a job as mundane as working in a call center. Every hour customers raise new questions and issues. The flexible corporate structure is more effective, but it also means that yesterday's yes/no decisions have become multiple-choice questions. To do their jobs effectively, workers require knowledge.

Google, as a private corporation, can share more information with employees than a publicly traded firm, including financials, deals in the making, and ongoing problems, says CEO Eric Schmidt.

"Most companies use employee portals as an HR mechanism. Here are your benefits, here are your vacation days, and so forth. That is the classic view and it is the wrong view. The right view is how can you spread information within the company that causes employees to solve problems without any executives needing to deal with them— sort of a work minimization strategy for executives. Get the employees to do the work. It is much more efficient. They're happier and I'm happier." Rather than knowledge management, Google's practice is more akin to knowledge liberation—the release of previously secret information to all employees.

Consider how modern corporations deal with something as seemingly finite as product knowledge. The IBM mainframe salesperson circa 1970 knew about the features and functions of the company's products in great detail but almost nothing about the firm's product strategy. IBM never "preannounced" products. The IBM account representative's job was to sell existing products—the more the better— and keep the competition out. The salesperson had no more knowledge about where the company was headed than did the customer. Nor did he need to. Technology was stable and fundamental changes to product strategy were rare. Customer requirements were generally straightforward. The salesperson delivered 85 percent gross margins on mainframe sales, enabling IBM to bundle extensive service and support with the product. Today, by contrast, the salesperson works in a volatile environment where customers have access to information about any competitor. Technology changes daily, as does the customer organization. The account manager needs to thoroughly understand IBM's business strategy, future directions, and views on emerging technology architectures to help customers plan and implement sophisticated technology applications. Today IBM is far more candid in discussing these critical issues with employees, who in turn release this information to the marketplace. Though competitors know more about the company's strategy, the gain from empowering its own employees is worth it to IBM.

The new salesperson needs much more than product information. Because he will not have a specific answer for every question, he needs a deep comprehension of IBM's architectural directions, philosophy, and principles. Often tricky issues arise regarding partnering with competitors, politics within the customer firm, media comments about IBM or stakeholder actions against it, or recent corporate disclosures. The salesperson needs to have the company's philosophy and values in his bones to say and do the right thing. No policy manual can cover every contingency.

Frequent and erratic shifts in core strategy have gone the way of the dot-com dodo. But thanks to continuing rapid-paced technology innovation and the pressure to entice ever more fickle consumers, competitive product cycles are as demanding as they have ever been. Managers must make more difficult decisions in less time. A decade ago, automakers took five to six years to bring a new car to market. Now it's usually three years, sometimes less than two, soon one. Rather than stockpile cars on dealer lots, automakers want to build a car within a week to a buyer's specifications and deliver it to her driveway. In consumer electronics, product cycles are measured in months. Even in the food industry the pace continues to pick up: have you checked out the tomato section of your local grocery lately (let alone frozen pizzas)? Producers of virtually all consumer goods and services face the twin threat of compressed development time and shorter shelf life.

Peter Senge was right when he argued that an organization remains competitive only if it learns faster than its competitors. Any firm can have the same technology as another; any product can be copied. Competitive advantage is ephemeral as firms constantly seek new ways to create value. Marketplace success hinges on the knowledge and creative genius of product strategists, developers, and marketers.

General Electric takes knowledge sharing seriously, applying unique ways to encourage this behavior. Steve Kerr, GE's former chief knowledge officer, says that many 1990s company meetings began with a round-the-table discussion where every attendee was asked to share something important he or she had learned. "You would be fired if you took company assets like money and hoarded them in your personal bank account. Similarly, if you hoarded information or ideas in your personal bank account you could be fired as well. Hoarding information is an integrity violation."

TRANSPARENCY AND EXECUTIVES

Corporate secrets occur when executives know something that employees don't. Blind spots occur when employees know something that executives don't. Knowledge liberation is about making the unknown known to both executives and employees.

Microsoft.com general manager Tim Sinclair supports an open enterprise. Since 1994 he has held one of the most challenging jobs anywhere—running the third largest Web site in the world. When he started out, the entire site ran on a single server that handled a million hits a day. As the Internet expanded, more groups at Microsoft added content. Today, more than 500 writers and developers in more than 70 locations around the world provide information for the Microsoft Web site. Five data centers manage its online traffic. Microsoft.com is the only corporate Web presence in the top 100, boasting 20 million page views per day and 5.5 million users per day. Along with the sites of the CIA and the FBI, it is one of the top targets for hackers. They itch to crack its security and embarrass the world's largest software company. Incredibly, Sinclair has managed a reliability score consistently in the top three on the Web today—99.78 percent uptime.

When asked how he orchestrates the human capital to achieve

such success, his mantra is transparency: "When there is good news, everyone knows. When there is bad news, tell everyone." If there is a problem with the system, if Tim has made a mistake, if his team is not performing well, rather than keep it a secret, he lets appropriate people in Microsoft outside his group know about it—including his boss. "When I open up with the bad news I get the support and resources I need." Tim says that at first this was counterintuitive, and it made his division look weak. Yet "rather than making me vulnerable, this philosophy of transparency strengthens me and my organization. People trust us because they know we're open and determined to deliver."

Tim is not alone. Firms like Johnson & Johnson and Seagate have adopted open book management policies where they share—in real time—the company's scorecard with employees and engage them in its development and in the attainment of its goals. Any employee of Seagate Systems can use the corporate intranet to see CEO Bill Watkins's objectives and how he is performing to achieve them. IBM has a scorecard on its intranet which captures internal metrics and how employees and departments measure up. It receives more traffic than any other part of the intranet.

TRANSPARENCY AND TRUST WITHIN THE FIRM

Open enterprises foster employee trust toward the firm. They also foster trust within the firm—among employees.

Samuel Johnson said, "Where secrecy or mystery begins, vice or roguery is not far off." Knowledge workers by definition aren't stupid. They know that the fewer secrets executives have, the more likely they can be trusted. Firms cannot be transparent unless they are trustworthy, or openness will harm them. Firms that are trustworthy can and should be transparent because openness helps stakeholders verify honesty, reliability, and consideration.

Opacity causes dysfunctional behavior within firms. A Xerox manager told us of an expression prevalent in the company in the early 1990s called "grin fucking." When certain mistrusted executives said things that subordinates thought were wrong or even ridiculous, rather than openly challenge the statement, employees just grinned back. Peer executives often treated one another the same way.

In 1998, Arthur Andersen told senior audit partners to implement its 2X strategy—bring in twice as much revenue from non-audit as from audit services. Then the firm increased the power of local office managing partners, each with his own revenue targets and balance sheets. It eviscerated the central Professional Standards Group—a panel of internal experts who handled tricky accounting questions—moving many of its members to local offices. The goal was to make it harder for auditors to deter clients from pushing the envelope on accounting standards. Enron became Andersen's most powerful client for both audit and consulting services. A Houston-based member of the Professional Standards Group, Carl Bass, complained in a December 1999 email to a colleague in Chicago that his advice that Enron take a $30 million to $50 million accounting charge for a specific transaction was being ignored. Four months later, he was removed from his Enron oversight role in response to complaints by Enron's chief accounting officer at the time, Richard A. Causey.

One former Andersen employee told us that in classes at the Andersen training facility in Chicago, if a student raised a problem or failing of Andersen in the past, teachers were known to reply "The past does not exist." Discussing problems from the past was prohibited—a big problem as those who fail to learn from history are destined to repeat it.

In both Xerox and Andersen a culture of uniformity and opacity undermined open discussion, free thinking, and challenges to the status quo—with disastrous results. When opacity reigns, organizational cultures include negativism, withdrawal, conformity, low commitment, risk aversion, lack of learning, organizational politics, defensiveness, and other symptoms not rooted in positive values.

Conversely, in open enterprises employees are engaged. There is greater loyalty and lower turnover, and employees are more likely to do the right thing. Employees in open and trusted firms are better motivated. Knowledge workers need to be fully motivated to succeed. Unlike an assembly line, where one can turn up the speed, management can't simply demand fifteen more bright ideas per month. But if we list the factors motivating workers, money is not the most important. It is concepts like mutual trust, respect, learning, ability to contribute and to see the big picture.

Michael Rice is working hard to create an open enterprise. As executive director of the Private Client Group at Prudential Securities, he is responsible for most of the company's business. In 2000 the company shut down its institutional and equity markets businesses. Today all its research is on behalf of private clients, eliminating the conflict of interest problems that other securities firms face. The 8,000 people in Rice's group generate $2 billion in annual revenue from more than 2 million clients and manage $120 billion of assets.

Prudential has constructed a "transparency architecture" to ensure an open spirit with stakeholders—from clients to regulators to stock exchanges. Rice says they seek to "live by the spirit not just the letter of the law." The company "opens the kimono completely" to employees, providing Financial Advisors (FAs) complete access to information about company strategies, financials, and operations. This is done via the corporate intranet and other communications tools, and also through an FA advisory council consisting of two FAs from each of ten regions. At FA meetings Rice reviews financial results in detail and discusses any issue.

"As first it was a food fight," he says, "but soon people realized we were serious about being open. Now they know more about the company, our problems, why we do things, how we make decisions, than I could have ever imagined." The process was extended to a branch manager advisory council that discusses issues ranging from strategy and operating style to communications and products. "The branches went from being outposts to being actively engaged in the company."

The transparency architecture resulted in engagement and loyalty. Rice says that in every organization he's seen, most employees think the home office doesn't get it. This was the situation at Prudential in the early 1990s. With a number of severe problems, the company had completely fractured trust. "Today," he says, "we have a culture of trust and that pays off." The firm is aligned around a clear strategy that employees cocreate. Loyalty has shot up. Prior to January of 2000 the firm's annual attrition rate was 23 percent. In 2002 it was 11 percent, dropping at a time when the firm cut FA compensation twice, laid off thousands of people, and reduced costs by $250 million in order to stay alive. "People knew our financial situation. We were always very up front about it." His advice is "Tell the truth. Tell the whole story.

Answer any question honestly and candidly. Do what you say you will. This is what builds trust and goodwill." Rice says that today the only gap between the field and home office is a geographical one. When the firm begins to grow again, he believes that a reputation of openness will attract the best and brightest. "I can't express the power of transparency," he says.

Numerous studies have shown that collegial trust and social capital are crucial for high performance. A culture of openness and trust drops internal transaction costs in three areas. First, an open culture reduces search costs—the costs of finding the right people and resources. Recommendations are made more often and considered more carefully among trusted parties. Second, an open culture reduces coordination or collaboration costs, as trust is the foundation of effective collaboration. Teams that lack trust are usually ineffective. Trust oils the mechanisms for collaboration, reducing friction or breakdown. Third, trust reduces contracting costs, eliminating the need for formal agreements, contracts, and resolution/litigation procedures. A handshake, even a wink, can speak volumes more than an elaborate document, and few documents anticipate all possible permutations of a relationship.

Conversely, office politics, turf battles, and the other games people play that undermine performance proliferate in a culture of mistrust. Openness is the antibiotic for such bacteria. As far back as 1990, Peter Senge wrote in *The Fifth Discipline* that transparency can reduce office politics and game playing:

> A nonpolitical climate demands "openness"—both the norm of speaking openly and honestly about important issues and the capacity to continually challenge one's own thinking. The first might be called participative openness, the second reflective openness. Without openness it is generally impossible to break down the game playing that is deeply embedded in most organizations.[3]

Games—real games, that is—can reveal a lot about the games people play in life. We have been advising a startup that has developed an online game called Office Politics that simulates and satirizes the antics of employees who try to climb the executive ladder. The game provides players with various devices and tools to "kiss ass, backstab, hire, and fire your way to the top." Since it's "only" a game, with few real-world consequences and online players who don't necessarily even know each other personally, you might expect that nasty, underhanded behavior would prevail. On the contrary. One winner's description of his secret of success is typical: "Making friends and alliances and playing a relatively clean game."

Transparency and trust within the workplace also change the customer experience. At Prudential Securities, in one minute an FA might be asked to explain the tricky issues regarding disclosure and conflict of interest in his industry and company. He might need to explain the rationale for Prudential's controversial decision to withdraw from investment banking. The next minute a client might wonder why Prudential has a national account center (for small accounts, $25,000 or less), asking if this is a step toward elimination of its branches. And when an important client asks why his niece was forced to deal with the national account center, the FA has the knowledge of corporate strategy on wealth management and the savvy to rectify the situation on the spot. As with all stakeholders, transparency, if handled right, leads to trust that leads to relationships and value.

Every year since 1983 the Great Place to Work Institute has catalogued the top 100 employers in the United States.[4] The program is so popular that the institute now collaborates with various publications to produce lists for more than eight countries, and as of 2003, identified the best companies in each of fifteen European Union countries as well.

The institute defines a great place to work as one where you trust the people you work for, have pride in what you do, and enjoy the people you work with. The institute argues that corporations should strive to be great places to work, not because of some warm and fuzzy notion of employees being happy and coddled but because this is the surest way for a company to be as profitable as possible. Institute research shows that companies that are great to work for capture a host of competitive advantages. A mutual fund comprising only companies from the institute's great place to work list would consistently and substantially outperform the market. These companies benefit from factors such as lower turnover, lower health care premiums, and more job applications.

Any company with more than 1,000 employees that has been in business for more than seven years can apply to be designated as a great place to work. In 2002 a total of 279 applied, and hundreds of employees in each firm filled out questionnaires about their feelings toward the company. Sample statements employees were asked to agree or disagree with were:

- Management keeps me informed about important issues and changes.

- People around here are given a lot of responsibility.

- Management involves people in decisions that affect their jobs or work environment.

- I am offered training and development to further myself professionally.

The institute says that trust between managers and employees is the most telling characteristic of the best workplaces. To assess a company's level of trust, the institute looks at three dimensions: credibility, respect, and fairness. Credibility concerns an employee's perceptions of management communication practices, competence, and integrity. Respect examines the support, collaboration, and caring employees see expressed by management's actions toward them. Fairness concerns the equity, impartiality, and justice employees perceive in the workplace.

The final two dimensions of the institute's model relate to workplace relationships between employees and their job or company (pride) and among employees and other employees (camaraderie). Pride is the feelings employees have toward their job, team or work group, and company, and camaraderie is the quality of hospitality, intimacy, and community within the workplace.

Great places to work retain their luster even during bad times. In "How to Cut Pay, Lay Off 8,000 People, and Still Have Workers Who Love You," an article accompanying the 2002 list of Best Companies to Work For, *Fortune* discussed the remarkable loyalty employees showed toward Agilent during a stressful period. The high-tech Hewlett-

Packard spin-off that builds measurement, testing, and communications equipment, placed 31st on the list of 100 best companies. At its peak in November 2000, Agilent employed 47,000 people, 12 percent more than the year before. Then came the 2001 economic downturn, compounded by the events of September 11. Agilent's sales plunged. Despite valiant efforts to avoid layoffs, such as across-the-board 10 percent salary reductions, in the end the company terminated 8,000 full-time employees and 5,000 temporary workers—about a quarter of its payroll.

Management worked incessantly to make the downsizing process as transparent as possible. Constant contact through email, intranet, and meetings—both group and one-on-one—kept employees informed as the process unfolded. Agilent CEO Ned Barnholt would frequently speak directly to employees through public address systems built into its facilities around the world. As a result, employees remained tenaciously loyal and supportive of management. "I knew that [downsizing] wasn't part of the HP Way, and it's not what Bill and Dave [Hewlett and Packard] would have wanted," one employee told *Fortune*. "But if they were faced with the same situation, they would have had to do the exact same thing."

Employee morale is essential to Agilent's survival. Companies today must nurture knowledge workers and provide the environment for extraordinary thinking—problem solving, innovating, and executing complex business functions. If Agilent's employees become angry, bitter, or afflicted with guilt—sentiments that often arise after large layoffs—then the company's capacity for innovation and creating value would suffer. Unlike industrial corporations of yesteryear, Agilent doesn't have mechanical assembly lines that ensure employees contribute regardless of their mood. By handling crises in a manner that doesn't undermine workers' faith in management, Agilent's leaders safeguarded the company's capacity to compete.

WHEN TRUST BREAKS DOWN: WHISTLEBLOWING

When companies violate trust, the consequences can be disastrous. Bad behavior not only undermines motivation, loyalty, and productivity; it makes companies vulnerable to problematic behavior such as whistleblowing or rebellion.

Sherron Watkins, Enron's vice president for corporate development, was an eight-year veteran of the company. Margaret Ceconi was a deal originator in the Enron Energy Services group and had been with the company less than a year. Like many employees, they knew about the questionable practices in the company's finance department and had raised the issue with their bosses. But unlike others, when they got no response, they blew the whistle. They could have gone to the *Houston Chronicle* or *The Washington Post*, but instead Watkins and Ceconi wrote letters to the CEO, Kenneth Lay, warning him of the pending implosion of accounting scandals that could devastate the company and the lives of its employees. Little did they know that their letters would set the stage for a who-knew-what-and-when platform from which the seventh largest company in the United States would take its death plunge.

Watkins became a celebrity after a congressional subcommittee released her letter and took her testimony on national television. She quit her job and joined the lecture circuit, speaking about the roots of Enron's collapse—talking about ethics at some of the nation's most prestigious business schools. She met with President George W. Bush and published a book on the Enron collapse.

In December 2002, *Time* magazine named Watkins, Coleen Rowley of the FBI, and Cynthia Cooper of WorldCom as its Persons of the Year. Rowley had written a memo to FBI director Robert Mueller about how the bureau rejected requests from her field office to investigate Zacarias Moussaoui, subsequently indicted as a September 11 coconspirator. Cynthia Cooper blew the whistle on WorldCom when she informed its board that the company had covered up $3.8 billion in losses with phony bookkeeping.

Observed *Time:* "Their jobs, their health, their privacy, their sanity—they risked all of them to bring us badly needed word of trouble inside crucial institutions."

The fate of most other whistleblowers is far less glamorous. In February 1999, three years before the world watched WorldCom drop to its knees, Geraldine Kelly, a cost management analyst working for the company in London, saw the writing on the wall. Frustrated by WorldCom's apathy regarding her concerns, she quit her job and spoke to the City of London fraud squad and the Department of Trade and Industry. Her claims were deemed unfounded.

In Richardson, Texas, twenty-two months later, WorldCom budget and financial analyst Kim Emigh blew the whistle on an internal policy change that he knew to be fraud, "pure and simple." When he got no response from his superiors, he began moving up the hierarchy, eventually reaching the chief operating officer, who told him: "On behalf of myself and corporate accounting, I want to thank you for making us aware of this (rest assured your name has never been mentioned)." He was fired ten weeks later. "It's hard to be the small guy and try to get the world to listen that this is headed in the wrong direction," says Janet Emigh, his wife.

Whistleblowing came to prominence as a phenomenon with the 1999 movie *The Insider* when Jeffrey Wigand (played by Russell Crowe) made huge personal sacrifices to expose the Brown & Williamson Tobacco Corporation and the entire tobacco industry for spiking cigarettes with nicotine. Whistleblowers have popped up at hundreds of companies, not just such infamous cases such as Arthur Andersen, Quorum Health Services, Xerox, Morton Thiokol, Halliburton, Smith Barney, Global Crossing, Tyco, and Duke Energy.

The federal government was the first U.S. organization to safeguard whistleblowing. Furious at unscrupulous suppliers saddling his soldiers with broken rifles and lame horses during the Civil War, Abraham Lincoln persuaded Congress in 1863 to pass the False Claims Act, also known as the Lincoln Act or Informer's Act. Lincoln was experiencing firsthand what Benjamin Franklin averred a century prior, "There is no kind of dishonesty into which otherwise good people more easily and frequently fall than that of defrauding the government." The law encouraged citizens to blow the whistle on companies swindling the public purse. Not only could diligent citizens feel good about helping their country, they also got 50 percent of the money recovered or damages won. The law's major failing, however, was that the whistleblower had to personally take the swindler to court in order to get the reward. For this reason, few citizens actually blew the whistle.

Five score and eighteen years later, in 1981, the General Accounting Office estimated the federal government was bilked tens of billions of dollars annually. The Department of Justice estimated that fraud consumed up to 10 percent of government expenditures. In response to the perception of rampant illegality, Congress strengthened the rewards for whistleblowing in 1986. It protected employees from reprisal by their employer and gave the whistleblower 15 to 25 percent of the funds recovered if the government took the swindler to court. Congress noted at the time that "if the Government can pass a law that will increase the resources available to confront fraud against the Government without paying for it with taxpayers' money, we are all better off. This is precisely what [the False Claims Act] is intended to do: deputize ready and able people who have knowledge of fraud against the government to play an active and constructive role through their counsel to bring to justice those contractors who overcharge the government."[5]

Citizens responded enthusiastically. More than 3,600 lawsuits have been filed since the 1986 revisions. In the 2000–01 fiscal year the government recovered nearly $1.2 billion, with more than $210 million awarded to individuals who disclosed the frauds. The General Accounting Office maintains a "Fraudnet" Web site where citizens can submit examples of fraud and abuse of government funds.

With so much money flowing to citizens blowing the whistle on companies trying to fleece the government, it's no surprise a small industry has grown up to encourage the practice. Dozens of Web sites, typically run by law firms, beckon potential whistleblowers with offers of comfort and guidance. The www.whistleblowerfirm.com site says:

> If you have found this Web site, then you have taken a significant first step. Our clients are current and former employees of companies that do business with the government, either directly or indirectly. They are highly skilled, ethical, and have already tried to bring the fraud to their superior's attention. Almost always, they are told (in some fashion) to mind their own business. We understand what you have gone through, or continue to go through. This is a pattern we have experienced through our clients over and over. We also understand what it takes to file and prosecute a proper and responsible . . . lawsuit. Give us a call. We can help you both in and out of court. All communications are replied to promptly and in confidence.

Such sites can be hugely comforting to a potential whistleblower. "To be a whistleblower," writes C. Fred Alford, "is to step outside the Great Chain of Being, to join not just another religion, but another world. Sometimes this other world is called the margins of society, but to the whistleblower it feels like outer space."[6] Now that employees have such ready access to support mechanisms, it's not surprising that the number of whistleblowing incidents increases yearly.

When *Time* asked its Persons of the Year whistleblowers if they would have done anything differently, Watkins replied, "I wouldn't not do it. [But] what I really failed to grasp was the seriousness of the emperor-has-no-clothes phenomenon. I thought leaders were made in moments of crisis, and I naively thought that I would be handing [Enron chairman] Ken Lay his leadership moment. I honestly thought people would step up. But I said he was naked, and when he turned to the ministers around him, they said they were sure he was clothed."

More than a decade before *Time* declared these whistleblowers heroes, Congress was so taken with the idea of exposing misdeeds *against* the government that it tried to expand the concept to misdeeds *within* the government, and granted protection to government employees who exposed wrongdoing inside the executive branch. The unanimously passed Whistleblower Protection Act of 1989 forbade reprisals against bureaucrats who revealed illegality, mismanagement, abuse of authority, gross waste, and substantial and specific danger to public health or safety. Subsequent court decisions undermined much of the protection that Congress promised bureaucrats, so in 1994 Congress repassed the law, again unanimously, with tougher provisions. However, the Department of Homeland Security legislation exempted its employees from the whistleblowing protection enjoyed by other civil servants.

Unfortunately, the impact of the Whistleblower Protection Act has been limited. The executive branch is not keen on publicizing misdeeds or incompetence within its ranks. Mismanagement or gross waste is often in the eye of the beholder. Not surprisingly, the bureaucracy prefers to deal with such matters quietly, away from the media spotlight, and in a manner that doesn't reflect on the current administration.

Taxpayer watchdog groups decry the way court decisions and executive branch behavior have gutted the intent of the Whistleblower Protection Act. In a letter to President George W. Bush, the Government Accountability Project lamented that "unless the whistleblower is a celebrity through media exposure like the FBI's Colleen Rowley, the bureaucracy routinely ignores, harasses or silences the messengers through career execution—most frequently by yanking their security clearances and branding them unfit to see classified information."

If public whistleblowers still do not have the protections that Congress has tried to grant, private sector whistleblowers have even less. Employees are protected from employer reprisals only in relatively few circumstances and industries, such as disclosures involving airline safety or violations at nuclear power plants. "We need to understand in this 'land of the free and home of the brave' that most people are scared to death," Dr. Alford said. "About 50 percent of all whistleblowers lose their jobs, about half of those lose their homes, and half of those people lose their families."[7]

But make no mistake: whistleblowing will not go away.

Corporate whistleblowers are typically young and often women. They are not a homogeneous group. Some have strong values that conflict with the behavior of management. Others see a personal risk to themselves in management behavior and make a calculated choice to whistleblow in order to protect themselves. Some financial managers, for example, have been asked to sign statements that they know to be fraudulent and have chosen to whistleblow rather than risk professional or criminal sanctions. Some, no doubt, are troubled individuals who have been isolated from the corporation. Others have less lofty motives such as revenge.

Down under, a group known as Whistleblowers Australia uses the Internet to encourage citizens to speak out about corruption, dangers to the public, and other social issues by encouraging self-help and mutual help among whistleblowers. The organization provides articles and leaflets to whistleblowers and publishes a newsletter. It also holds meetings of whistleblowers and supporters and provides contacts with like-minded individuals and groups.

Corporations pay a heavy price for opacity and for reprisals against whistleblowers. If employees suffer an injustice and feel that they have no place to turn or that the mechanisms supposedly in place are ineffectual, and if they blow the whistle, word spreads like wildfire. If they are still not taken seriously, morale will suffer throughout the organization.[8]

The upshot is that some companies are turning to third parties to operate confidential telephone hotlines or intranet sites that employees can turn to if they want to blow the whistle on improper behavior. The goal of these services is to make employees confident that an indifferent management won't brush their complaint aside. National Hotline Services and The Network each has hundreds of corporate clients. They provide a safe outlet for employees to raise ethical concerns ranging from allegations of sexual harassment, fraud, and kickbacks to safety violations.

Better still, of course, are companies that create cultures of trust, where whistleblowing is unnecessary. Yet every company needs to offer employees an ombudsman, telephone hotline, or other procedure to voice their concerns that is easy to use, well known, and demonstrably free from retaliation. Mistrust is infectious and travels fast.

CORPORATE CHARACTER

How can companies improve their cultures through active transparency? Social scientists and business researchers have argued that high-trust societies more easily spawn large corporations. Francis Fukuyama notes that societies with associations based on family or kinship, religious, or governmental ties but lacking generalized trust (such as China, Hong Kong, Taiwan, France, and Italy) have tended to create smaller, less successful enterprises. High-trust societies like Japan, Germany, and the United States have been more successful in building large-scale enterprises.[9]

Yet corporate cultures vary dramatically among and within Japan, Germany, and the United States. We've spent over a decade showing how focused, networked firms perform better than traditional vertically integrated corporations.[10] In such firms as Kroger, HP, Johnson & Johnson, Herman Miller, Google, and Progressive, bonds of informal trust become more important than formal bonds or hierarchy. Command and control models, typical in Japan and Germany, tend to be less effective than the empowerment models of the United States, Canada, and Scandinavia.[11]

Trust is critical to distributed knowledge work, but the trust of U.S. workers in their employers has soured since the economic downturn began in 2000, and the upbeat can-do attitude of the 90s has largely evaporated. Workers are depressed by the weak economy, the high-profile bankruptcies such as Enron and WorldCom, and the lavish compensation packages many senior executives have enjoyed.

A *New York Times*/CBS News poll found in October 2002 that U.S. workers were more anxious about the economy than at any time since 1993. The survey found that 56 percent considered the economy fairly bad or very bad. Thirty-nine percent said they thought the economy would get worse, and only 13 percent predicted it would get better.

The *Times* noted that "in a strong departure from the 1990's, when CEOs were often hailed as heroes, workers are voicing a sense of anger, even betrayal, toward top executives. Among experts in human resources, a sharp debate is under way about whether workers' commitment to their employers has waned in response to corporate downsizing and a sense that many top executives have betrayed workers and investors."

According to a Rutgers–University of Connecticut poll, 58 percent of workers think that most top executives are interested only in looking out for themselves, even if it harms their company. For the first time in two decades, most workers surveyed said they would join a union if they could, seeing this as a path to greater job security. Unions are capitalizing on this receptive mood and using technologies such as the Web to speak directly to workers in ways that were not possible previously.

America's nonhierarchical businesses feed on trust, and relatedly, are more vulnerable to crises of trust. Traditional corporate hierarchies have stronger mechanisms for control. In Japan, for example, there is reverence for authority. Obedience, fear of punishment, and status based purely on rank help ensure stability. Many individuals have enjoyed lifetime employment at one company. Promotion has often been based on seniority rather than on merit. Employees work in the offices of their corporation and rarely remotely or at home.

In networked, distributed firms such as those in the United States, trust is more implicit and not as formally baked into organizational structures. As such it is fragile. Corporate cultures are more merito-cratic.[12] Trust is based on the tacit understanding that if you play by the rules and perform well, you will succeed. When trust breaks down, the results are typically disastrous and swift. Today, businesses face a clear and present danger: a decline of generalized trust in society, combined with behavior that undermines trust in the workplace. People who performed well in many failing companies nonetheless lost everything. Some who failed to perform made out like bandits (and some *were* bandits).

Firms need to be of good character, not unlike people. When we think of individuals having character, we conjure up traits like honesty, reliability, benevolence, and integrity. Persons of good character are forthright, straight shooting, and open in their interactions with others. They abide by their commitments. They conduct their lives on the basis of ethical values. These are the same traits that characterize the open enterprise.

The people in a firm determine its character. But a firm can also shape the character of its people. Most assume that a person's character is formed long before that person becomes an adult and enters the workforce. Some economists might even argue that work and competition bring out the self-interest in people and that the influence of the workplace on character is somehow negative. But Ralph Larsen, CEO of Johnson & Johnson, argues that work in the modern firm can be a character-building experience.

> I contend that the influence does not have to be negative. Indeed, our corporations and free enterprise system are surely in jeopardy if it is. On the contrary, it is our experience that the modern workplace can be an extraordinarily powerful and positive character-building institution. I feel that character—both personal and corporate—is a company's most valuable resource and attribute.

In the 1930s during the Great Depression, Johnson & Johnson CEO Robert Wood Johnson wrote *Try Reality*, a pamphlet that asked business to adopt a "new industrial philosophy." He said, "Industry only has the right to succeed where it performs a real economic service and is a true social asset." He went on to order the responsibilities a company has to its various stakeholders. Johnson believed that if companies were going to be allowed by governments and society to operate in a free market system, unencumbered by burdensome laws and regulations, then they needed to act in socially responsible ways. A few years later he expanded this view into the J&J Credo.

Of course, corporate character is not defined by a document. It is defined by the actions of people. No document can foresee all the choices that employees face in an increasingly complex and transparent world. Values need to be in the DNA of the firm. Johnson & Johnson awkwardly but aptly calls this "credo-ization."

A salesperson is invited to a competitor's suite at a trade show. A manager must lay off someone, and the lowest performer is the only woman in his group. An employee receives a funny but sexually explicit email from a colleague. An executive can increase share price and short-term investor confidence by deeply cutting head count. A client manager has an opportunity to overcharge a customer and make his bonus. A salesperson is asked by a government official for a "favor." A manager is congratulated by the CEO for someone else's accomplishments. A freshly hired M.B.A. is explaining disappointing quarterly results to an institutional shareholder. A purchasing agent gets offered courtside seats by a key vendor.

When J&J employees face such dilemmas, the credo provides a guide to do the right thing. According to Larsen, "It helps good people be the best they can be. In this sense . . . it is a character builder."

Increasingly, in a transparent world such corporate character is critical to business success. Says Larsen, "We have learned that principled action is not only the moral thing, it is the correct business decision. With each right decision we make we reinforce the trust people have in our products and us. And conversely with each transgression we erode the special character so critical to our success." When Tylenol's integrity was violated by the 1982 lid-tampering scandal, Johnson & Johnson's stock immediately dropped 18 percent. But it recovered quickly. Larsen reflects on the experience: "It has been my experience that people who make it a habit to work at making the correct ethical decisions in the countless small choices we face in life are most often those same people who can be counted on to make the ethically correct decisions on the big things—when a crisis hits and the pressure is on."

The character of an open enterprise starts with the CEO. Tony Comper is the CEO of the BMO Financial Group, a financial services organization with $250 billion in assets and 33,000 employees. BMO provides a broad range of retail banking, wealth management, and investment banking products and solutions in Canada and, through Chicago-based Harris bank, the United States.

As in any company, tricky situations arise continually. Comper handles these differently than many CEOs. When information comes to light that might embarrass the bank, his staff reports they've never heard him ask "How do we get out of this mess?" Rather he poses the question "What's the right thing to do here?" This is now part of the bank's folklore; a culture of doing the right thing has developed. It seemed to make short-term business sense to turn off the credit tap to small businesses during the 2001–02 downturn. But Comper decided to be loyal to small business and take some short-term risks. Doing the right thing in this case meant standing by customers through tough times. The result: BMO more than doubled its market share.

Persons other than a CEO can, of course, influence a firm's character. Mahatma Gandhi said: "You must be the change you wish to see in the world." When individuals show character in a transparent world, it can be infectious.

THE POWER SHIFT

While increasingly essential to business success, transparency is a double-edged sword since it also creates an unprecedented power shift in favor of employees, particularly those who are strong contributors. This promises to shake the foundation of the corporation as much as the original trade union movement of the early industrial corporation. Considering the tough job market and the huge increases in executive compensation over the past years, it may seem that employees are losing ground. But there's more here than meets the eye.

Transparency brings market forces to bear on labor markets. The friction in labor markets is melting as salaried personnel have newfound access to information about jobs and employers through companies such as Vault.com and Monster.com. When unemployment is high (as in the case of Silicon Valley today), knowledge of labor markets is less useful. But with normal levels of unemployment, knowledge is power—especially for people with in-demand capabilities.

CGI is a rapidly growing information technology services firm with more than 21,000 employees worldwide and revenues of more than $2 billion. More than 80 percent of employees—which it calls members—are shareholders. Members can change management behavior in various ways. For example, in each region there is an annual meeting/dinner that all members attend. Here they can challenge corporate management in what president Mike Roach refers to as a bear pit session. Says Roach, "This is not just about management accountability but member accountability. If you're an owner of the company, as most members are, you have responsibility to provide leadership." Like many firms, CGI surveys employee satisfaction each year. The difference is that management compensation depends in part on the results. "If you treat employees as owners, you have a higher responsibility to them, and they have responsibility to you. Profit sharing encourages transparency," says Roach.

IBM, though, generally viewed as one of the best employers, and a leader of the digital revolution, has experienced the effects of the shift to employee power. It is closely scrutinized by a number of online employee groups who are worried about the company's attempts to reduce pension and health care benefits. In May 1999 IBM announced a plan to move from a traditional pension plan to a cash balance plan, saying that only 30,000 employees near retirement age could remain with the older, more generous scheme. Within months, however, the computer giant was forced to more than double the number of employees who could remain with the traditional plan as angry workers organized via the Internet on Yahoo! discussion groups and other Web sites.

IBM, to its credit, faced a difficult problem with its pension program, where it needed to shift resources toward stock ownership in order to attract talented workers during the technology boom. When it was clear that the new program wasn't going to fly, IBM took the right approach in dealing with this crisis. It engaged with the employees to address the situation. Says IBM executive Jon Iwata, "We focused on creating a dialogue. We have a rich tradition established many decades ago to allow employees to express how they genuinely feel about things through many channels. We have a speak-up program, we have the open door program, different programs to allow employees to express how they genuinely feel about things to the very top of the business, and believe me, sometimes they utilize those channels to express grave dissatisfaction." Iwata today doesn't view this as "one that management lost." Rather, "We think that to be consistent with our values and our relationship with our workforce we needed to make the required adjustment."

McDonald's is quickly learning the power of increased transparency to its workers and the general public. Until recently, the company was pretty much having transparency forced on it.

McDonald's scattered structure has long frustrated attempts to unionize its workforce. Often when a store is unionized, the company retaliates by shutting it down. But with the Internet's arrival, McDonald's employees can now contact one another, share information, and organize in a manner that was previously undreamt of. One of the best-known employee sites is the McDonald's Workers' Resistance.[13] According to its Web site, the Resistance doesn't have "any leaders, paid campaigners or anything like that, we're all just crew members like you. MWR will only be successful if workers keep getting involved, that means you! If every McDonald's worker who read this site and agreed with us got involved then together we would be able to do wonderful things. We need your help!"

The oldest and most popular anti-McDonald's Web site is McSpotlight, operating since 1996 and offering more than 120 megabytes of the inside scoop on McDonald's operations. It is designed for the general public, not just employees.

McSpotlight does more than could any union. It created the McInformation Network, a U.K.-based group drawing on volunteers from 22 countries on four continents. The network is dedicated to "compiling and disseminating factual, accurate, up-to-date information—and encouraging debate—about the workings, policies and practices of the McDonald's Corporation and all they stand for. The network also highlights opposition to McDonald's and other transnational companies."

Borrowing a page from the environmental movement, McDonald's protest Web sites encourage citizens to think globally and act locally. By sharing experiences from around the world, protesters realize that they are part of a much larger movement and that their local efforts matter. If you want to stop a McDonald's from being built in your

neighborhood, you can take heart that hundreds of other neighbor-
hoods in dozens of countries are doing the same.

To what does McDonald's owe the pleasure of being the target of
strident, state-of-the-art vigilante Web sites? McSpotlight explains:
"Yes, we appreciate that McDonald's only sell hamburgers and loads of
other corporations are just as bad. But that's not the point. They have
been used as a symbol of all multinationals and big business relentlessly pursuing their profits at the expense of anything that stands in
their way.

"McDonald's were chosen for this dubious honor because a) everyone's heard of them, b) they're bullies who threaten legal action on
almost anyone who dares criticize them, c) there's stacks of in-depth
information available about them (thanks to the research that's gone
into the McLibel Trial), d) the nature of their business means loads of
contemporary issues are relevant, e) they pioneered various unwel-
come practices which other companies have followed and f) they take
themselves far too seriously."

The site attracts more than 1 million visitors per month, with no
facet of the company's operations left unexplored. Before the World
Wide Web arrived, most protesters measured success by the amount
of media coverage they attracted. Much like the tree falling in the forest, if a protest doesn't get television time or column inches in a newspaper, it didn't really happen. But increasingly protesters don't care
whether the local newspaper gives them publicity; they can achieve
exposure on their own.

October 16, 2002, was the eighteenth annual Worldwide Anti-
McDonald's Day, and McSpotlight claims it was the most successful
so far. For the first time, the McDonald's Workers' Resistance encouraged employees to join the protests. Employees were asked to not
show up for work or to go to work and sabotage operations. Accordingly to the Resistance Web site, it had reports of local protests from
Australia to Mexico, Russia to South Africa, Brazil, and the United
States, and throughout eastern and western Europe, including Ireland
and the United Kingdom. As described by the site:

On the day itself, according to reports received, action included: strikes
in stores in Paris and Norfolk; a stoppage in Moscow; attempted strike

at a store in New Zealand and London, England; a walkout in Nottingham; collective resignations in Glasgow; many acts of absenteeism, defiance and disruption by individuals and small groups of workers in many countries including the US, Ireland, Australia, Canada, Denmark, Madrid, and Germany. In addition there were solidarity actions by protestors in support of McDonald's workers in the North of Ireland, Germany, Australia, Scotland, Sweden, Serbia and England and especially in Italy (including a blockade in Milan).

In six Paris McDonald's controlled by CNT France they went on strike around specific demands related to full time employment and standardized pay rates. They gathered at 10:00am by the 'Fountain Of Innocents', at 3pm they were due to meet with McDonald's representatives and they arranged a public meeting in the evening.

In Norfolk a strike crippled a restaurant, there was a picket that held for most of the day. At one point a manager came out to moan pitifully, "Why are you doing this?" "Read the leaflet." "I'm not reading that," he raged, ripping it up. When McDonald's head office was asked why the store was virtually unstaffed they replied that it was because of "some sad individuals trying to take McDonald's down."

And then there was the magnificent news from Moscow. As far as we can understand, they negotiated with a "friendly" manager to be allowed to stop work for a short time without the matter being taken further. Although lacking much common language, the feeling of international solidarity as we talked on the phone was amazing.

You don't need to form a workers' movement to set up a Web site to criticize your boss. Some frustrated workers go ahead and do it themselves. Consider the battle between pharmaceutical firm Wyeth-Ayerst Canada Inc. and Louise Phaneuf, the company's former manager of training and development. Phaneuf, a single mom, established a Web site to publicize her continuing efforts to receive long-term disability benefits because of chronic pain that she says started while employed by Wyeth-Ayerst.

"Their callous treatment of me during a time when I was seriously ill makes for interesting and enlightening reading for anyone who has Wyeth-Ayerst in mind for a career, is using their products or is presently in their employ," Phaneuf says on the site. Wyeth-Ayerst says such material causes irreparable harm and hurts its ability to attract new staff. Doubtless this is true, if only because some visitors to the site believe where there's smoke there's fire. The drug company asked the Quebec Superior Court to shut the site down and order Phaneuf to pay $100,000 in damages for slander and violating the privacy of Wyeth-Ayerst executives by posting their email addresses. The case was dismissed, and Phaneuf promptly updated her Web site with all the new material generated by the legal proceedings.

The power shift is so pronounced that even unreasonable, marginal employees can reach an audience and cause PR headaches, perhaps sending a firm into a trust crisis. If they can do it, reasonable men and women can do much more.

Knowledge is power and employees have more if it. Memo to managers: get used to it; this is ultimately a good thing. This is the same kind of power that drives innovation and competitive advantage. Rather than fight or flee, engage.

CHAPTER 5

TRANSPARENCY AMONG
BUSINESS PARTNERS

A greengrocer just off the Boulevard St. Germain in Paris offers a modest, carefully displayed variety of vegetables and fruit. Behind each display is a sign listing the product's town, maybe even its farm of origin. It's quite possible that the *patronne* knows the grower personally; maybe he's her brother-in-law or she herself bought the produce from a farmer in a market on the outskirts of Paris.

Your local Stop'n'Shop doesn't offer anything like this, but it may have a decent enough selection of wines from around the world. The best labels name the estate on which the grapes were grown, fermented, and bottled. *Appellation d'origine contrôllée* is France's invaluable branding gift to the global wine industry. It vouchsafes that what's in the bottle has the personal touch of a grower with a name and nuanced reputation.

Such trustworthy transparency at the cash register seems charmingly anachronistic in a mass market world, and we willingly pay a premium for it. We are more accustomed to hearing that a single fast food hamburger contains meat from dozens to hundreds of different cattle from several nameless ranches[1] or that an inkjet printer was designed on three continents, includes parts and materials from four, has been assembled in two, and was altered by three dozen or more companies before it plopped down at our local retailer. Country-of-origin product badges mask a global complex that we can only imagine.

Indeed, the inkjet printer is a miracle of the global supply chain. Its efficient choreography lets Hewlett-Packard, Canon, Epson, and Lexmark profitably price these printers cheaper than many a bottle of wine.[2]

Such modern miracles still leave many in the supply chain grumpy:

they continue to wrestle with the subtleties of simultaneous collaboration and competition. Retailers and vendors tussle about outmoded costs and time-consuming screwups. Brand name companies argue with their outsourced suppliers and distributors about who pays for mistakes and crossed signals. Innovators wrestle with collaboration and intellectual property issues. Employees wonder when employers will smarten up. Consumers don't trust what they buy, whether for value, health and safety, environmental, or ethical reasons.

Old habits die hard: mistrust, combativeness, and high-handed buying practices characterize most supply chains in 2003. Despite vaunted progress by innovators like Wal-Mart, Procter & Gamble, and Cisco, supply chain cheerleaders—trade association executives, academics, and consultants—still find themselves pleading for more collaboration, trust—and transparency.

TECHNOLOGICAL REVOLUTION

Despite the failures of the 1990s e-business mania, technology continues to change the way businesses work. Indeed, manufacturing, retail, and many service industries are in the midst of an information revolution that will extend transparency to the smallest, most granular business events. It's the product of Auto-ID technologies: radio-powered microchips, each tinier than a grain of sand, that broadcast a unique serial number like a talking bar code.[3] The most common Auto-ID tool will be the radio frequency identification (RFID) tag. Once costing $50 each—and currently about 5¢ to 10¢—these smart little communicating tags will soon cost almost nothing. It will be good business to stick one on or in nearly any foodstuff, part, finished item, package, pallet, or container that moves through a supply chain. Also tagged will be every working object in the supply chain, from dolly cart to sorting machine to precision robot. Of course, all workers will carry Auto-ID tags too. Bits and atoms merge; soon every thing will be connected.

RFID tags aren't mere passive bar codes; they're smart and they can talk. Each contains a tiny microcomputer that exchanges information wirelessly with RFID readers in production lines, trucks, retail stores, homes, and handheld devices. A food item tag at the grocery store could tell your user-friendly personal digital assistant (PDA) about its calorie and cholesterol count (for dieters and diabetics), allergy alerts (e.g., peanuts), organic or genetically modified content, and so on. On the spot, if you wished, you could get a product rating from a trusted adviser, whether a favorite chef, consumer group, or environmental organization. Some growers will use this transparency to differentiate their tomatoes or lamb chops. *Apellation d'origine contrôllée* could very well become a new force in the supermarket.

The oft-predicted no-checkout grocery trip may finally come true: a reader at the exit instantly totes up the prices from all the tags on your cart, you authorize payment with the wave of a key fob, and off you go. The system loads a detailed receipt into your PDA and personal Web site.

Why would producers and retailers spend money to provide such risky transparency to consumers? Retailers and their suppliers will install Auto-ID to save billions in the supply chain. Once the system is in place, they can hardly deny consumers the transparency that is so readily available. Indeed, consumer visibility into the supply chain will become a competitive differentiator.

What benefits will sellers get? The supply side of Auto-ID is even more dramatic than the consumer side. As you toss a bird into your grocery cart, a nearby store reader will set off a process that tells staff when to refill the shelves. The reader also advises the grocer's automated replenishment system of your purchase; when a trigger number is reached, it will order more of your favorite kind of chicken: "aerobic" free range, A-1 organic corn fed, and purebred non-GM lineage (naturally!). Auto-IDs will be everywhere in the supply chain. Every chick will get one at birth. Auto-ID will track its diet, activity levels, protein-to-fat ratio, weight, body temperature, and other key indicators: it can also alert the grower to most health threats. As the bird moves from slaughter through processing and delivery, its existence, location, temperature, and humidity will be monitored continually. No need to open cases of packaged chickens when they arrive at the retail distribution center; the networked distribution management system will describe the cargo, report on the health indicators of each carcass, and divvy the cargo out to trucks bound for various grocery stores. Same at the grocer's: no need for manual checking; wireless data capture updates the inventory.

Retailers and suppliers across a wide variety of industries from commodity raw materials to custom luxury goods will justify their investment in Auto-ID on cost savings alone. Thanks to automated replenishment, costly "safety volumes" of goods in stores or distant warehouses will no longer be needed. Just-in-time production, logistics, and assembly, while not quite fully realized, will be within reach for even the most complex and unpredictable goods categories. Inventories will be cut by 5 to 25 percent depending on the product category.[4] Shrinkage due to loss, employee theft, and shoplifting will be slashed. Initially most savings will go to consumers due to fierce competition; some of this will later be recovered as profit because Auto-ID enables new services and tailored offerings for premium customers.

New efficiencies will abound. Trucks, containers, and shipping pallets will keep the supply chain informed about where they are and what they are up to; utilization rates and security will improve dramatically. RFID tags will automate recycling. Some items will route themselves back to their original manufacturer for reuse. For others, much finer sorting—for example, by various formulations of glass and plastic—will be performed at the start of the recycling process.

Transparency is the watchword of the Auto-ID-based open business web. On the rare occasion when, for example, an infected chicken gets through to a consumer, the source of the problem will be pinpointed quickly and precisely. Managers at all points of the supply chain, from raw materials production to logistics and consumer retail, will share real-time visibility into customer demand, inventories, production flows, and any problems that can affect the chain's performance. Winning business webs will abandon adversarial nickel-and-dime negotiating and operational opacity in favor of collaborating to maximize efficiency, market share, revenue, and competitive advantage.

Indeed, managers will have no choice, because human beings can't keep up with the volume of information that Auto-ID networks generate. They will depend on sophisticated computer programs that make decisions by combining new information with historical data, performance goals, predictions, and complex optimization algorithms. Supply chains will compete on the basis of information intensity. Transparency and trust will not just be good manners. They will define the difference between winning and losing.

Pundit Dreams?

Many leading companies are promoting Auto-ID as the wave of the future. Indeed, there is more disciplined commitment to this technology—in high industry places—than we saw in the two or three years after the appearance of the Web.

The Auto-ID Center is an industry-funded research program head-quartered at the Massachusetts Institute of Technology in Cambridge, Massachusetts (U.S.), and at the Cambridge Institute for Manufacturing in Mill Lane, Cambridge (U.K.). Its vision is to "revolutionize the way we make, buy, and sell products by merging bits (computers) and atoms (humans) together for optimal mutual communication. Everything will be connected in a dynamic, automated supply chain that joins businesses and consumers together to benefit global commerce and the environment."

The center's sponsors include companies and government departments that would use Auto-ID (like Canon, Coca-Cola, the U.S. Department of Defense, Gillette, Johnson & Johnson, Target, Tesco, and Wal-Mart) and technology vendors (like Accenture, AC Nielsen, IBM, Intel, NTT, Philips, SAP, and Sun).

This initiative faces the usual hurdles of industrywide innovation: technology standards, organizational and process change, business case development, competitive parochialism, regulatory hurdles, and sheer inertia. But the initial steps—and the associated names—are promising.

- In November 2002 Gillette announced plans to buy 500 million RFID tags for use on its razors from start-up Alien Technology. The company plans to use them in stores for inventory management and theft prevention (if the shelf notices that lots of razors have left at once, it will notify store security), and also to track products as they move from factory to supermarket. Prior to this announcement, the largest order ever for RFID tags was 30 million for use in Star Wars toys produced for Hasbro.[5]

- Marks & Spencer replaced printed bar codes with RFID tags on 85 million returnable plastic food trays that suppliers deliver to its six distribution depots. The company will save money on printing, labor associated with attaching and reading labels, and a variety of other inefficiencies. Its goal is to displace $8.5 million per year.[6]

- RFID improved transparency, health, and safety for 37,000 runners in the 2002 Chicago Marathon. All racers stuck the ChampionChip RFID on their shoes. With a few readers strategically placed along the route, for the first time the marathon could record each runner's precise start, finish, and split times. The readers also discouraged cheating. An unintended health and safety benefit happened at the end of the race. Before, many runners who waited in line for official finishing times—instead of properly cooling down—ended up in a medical tent. Now that they get results as soon as they cross the finish line, they can begin cooling down immediately.[7]

- In June 2003 Wal-Mart told its top 100 product suppliers to put RFID on all shipping pallets by 2005. Its CIO, Kevin Turner, said, "RFID will give new meaning to the notion of real-time management. We see opportunities in everything from global supply-chain visibility to tracking on-shelf product availability to replacing our current antitheft tags to allowing customers to check themselves out when they leave our stores."[8]

- The CEO of the Grocery Manufacturers of America strongly endorsed Auto-ID, saying Procter & Gamble hopes to use it to cut inventory by 40 percent, or $1.5 billion, per year.[9]

The transparency imperative in the supply chain is unmistakable. But this is neither your grandfather's supply chain nor your grandfather's firm.

THE RISE OF BUSINESS WEBS

By the beginning of the twentieth century Adam Smith's vision of compact, owner-operated businesses had given way to a capitalism of large scale, vertically integrated joint-stock corporations. These firms operated with supplier-driven, command-control hierarchies, division

of labor for mass production, lengthy planning cycles, and stable
industry pecking orders. Ford Motor Company didn't just build cars. It
owned rubber plantations to produce raw materials for tires and
marine fleets for shipping materials on the Great Lakes. Hearst didn't
just publish newspapers. He churned out newsprint from his millions
of acres of pulpwood forest. IBM's most profitable products during
the Great Depression were cardboard punch cards; it built and sold
clocks until well into the 1970s.[10]

While big, do-all corporations seemed natural in the middle of the
twentieth century, they run counter to a core principle of liberal economics: that the open and competitive marketplace is the best source
of value for money. Could Ford's private fleet outperform specialized
merchant marine companies like American Steamship? If not, why did
Ford enter the shipping business when it could get better, faster, and
cheaper services from outside parties? Pushing the issue, isn't vertical
integration eerily similar to Soviet central planning? The economist
(and disillusioned socialist) Ronald Coase considered these issues during the 1930s and asked an even more fundamental question: "Why
does the firm exist?"

His Nobel prize–winning answer was transaction costs, which arise
when entrepreneurs expend time and money to find suppliers, write
contracts, handle the complexities of working with other parties, coor-
dinate their activities, and check the quality of their work. Coase
argued that a firm will expand as long as costs inside are lower than
outside.[11] In the 1930s, the era of manual typewriters, telexes, and
telephones (and no computers or Internet), transaction costs were so
high that vertical integration made sense.

Beginning in the 1970s, information and communications technologies caused transaction costs to plunge so low that Coase's law
put the engine of corporate expansion into reverse as firms began to
outsource activities to the competitive marketplace. Faster, better, and
cheaper information—in a word, transparency—resulted in lower
transaction costs and the emergence of a new kind of firm. We
described this new sort of firm—or collection of firms—with coauthor
Alex Lowy in our book *Digital Capital*.

Researchers have given such groupings various names—virtual corporation, business ecosystem, business web (our preferred name),
value network, process network, or (more prosaically) outsourcing.

Whatever you call it, most observers agree that organizations increasingly focus on what they do best and rely on partners, suppliers, and customers for the rest.

Economists who built on Coase's thinking pointed out that one cost of going outside is the business risk of dealing with outside agents who might end up competing with a firm's core business or make it a hostage to their unique competencies. Such risks apply especially where a supplier can monopolize a unique capability that is central to what a firm does. This happened to IBM after it launched what was to become the main design for personal computers in 1983. Its somewhat "open" design sourced the operating system from a new company called Microsoft and the main processor chip from Intel. By the end of the decade, IBM lost control of the PC market to Microsoft and Intel, which came to dominate the industry and capture most of its profits.

Such risks apply particularly in areas that are highly strategic to a company. Some might argue that strategic activities—the essence of what makes a particular firm unique and competitive—should always remain inside the firm. But who's to say what's truly strategic? Competitive conditions, as well as the new flexibility that results from declining transaction costs, can justify outsourcing just about anything.

As its 2001 annual report says, "IBM used to be the poster child for closed, proprietary computing," once at the heart of its ability to dominate its industry and control its customers. Then it lost the PC to Microsoft, while its homegrown software for big computers fell to the nonproprietary Unix. After a few short years, IBM was gasping for breath. Then, under Lou Gerstner, it came to terms with these changes and the new economics of the computer industry by shifting to professional services and business software. It dumped its operating systems business in favor of Linux. Now IBM touts an operating system produced by a business web: an industry-spanning self-organized collection of individuals and companies (including itself, of course).

If IBM can take such risks, then perhaps anything can be outsourced except strategic and operational oversight and coordination. A multibillion dollar firm might consist of little more than a board of directors supported by a CEO, a CFO, and a small staff.

Business webs are everywhere. The most striking are led by Internet-based companies that defied the cynics and sustained huge growth with minimal physical assets and vast quantities of market partners. A quintessential example is eBay, an exchange marketplace for millions of sellers and buyers and now a mainstream retail industry player. While its reported revenues in 2002 were $1.2 billion with a $250 million profit, its retail marketplace facilitated overall sales of $15 billion. With 4,000 employees, this means that eBay facilitated $3.75 million in auction sales per employee and got $300,000 in company revenues per employee. Compare this to Wal-Mart, with sales of $220 billion and a profit of $6.7 billion (a 3 percent overall profit versus eBay's 21 percent) and 1.3 million employees; it got $169,000 in company revenues per employee.

Business webs aren't just for specialized e-commerce firms; they are also widespread in traditional industries. Young technology companies like Cisco and Dell were early adopters of the Internet to spike efficiency and innovation in their partner networks. Notoriously, neither makes much of what it sells.

Older companies with legacies of vertical integration have also become business web choreographers. Detroit's Big 3 focus increasingly on stick handling the complexities of the car business, using business web partners for everything from design and color selection to information technology services and parts manufacturing. Daimler-Chrysler even lets Magna International assemble entire vehicles. For cobbling none of the shoes it designs and sells, Nike is put down by some as a hollow brand. Wal-Mart's logistics feats with firms such as Johnson & Johnson enable it to crush competitors like a Sherman tank. Everywhere, outsourcing is hot, spawning the exceptional growth of companies like Accenture and CGI (information technology and business processes), Celestica and Solectron (electronics manufacturing), UPS and DHL (logistics), and Biovail and GCI (clinical drug trials).

Transparency both enables and is required for networked business models. CGI's Michael Roach explains: "We're positioning ourselves as an extension of our clients' capability value chain. Their business processes are our business processes. Just to get an outsourcing partnership going, each party needs vast information about the other— their capabilities, their history, processes, systems, even culture."

Because 70 percent of CGI revenues come from such long-term relationships, transparency is a permanent condition. Says Roach: "If
you're going to be an extension of a client's business you need to be
open in fact, aligning your strategy and behavior with your client's. If
your clients are doing well, you do too. If your clients are doing badly,
so do you. Pain and gain are shared across the value chain."

S-WEBS IN THE B-WEB

As a piece of working computer software, Linux is a tangible, albeit
"virtual," product. But not all value comes from tangible goods,
whether hard, soft, or virtual. Also important—increasingly so in a
knowledge-based economy—are exchanges of *intangibles*, what we
have previously called digital capital[12] and what others describe as
knowledge assets or intellectual capital. Knowledge, relationships,
ideas, processes—and trust—are assets that compare in importance to
goods, services, and cash. Many Linux developers vigilantly defend the
intellectual commons of open source and expect megaplayers like
IBM to abide by the community's rules. Thus, the Linux open source
community is, for IBM, both a business web (which develops a
product that it takes to its customers) and a stakeholder web (which
scrutinizes IBM's behavior as an industry "gorilla"). In this sense, a
stakeholder web, which we described in Chapter 2, is a dimension of
the business web. Aligning the hopes, expectations, and demands of
the s-web with the economic imperatives of the b-web is a winning
strategy.

Hewlett-Packard has recognized that its s-web extends beyond
obvious cash nexus relationships, and also sees the s-web as facilitating
growth of its b-web. Its e-inclusion program is a "vision of empowering
and enabling all the world's people to access the social and economic
opportunities of the digital age." The program relies on partnerships
with companies, governments, development agencies, nonprofit organizations, and individuals. In fact, an explicit goal is to turn such partnerships into an ecosystem. Hewlett-Packard embraces organizations
like McKinsey & Company, Grameen Bank, the U.S. Department of
Commerce, Freedom from Hunger, and the World Resources Institute
to align its business web with an extended stakeholder web. Sample

projects include a microfinance initiative, which provides small loans ($50 to $750) to poor women to help them build businesses and bring their families out of poverty; DevelopmentSpace Network, which uses technology to link donors (including HP employees) to social entrepreneurs; and the Global Digital Divide Initiative, a World Economic Forum project aimed at fostering technology-driven economic growth and entrepreneurship in developing countries. In all these projects, HP expects to simultaneously develop new capabilities, products, and services; expand its markets in emerging economies; and help build a better world.

Debra Dunn, HP's senior vice president of corporate affairs, comments, "We do this for two reasons. One, to grow revenue. The other is that we need a stable global context for our business to thrive. The world has never been more unstable in the past 18 years of my career at HP. As a company, we need to be part of solving these problems."

The flip side of all this is that companies should recognize that even s-web opponents can turn around to contribute to the economic goals of the b-web. As we describe in Chapter 6, People for the Ethical Treatment of Animals (PETA) forced its agenda onto the fast-food industry during the late 1990s. Some tried to ignore the organization with negative impact on their reputation and customer loyalty, while others (Burger King in particular) engaged with it—to their benefit.

The business web is an expansive concept. Depending on the initiative or the issue, its s-web dimension—dependent, of course, on transparency—can include millions of people, all sorts of stakeholders, and a vast array of issues.

TRUST AND TRANSPARENCY IN THE BUSINESS WEB

The Potential

Where transaction costs are low, a business web gets going more easily and performs better. Trust lowers transaction costs; transparency boosts trust. Transparency in a business web also improves operational efficiency. This becomes apparent when companies use new techniques to wring costs out of their supply networks.

We do not propose a one-size-fits-all, totally naked view of the world. As with all good things, transparency has a law of diminishing returns. Exposing proprietary trade and competitive secrets, or private employee and customer data can severely damage, even destroy, a company and its stakeholders. There are obvious examples: a bank should always protect the secrecy of its customers' account balances. But sometimes the right answer is less than obvious: Is it in Microsoft's interest to publish the proprietary source code of the Windows operating system? Resolving such trade-offs, as we shall see, is the art of competitive strategy in a world of business webs.

In the old economy, supplier relationships were routinely combative. Companies told suppliers to cut prices or lose their business. Buyers and sellers used whatever privileged knowledge they had (what economists call information asymmetries) to gain short-term price, timing, or quality advantages over one another. Now, suppliers *participate* in the business web. Competition is often business web versus business web rather than merely firm versus firm; in these situations, suppliers function as partners rather than adversaries. Undue secrecy, win-lose negotiating, and an insistence on exclusivity become counterproductive.

Cisco, for example, knows what its suppliers pay for components, labor, and facilities. It sees through the value chain, negotiates appropriate margins with partners, and balances its short-term interest in minimizing costs against its long-term interest in the robustness of its suppliers. Cisco's suppliers have a new kind of power derived, ironically, from their vulnerability. Transparency liberates them to detail the costs of their operation so they win fair treatment on strategic grounds.

"We are removing the boundaries of the firm. Everyone's business is everyone's business," says Celestica CEO Eugene Polistuk. Celestica, along with its competitors like Solectron, provides contract manufacturing to Cisco and other name brand electronics companies. "Before, we had networks of data: now we have intelligent systems based on standards. The openness, the pervasiveness, the speed and the sheer volume of information is redefining the way we work together."

The faster the information the better. Instantaneous information about demand, special promotions, quality, availability, and any glitches that happen along the way, all enabled by next-generation information systems, ensures that the right products appear at the right place at the right time, while keeping inventory to a minimum.

Managers who either hide or lack information about their own firm's operations cannot manage human capital and transparent relationships within a b-web.

Bill Watkins is president and chief operating officer of Seagate Technology, a company that builds hard disk storage devices for computers. It's a highly competitive business. "Our product cycles last six months to a year, but they take two years to develop. Price is constantly dropping and storage capacity is constantly increasing. So to survive it takes a culture where you can't hide problems. We don't have time for that." The company must be honest with customers when problems occur, which can be a challenge when other companies practice deception. "There are always issues, but we can explain that they are issues we can control. So we say, 'We have a problem here, but don't panic.' How do you communicate that when others have the tendency to massage data to hide problems? Some customers will overreact. Most respond properly. In our long-term relationships, our customers know to trust us. Openness builds trust."

This is the theory and potential of transparency in business webs. The reality proves the potential often enough, but not always.

The Reality

United States labor productivity growth began to accelerate in 1995 in tandem with the growth of the Internet. Productivity increased from an average annual growth rate in the 1.5 percent range to better than 2.5 percent. In the recession of 2002 companies tightened spending and used what economist Robert Samuelson described as Darwinian techniques to get more out of fewer employees and tighter information technology investments; the growth rate jumped to a remarkable 4.8 percent.[13]

Transparency and trust in the business web were critical in industries, like retail and wholesale distribution (led by Wal-Mart), semiconductors (Intel), and computer assembly (Dell), that enjoyed some of the biggest productivity breakthroughs. It may seem strange that trust mechanisms are only now being formalized in various industries.

But the legacy among most trading partners is mistrust and conceal-ment. Only in the late 1980s, says P&G global external relations officer Charlotte Otto, "was there a mindset shift from thinking of retailers as a necessary evil to thinking of them as our partners." Indeed, Wal-Mart's supply chain transparency in the aid of efficiency does not protect it from charges of unfair labor practices from union-ists, media, and human rights proponents, while many suppliers grum-ble about its stubborn demands across the negotiating table.

Mistrust—if not open warfare—still dominates many business-to-business relationships. According to a 2001 cross-industry survey of suppliers (like Allied Signal and Monsanto), manufacturers (like IBM, Steelcase, Whirlpool, etc.), and retailers (like Amazon, Eddie Bauer, and Wal-Mart) by the Center for Advanced Purchasing Studies:[14]

- No one manages the entire supply chain from end to end.

- Most respondents view supply chain management as strategic, but are cynical about efforts to make it work. They lack management support internally and influence over trading partners externally.

- Many still operate in an adversarial mode, focused on gaining the upper hand on price or fooling competitors. Doubt and suspicion are widespread.

- Most companies participate in many different supply chains. The resulting complexity is a big problem.

- Managers are loath to share vital information even within their own firms—let alone with trading partners.

- Tools, technologies, and techniques for collaborating, sharing infor-mation, and streamlining business processes have yet to be widely adopted. Technological solutions that have been implemented are often insufficient, particularly in the absence of trust-based rela-tionships and changes in daily operations.

The cynic might ask, why not? After all, if firms want trust-based relationships, they can have them inside their own walls. If transaction costs are low enough to let firms procure goods and services externally, surely this doesn't mean firms should forgo their negotiating power. Getting the most for your money is what a competitive marketplace is all about. Outside suppliers (and, for that matter, customers) are market "agents" whose legitimate goal is to use information asymmetries to maximize their own self-interest, making as few concessions as possible.

Yet whatever the industry, from retail to automotive to pharmaceuticals, the cards-close-to-chest alternative leads to the notorious *bullwhip effect*. Procter & Gamble executives coined the term after studying the demand for Pampers disposable diapers. Babies naturally use diapers at a steady and predictable rate, resulting in uniform retail sales trends. But retailer and distributor orders varied, and P&G's own orders to its materials suppliers fluctuated even more. Small events—for example, a postponed order followed by a larger order than usual—were amplified wildly as they moved up the chain. Hence, the bullwhip.

The result is a costly collection of inventory and timing imbalances: too much pulp or plastic in a supplier warehouse and too few diapers at your local store. In industries (like diapers) where profit margins on sales are typically in the low single digits, such foul-ups really stink. In others (like consumer electronics) where a product's entire shelf life can be six months, the bullwhip effect can be catastrophic.

It gets worse. The great fiasco of the telecom supply chain in 2000–01 was the result of overoptimistic projections up and down the line. Distributors like Techdata, Ingram Micro, and Merisel passed big forecasts to manufacturers like Cisco and Nortel, who in turn ordered more finished assemblies from suppliers like Celestica and Solectron. Much of the overoptimism was defensive in nature: each distributor was "reserving" production on spec, to stay ahead of everyone else. Similarly, Celestica and Solectron hedged their bets with big forecasts to component suppliers. Everyone wanted to make sure they had enough goods to meet anticipated demand, and no one realized that the total volume being stocked across the industry was many times what the market would bear. When demand wilted, an entire industry went down the chute. Here and elsewhere, the fundamental cause of the bullwhip effect is opacity: supply chain participants failing to share information in a timely fashion.

Leaders Lead with Transparency

A McKinsey study illustrates how industry leaders apply transparency to such problems. It found that the top productivity driver is well-targeted technological innovation, typically in the form of applications like customer databases, inventory management, interactive voice response systems, and in the example of the semiconductor industry, clever tools for microprocessor design and manufacturing. Several of these applications increase information flow.

A new approach to transparent, trust-based partnering is very slowly spreading from retail into other industries. Collaborative planning, forecasting, and replenishment (CPFR as it is called) relies on three principles:[15]

1. The process focuses on consumer demand and value chain success, rather than on the parochial interests of individual participants.
2. Trading partners jointly develop a single shared forecast that they use to plan activities across the supply chain. All parties are accountable for the defining terms of a transparently shared forecast.
3. All parties commit to the forecast by sharing the risks entailed in removing constraints, such as access to current sales information or advice on changes in market conditions. Shared accountability for transparency strengthens short-term performance and long-term trust.

With transparency in place, retailers can confidently tackle other areas for productivity improvement. One is more precise merchandise planning that enables them to have the right product on the right shelf at the right time. Another is revenue management, which lets them set list and sale prices with precision. Major players use sophisticated software for both merchandise planning and revenue management. But all these are for naught if the b-web falls victim to the bullwhip effect. Without trust and transparency, retail performance can be iffy. However, only a handful of companies are succeeding with CPFR. Most retailers don't want to tip their competitors to next week's Pampers promotion. So they play it close to the chest, while Wal-Mart beats them on volume with "everyday low pricing."[16] Johnson & Johnson supply chain executive Mark Letner describes the dynamics of transparency and trust among b-web partners:

> We have two supply chains. The most elaborate, sophisticated, and heavily invested is the supply chain for direct materials—things that go into the finished product. The end objective is for everyone along the supply chain to understand the end unit forecast—how the product is going into the market, to mitigate their risk. We share scheduling and forecast information with them. They share quality, sometimes cost information with us—all this is essential to support a flow of continuous daily supplier deliveries rather than the old approach of once-a-month deliveries. For indirect materials—carpets, chairs, construction, information technology that make up 2/3 of what we buy—we are looking for the supplier to provide the product and add some value, like installing the carpets and setting up the computer drops. There, the level of sophistication and control is lower. Not crude, but we share much less tactical information.

Transparency changes the dynamics of price negotiations.

> The last thing we want is our suppliers not making money, and the J&J Credo says our suppliers should have an opportunity to make a profit. In the ideal negotiation, we all know what it costs—or should cost—a supplier to deliver something based on historical information, experts and so on, and we negotiate price based on that. Reverse auctions help us get even clearer on what is the lowest price a supplier can afford. I'd rather pay 8 cents more in profit rather than have a supplier bury it in a supposed cost structure.

Transparency, especially with direct materials suppliers, goes much deeper—into supporting a group of special relationships.

> The word partnership is overused. Less than a hundred of our 30,000-plus suppliers, I would say, are true partners. But where we have these partnerships, we might review forecasts, clinical research such as new claims we are trying to develop for a medication, even advertising. We're trying to get them excited about our business.

It also motivates a courageous company to help raise the quality of competition across its industry.

> We will use any expertise we have, including process expertise, technology, and so on, to help a key supplier be successful. Because if they aren't successful, we won't be successful. What really makes us happy is when they take what we've taught them and they go off and market it elsewhere—even to our competitors. Because at the end of the day, we don't compete on price or a particular packaging or technique, but on our ability to execute.

We could tell similar stories about transparency leaders in other industries—companies like Southwest Airlines, General Electric, Charles Schwab, Federal Express, and—not surprising when you think about it—the U.S. military. Typically, these organizations have achieved lopsided advantages relative to their competition, whether on price or innovation, and sometimes on both, by focusing especially on real-time information systems that deliver up-to-date news and decision-making support to anyone in the business web who needs it. Using their knowledge to be demanding of their suppliers on quality and price performance, they also typically do the most to help their suppliers succeed. Once present, such advantages become "mission critical." For winners, transparency is increasingly a matter of survival.

STANDARD FITTINGS

A special kind of transparency reduces the likelihood of the trauma that IBM endured during the 1980s when it lost control over the PC marketplace to Microsoft and Intel. This is the transparency that open standards make possible. Open standards are nothing new. They have been part of industrial society since its inception. The humble electric plug is a perfect example. You can buy any electric appliance with the confidence that it plugs into and runs on any standard wall socket. No one "owns" the rules for making electric plugs or designing electric products that use them. In the United States, Underwriters Laboratories, an independent, not-for-profit organization, tests and certifies the safety of electric products. When the electrical code changes, for example, with the rise of three-pronged grounded plugs, they change for everyone. No company "controls" the three-pronged design.

Such open rules are more widespread than you might think. Industrial plumbing and lighting, automotive components (such as spark plugs and tires), telephone networks, auditing (generally accepted accounting principles), and many other goods and services rely on open standards. With such standards, manufacturers and service providers know that piece parts from various sources will plug into and play with one another. Standards are mechanisms for certifying compliance (i.e., transparency) and provide a level playing field for innovation.

Computer manufacturers' shift to Linux is a competitive strategy, a lesson learned from the PC debacle. Hewlett-Packard and IBM chose to deemphasize homegrown "legacy" operating systems in favor of Linux. This meant treating the operating system as a neutral, standard "fitting" rather than as a differentiating basis for competitive activity. Many parts of the Internet (like email) and technologies that connect to the Internet (like Wi-Fi networks) are similarly open and standards-based. The benefits of an open Linux are many:

- By taking operating systems off the table as a basis for making money, IBM and HP gain a potent weapon for competing against archrivals—Microsoft and Sun—both of which depend on operating systems (Windows and Solaris respectively) to make their financial targets. A collateral benefit is a shift in focus to other areas of strength (services, business software, and hardware).

- Historically, IBM and HP produced and maintained various operating systems for large-scale and specialized computers. Linux provides the cost-saving prospect of simplicity: one operating system for everything. This does not come at zero cost: both companies spend heavily to improve and adapt Linux. Nevertheless, they also get to draw on the free services of outside volunteers who add features and credibility to Linux.

- Hewlett-Packard and IBM gain economic and moral high ground with customers who are happy to pay little or nothing for a key technology. Linux plays well with governments and in emerging markets; it's also winning on Wall Street and in the manufacturing companies of the Midwest.

- Linux helped these companies learn to pick up on innovative, next-generation concepts like grid computing, which (like Linux) originated at the bohemian fringe of the computer industry.

Linux is one of many standard fittings in today's computing environment. But transparent standard fittings—already a given in many industries from railways to meat packing—continue to appear in new arenas to support innovation and cost reduction while meeting the needs of diverse stakeholders:

- RFID tags and their low-tech precursor, bar codes, are standard fittings for retail and logistics companies. Neutral industry bodies, like MIT's Auto-ID Center and the Uniform Code Council, develop and manage their rules of use as open, nonproprietary standards.

- The genetic code is a standard fitting for life. Celera Genomics, after a brief and passionate fling at privatizing the human gene sequence, backed out of the business. It left the field to the public science Human Genome Project, many of whose leaders kept the overall sequence in the public domain. Meanwhile, companies and universities have quietly patented many individual human genes. The U.S. Patent and Trademark Office has a backlog of thousands of new gene patent applications. Should genes be patentable?

- Fundamental to the entire economy are rules about money, the standard fitting of commerce. Though the underlying dynamics may be difficult to fathom, key assumptions—exchange and interest rates—are usually well known and set through an ultimately visible process. Central banks, like the Federal Reserve, set interest rates, while currency exchange rates, set by traders in an open market, are known to all.

Firms support transparent and shared ownership of standard fittings when they see a business case. IBM put its market and brainpower behind Linux for competitive reasons. Wal-Mart and P&G back

RFID because lean high performers (like them) will be best at gaining competitive advantages from the industrywide initiative. Defeat caused Celera's retreat: unable to make money from the genome, the company shifted to pharmaceuticals.

Peer Production

The examples we've been discussing all illustrate a special and powerful kind of production mechanism, one whose continuing vitality depends on transparency in the intellectual commons. We tend to think of production and supply chains as being either inside an individual firm or the result of marketplace transactions—in either case, hierarchically managed by a boss or a buyer. Yet neither in-firm nor firm-market hierarchical transaction truly describes the production mechanisms for Linux, RFID standards, the human genome sequence, or the evolution of basmati rice over centuries (see Chapter 1). In all these cases, a self-organizing, transparent and trust-based cooperative mechanism is at work, whereby individuals and businesses carve out pieces of a problem, work on them a bit, and contribute the results to a larger, more or less self-managing group. Out of the agglomeration and integration of these individual contributions, a new outcome takes shape.

Linux, a complex, industrial-quality operating system may be the most striking, but it is neither the only nor the most recent example of what some call "peer production."[17] We described such models in *Digital Capital* as the "alliance" form of business web.[18]

Alliance production is especially good for knowledge endeavors, particularly collective innovation and the social arts (like jazz and multiplayer games). Alliances often produce better results than hierarchies or markets, especially when a project is broken into modules to be worked by several or many peer individuals or companies. Why? Alliances draw on the varied capabilities to be found among a self-selecting collection of contributors. Rather than assign a task to someone because it's that person's job or because of a contract, people select themselves on the basis of their belief in their own suitability for the task at hand. Then, peers assess each contribution for adoption into the larger whole on the basis of merit—only after the contributor produces it. Does *stockholder web* work for us as a new bit of business jargon? Does this chunk of Linux code really do the trick? Is this gene sequence description scientifically credible? Do we agree on how to use RFIDs to describe the contents of a shopping cart?

Such mechanisms can only work if information flows transparently and relationships embellish trust. Peer production is especially useful when creativity and collaboration are at a premium. With the technology revolution, information has become a readily available factor of production. Unlike physical resources like machines and electricity, knowledge and culture have the unique property of being nonrival: the use value of knowledge (a pop tune, a piece of computer software, a new way to manage inventory in a retail store) is not diminished when it is shared. In other words, knowledge doesn't wear out. Meanwhile the physical resources for knowledge production—computers and communication networks—are cheap and pervasive. Today's scarce resources are human creativity and collaboration, and it is here that peer production shines.

Critically, in peer production, the outcome of work is shared among contributors, sponsoring patrons, and sometimes beyond, whether exclusively among paid-up members of an industry consortium (as with MIT's Auto-ID group) or with the general public (as with Linux or the genome sequence). As we discuss in the next section, such "commons" are the lifeblood of peer production. Arguably, the entire World Wide Web is a peer production extravaganza whose best reference tools (Google) rely on peer review mechanisms.

Because outcomes are shared, only some companies make money from peer production. The Internet's transparency-enabling facilities make it easier. Not only Google but also Amazon and, to a degree, eBay, use peer production techniques. Other examples include online games, chat groups, Weblogs, mutual help and support (whether of a personal, technical, or medical nature). Companies that "host" such services can make money directly from the peer production (selling access or the results) or from related sources (advertising or product sales).

Others invest in peer production to provide a foundation for related money-making activities. When an IBM, Hewlett-Packard, or Oracle works for free to help develop Linux as a "standard fitting," it does so with the prospect of selling related software and services. When Wal-

Mart and P&G contribute people and money toward next-generation RFID standard fittings, their game plan is to profit from a more efficient supply chain. When Pfizer contributes its scientists to help decode the human genome, it hopes for a payoff in new drug patents.

But money isn't the only reason for helping out. People—even firms—may engage in peer production for nonmaterialistic reasons, like fun or fame. Often that is enough, especially if the activity is part time and doesn't interfere with necessary materialistic pursuits. Software developers contribute to Linux because they enjoy writing code (fun), while hoping to gain stature and trust from their peers (fame). Some (profit) also monetize their stature via consulting contracts, jobs, publishing, and so on. For academic researchers, the economics of peer production are tried and true. (Social capital can sometimes lose value when dollars cross. "An act of love drastically changes meaning when one person offers the other money at the end, and a dinner party guest who will take out a checkbook at the end of dinner instead of bringing flowers or a bottle of wine at the beginning will likely never be invited again.")[19]

What's exciting is that, mainly because of the Internet's pervasiveness as a transparent collaboration tool, peer production is on the increase. Our main examples—Linux and the Human Genome Project—are among the most powerful. Linus Torvalds, originator and leader of the Linux initiative, says that without the Internet, a self-organizing, motley crew of hackers from around the world could not have created an industrial-strength operating system to challenge Microsoft and gain the allegiance of IBM and Hewlett-Packard. Dr. Eric Lander, director of MIT's Center for Genome Research, told us that the Internet chopped many years off the Human Genome Project.

Transparency in the Commons

Alliance–peer production depends on trust and sharing. When you freely contribute your best, you must be confident that it will not be stolen or used against you. You must have full use of the outputs. Free riding must be rare. Evaluation and integration of your and others' inputs must be fair and effective. Reciprocity engenders trust; the outputs will be available to everyone in the club.

We are describing a "commons." The *Oxford English Dictionary* (another big peer production project) equates the "commons" to a resource held "in common"—"in joint use or possession; to be held or enjoyed equally by a number of persons." As digital commons advocate Lawrence Lessig suggests, a resource held in common is "free" to those "persons." Free, in this sense, does not mean that the resource is handed over for no payment. Rather, "a resource is 'free' if (1) one can use it without the permission of anyone else; or (2) the permission one needs is granted neutrally. . . . The commons is a resource to which anyone within the relevant community has a right without obtaining the permission of anyone else."[20] Common information is transparent, and transparent information is common.

It isn't easy to protect a commons, whether physical or informational. Free riders try to use it up. Encroachers seek to privatize it. When this happens, trust and sharing decline.

Battles over commons mean work for lawyers. Linux and other open source software find protection in a special copyright that all their users must sign. Called the General Public License (GPL), it makes Linux available at no cost (including its inner workings, or "source code"), but requires all users to share—also at no cost—any changes or improvements they make to it. Anyone can have it and anyone can make it better, as long as they share.

You might think that the Internet would always broaden the commons. Lessig (himself a lawyer and law professor) focuses on threats to the commons in large-scale, highly visible peer production and cultural phenomena like music, books, and computing. He argues, and we agree, that while creators and publishers require copyright protection as an incentive to produce, such protection should be limited in time and scope. In the 1790s, 13,000 titles were published in the United States, but only 556 were filed for copyright and these enjoyed limited protection. Now, all works are copyrighted automatically. Initially, a copyright lasted only 14 years and could be extended only if the author were still alive. Since then, the U.S. Congress has gotten into the copyright extension business. It has retroactively extended copyright laws 11 times since the early 1960s.

The 1998 act extends the copyright to 70 years (from 50) after an author's death and to 95 years (from 75) after publication for works owned by firms. (The act is named after Sonny Bono, the late pop singer and congressman who said, "Copyright should be forever minus a day.") Walt Disney and other media companies were major lobbyists for the bill, without which Mickey Mouse would have begun entering the public domain in 2003. Music swapping based on Napster and its successors on the Internet has only made the industry more passionate about protecting copyrights.

As Lessig argued in April 2002 before the U.S. Supreme Court, such repeated copyright extensions threaten to keep culture in private hands forever. These practices reduce culture to a private commodity. But creativity thrives in an open, free space. Every creator stands on the shoulders of other artists and our communal heritage. In this sense, culture is in part a peer production phenomenon. Disney, says Lessig, "ripped, mixed and burned" centuries-old legends like Snow White and Sleeping Beauty. Walt himself "stole" Mickey's precursor, Steamboat Willie, from Buster Keaton's Steamboat Bill movie character in 1928. Lessig's—and our—preferred approach is to return to the standard of the Founding Fathers: copyrights should last 14 years or thereabouts. Sadly, in January 2003 the Supreme Court turned down Lessig's plea to quash the 1998 copyright extension.

Such problems are not limited to pop music and movies. The U.S. Patent and Trademark Office has been issuing patents for naturally occurring human gene sequences since 1980. By 2003, over 2,000 human genes were patented internationally by private companies, universities, hospitals, and government agencies. Tens of thousands of additional applications were before various patent offices.

The result: a widening battle over whether genetic information will be accessible to stakeholders—patients, caregivers, funders, and researchers. One important case involves Utah-based Myriad Genetics, which in 1997 patented BRCA1, a gene that predicts the likelihood of breast cancer. The patent gives Myriad the right to decide how other companies use the gene for diagnosis and treatment, to charge royalties for using the gene in research and development, and to bar its use. The company also patented (much more reasonably) a test that it invented for BRCA1 and a related gene. It actively enforces a near-monopoly on breast cancer tests that rely on the gene and dictates terms to academics who want to do new research and develop new treatments. Myriad is fiercely protective of its multimillion dollar testing business, which it markets aggressively to doctors and hospitals.

Several researchers, in the United States and elsewhere, have identified new avenues of research based on BRCA1, but the company has stymied their visions of improved therapies. It refuses to approve—or to perform—new, sometimes cheaper tests that rely on "its" genes.

In January 2003, the normally probusiness Conservative government of Ontario decided to defy Myriad and use a much cheaper competing test. Provincial health minister Tony Clement called gene patenting "abhorrent," saying, "We do not accept their [patent] claim and we are disregarding their claim. This is a fight for access to women who might have a predisposition to breast or ovarian cancer." He said he was prepared to fight Myriad's Canadian patent "to the highest court of the land." Ontario was neither alone nor the first—challenges to Myriad's European patents began in 2001.

How could this happen, you may ask? How can any company gain patent rights over the genetic code of the human body, the defining essence of our common heritage? Typically, patents are granted for inventions of new things, not for discoveries of existing things. Patents are normally granted only to inventions, not natural phenomena; for example, you can't patent a new insect species that you find in the wild. Surely if anything is part of the "commons," it must be our genetic code. What was the Patent and Trademark Office thinking?

Proponents of gene patents argue that the genomic revolution is now the basis for the design of drugs and tests for most diseases. The cost of bringing new drugs to market can be in the hundreds of millions. Without patent protection of gene sequence discoveries, drug companies risk losing their inventions to copycats. They will be less inclined to invest and humanity will be the loser.

To receive a patent, the invention must be novel, nonobvious, and useful. Drugs and tests meet this standard. But genes? Initially, the Patent and Trademark Office was fairly quick and cooperative in granting patents. It justified the decision to treat gene sequences as inventions because their proponents synthesized the sequences separately from their presence in the genome strand. Also, until the late 1990s, isolating a gene was slow, expensive, manual test-tube work: Myriad spent millions to isolate BRCA1. The gene "find" was clearly of value in preventing disease. Under these conditions, the argument that the "invention" was novel, nonobvious, and useful stood up.

However, thanks to technology all this has changed. Now, most gene research is conducted on computer models—*in silico* rather than *in vitro*. The research uses standardized techniques, tools, and databases. Rather than a scientist with a Ph.D., a trained technician can do it. A gene sequence is no longer a nonobvious novelty. It does not require big investments. Many, if not most, applications in front of the patent offices are defensive in nature: the applicants don't necessarily know the functions of the purported sequence, nor can they explain how the patent will be made "useful." Believe it or not, most human genetic information is useless "junk." But the more patents a company owns, the more likely it is to own some useful ones, while fewer useful patents will go to competitors.

The problem is that, as the Myriad example illustrates, rather than promote innovation and the cost-effective delivery of health care services, gene patents retard innovation and increase costs to patients and providers. Gene patents are a force for opacity.

Research by Mildred Cho, a bioethicist at Stanford University, shows that patents of gene sequences deter new research and the design of new clinical tests. Other research reveals that growing numbers of university scientists engage in knowledge hoarding: concealing or slowing the publication of their research results. Even worse is the threat of a patent in the form of a patent application. Cho comments, "the number of people who are affected by an existing patent is smaller than those who might be affected by a future patent, because there are more unknowns."[21] When a gene sequence becomes frozen due to a patent application, other researchers tend to await the outcome of the application before working with the sequence. This is a further detriment to innovation.

Thanks to the 1980 Bayh-Dole Act, which gave U.S. universities the right to hold patents, the industrialization of academia is replacing open science. One analysis of this problem, published in the *Journal of the American Medical Association*, presents it as essentially a transparency issue:

> Openness in the sharing of research results is a powerful ideal in modern science. . . . Communalism, the shared ownership and free exchange of research results and approaches, [is] a fundamental norm underlying the social structure of science. Such sharing is critical to the

advancement of science, for without it researchers unknowingly build on something less than the total accumulation of scientific knowledge, and scientific work is slowed by problems for which solutions already exist but are unavailable. The power of the ideal of openness is reflected in the following quotation from Albert Einstein, inscribed on his statue in front of the headquarters of the National Academy of Sciences: "The right to search for truth implies also a duty: one must not conceal any part of what one has recognized to be true." Nevertheless, strong pressures, both personal and external to researchers, may result in their breaching of the ideal of openness. Personal pressures include competition between researchers for priority and recognition. External pressures include the requirements of the promotion process, competition for funding, and processes and procedures related to the commercialization of university research.[22]

What's the solution? In September 2002 the U.K.-based Nuffield Council on Bioethics published recommendations from an international panel of experts. It noted that many existing patents over DNA sequences are "of doubtful validity." The group recommended that in future, the granting of patents over DNA sequences should be the exception rather than the norm. Instead, the council suggested that patents could and should be granted for specific diagnostic tests based on DNA sequence knowledge. It called on the patent offices of Europe, Japan, and the United States to join forces in order to fix the situation. Another approach was a 2002 motion by Congresswoman Lynn Rivers to protect medical researchers and genetic diagnosticians from patent infringement lawsuits.

Clearly, not everything should be in the "commons." Standard methods for using RFID tags across retail supply chains should be. Competitive customer information and logistics techniques should not. New tunes and books should not, but after a while, they should. Our common human heritage—the genetic code—should remain in the "commons." But newly invented health tests, treatments, and medicines should not, at least not for their first 20 years or so. We are all stakeholders of the scientific and cultural artifacts on which creativity and invention depend. We must be careful in managing what shall be transparent and what opaque, and for how long.

CHAPTER 6

CUSTOMERS IN A
TRANSPARENT WORLD

We have spoken of a power shift to employees. There is another shift, thanks to transparency, to customers. But it cuts both ways. Companies know even more about their customers. In the past, firms relied on surveys to discern customer preferences. Today massive, exquisitely detailed databases track customer behavior. At any time a large retailer knows which models of jeans sold in the Cleveland store in the last hour. If purchased with a credit card, the company also knows the buyer's purchasing habits—information tailor-made for custom marketing campaigns. For years, customers have been on the wrong side of a one-way mirror.

Today all that is changing as customers peer back and take action on what they know—with seismic effects. Customers have increased access to knowledge about products and services and they can discern true value more easily. To compete, firms need truly differentiated products, better service, or lower cost more than ever because deficiencies in value cannot be hidden as easily. Companies can't make garbage smell like roses. And increasingly they need business integrity because it becomes part of a brand. Customers can increasingly hold corporations accountable for everything from integrity to product and service value. Open enterprises understand this power shift and embrace it.

A vignette from a business where customers were completely in the dark makes the point. Some mail-order camera merchants are notorious for sleazy sales tactics and fraudulent behavior. They typically advertise jaw-dropping bargain-basement prices on the back pages of photography magazines. The goal is to get the customer to nibble the bait, that is, dial an 800 number. Once on the line, their salespeople employ time-tested techniques to hook the gullible buyer. They range from bait and switch to a higher-priced product to stripping out accessories that normally come with a product and selling them for inflated prices. Sky-high shipping charges are another favorite tactic.

For these crooked companies, the Internet is a godsend. No longer forced to buy pricy magazine ads, these companies build attractive Web sites at relatively little cost. They claim to be among the country's busiest dealers. They rely on price comparison Web sites to hook the suckers for them, since their ultralow prices beat any legitimate competition.

The only recourse consumers really have is to use the Internet to warn one another. A popular site for intelligence gathering and sharing is www.photo.net, where thousands of customer horror stories

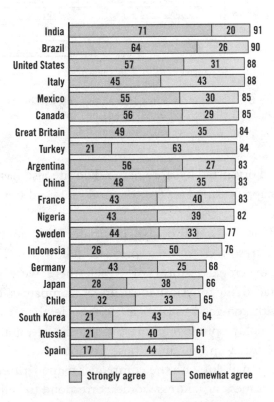

Figure 6.1 Gather Information Prior to Major Purchase

Source: Environics International

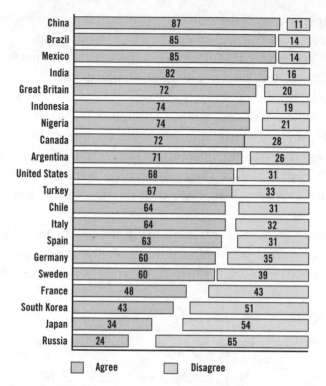

Figure 6.2 Consumers Have Power to Protect Themselves
Against Unfair/Dishonest Practices by a Company
Source: Environics International

are posted and organized by store name. The site also has hundreds of
stories from happy customers who got good value and service from rep-
utable stores.

In 2001 Don Wills, a Brooklyn computer programmer and avid
photographer, resolved to help prevent fellow shutterbugs from
being taken by crooked stores, of which there were many in his
city. Wills traced the physical location of companies that ran the
Web sites with too-good-to-be-true prices. He then rode his bicy-
cle around Brooklyn photographing the ramshackle, graffiti-adorned,
sometimes boarded-up buildings these companies used. Often there
would just be a mail slot with the company's name written beside it in
felt pen. Sometimes one address would correspond to half a dozen different online camera stores. Wills posted the photos at (the now
defunct) photopoint.com. The photos were a smash hit and instantly

became part of Internet folklore. Wills used the same tool—the Internet—to expose the crooks that the crooks used to perpetrate their crimes.

Throughout the economy the transparency-opacity battle rages on. Food companies resist labeling their products as genetically modified. Old-style firms hide product inadequacies. Companies with high-price structures work to keep customers ignorant. But the forces of opacity are in retreat. And smart firms know this.

Customers have a growing sense of their own power. Most people in G20 countries feel empowered as consumers according to a 2001 survey by Environics International.[1]

Two-thirds of those surveyed believed that consumers have the power to protect themselves against unfair or dishonest practices by a company. In Russia, Japan, South Korea, and France only a minority of

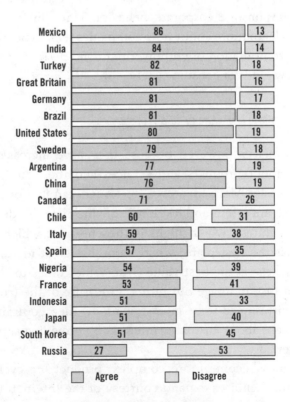

	Agree	Disagree
Mexico	86	13
India	84	14
Turkey	82	18
Great Britain	81	16
Germany	81	17
Brazil	81	18
United States	80	19
Sweden	79	18
Argentina	77	19
China	76	19
Canada	71	26
Chile	60	31
Italy	59	38
Spain	57	35
Nigeria	54	39
France	53	41
Indonesia	51	33
Japan	51	40
South Korea	51	45
Russia	27	53

Figure 6.3 Do Not Hesitate to Complain to Companies

Source: Environics International

consumers felt empowered. People aged 65 and higher also tended to feel less able to protect themselves.

Seven in ten people do not hesitate to complain to companies that produce or sell the products that they use. Over one-third of respondents are adamant about this aspect of their consumer behavior. Better-educated people, those with higher levels of income, and Internet users are more likely than others to be ready to take companies to task.

Historically customers care about price and value (product utility, quality, innovativeness, service(s), and safety). They also care about brands—in the past an "image" or promise of a product or company. Increasingly there is a new kid on the block—values—as customers want to buy from companies they consider to be "good" and give back to the community.

Nearly eight in ten U.S. consumers say they can make a difference in driving responsible corporate behavior. Three in four consumers also want to learn more about how companies seek to be more responsible.[2] This combination of empowerment and desire to learn sets the stage for new kinds of consumer behavior.

TRANSPARENCY AND VALUE

Consumers feel empowered because they have increased access to knowledge about products and services and they can discern true value more easily. More than ever, customers can find out which cars perform best, are safest, and last longest; which laundry detergent gets clothes the whitest; which flight is the cheapest; which cell phone company has the best plans; which book has great ideas; and which vacation package is the best value. True value comes to the fore, and brand is not just an image but rather a measure of the trust and relationships.[3] Firms need to be honest, abide by their commitments, and show they care about customer interests by providing superior products or lower cost.

As products become more complex, product life cycles shorten, and consumers' choices expand courtesy of the Internet, the public's appetite for timely and dispassionate advice continues to grow. Debates have long raged in online newsgroups in areas such as photography, audio components, and cars, as to which companies make the best products. But few participants purport to be impartial observers; most act as tireless brand advocates, staunchly defending buying decisions they made and why professionals choose, say, Canon over Nikon, or Porsche over Corvette.

In the late 1990s a number of dot-com companies sprang up to provide more neutral and structured forums for consumers to share views on products and services. The largest, Epinions.com, covers over 2 million products and services in over 30 different categories. Along with the standard consumer electronics fare of camcorder and computer reviews, Epinions contributors offer advice on more exotic products such as wine, men's cologne, movies, and athlete's foot remedies. The goal is to give the consumer knowledge and confidence based on hearing the first-hand unbiased experiences of other consumers, rather than the opinions of a single so-called expert.

Epinions encourages opinion givers with money and flattery. If you consistently submit high-quality reviews of products and services that buyers find useful, Epinions will pay you. You will also be acknowledged in the community as someone whose opinion should be respected.

The company says it goes to great lengths to highlight the people behind the reviews so that visitors know exactly whom to trust. In addition to user biography pages, review lists, and the ability to comment on reviews, users can flag reviewers they don't like and their reviews will be deleted from view. Conversely, Epinions allows all users to build a "Web of Trust"—a personalized network of reviewers whose reviews and ratings they consistently find valuable.

The company works hard to assure visitors that the opinions are unbiased. Traditional trade magazines that review products such as cameras or cars often refuse to publish negative reviews. If a product is shoddy, the editors claim they will "work with the manufacturer" to improve the product rather than publish a negative opinion. They won't even tell readers that the review was commissioned. They insist this ignorance-is-bliss policy serves the buying public better in the long run. The truth is, the typical car enthusiast magazine depends on ad revenue from car manufacturers, and it cannot afford to alienate any of them. Increasingly, media-savvy readers see such policies for what they are—editors' groveling at their advertisers' feet. Some publications, such as *Consumer Reports*, feel the only way to avoid this potential conflict is not to accept advertising.

A competitor of Epinions is ConsumerSearch.com, which aggregates product reviews from other Web sites and traditional publications. "We begin by looking for the best reviews, both on and off the Internet, and then we rank them according to how well they identify the category's best products. Next, we develop our Full Story report, analyzing whether the experts agree or disagree. When they disagree, we try to determine whose work is more credible. Finally, we distill the results about which products are top-rated and best in their class into our Fast Answers."

Epinions and ConsumerSearch deal with a large array of products. Some aggregation Web sites deal with just a handful of products, such as www.rottentomatoes.com, which specializes in movies. Created by movie buff Senh Duong in 1998, Rotten Tomatoes had 2.7 million readers each month in early 2003. With more than 87,000 titles and 200,000 review links, Rotten Tomatoes offers a fun summary of the critical reaction on movies from the nation's top print and online film critics, summarized by the Tomatometer. If more than 40 percent of reviewers pan a movie, it's dubbed a rotten tomato.

Rottentomatoes.com is a much-needed antidote to studio advertising. In the ads, every film is a hit and "must-see"—often backed up by a half dozen film critics. No matter how bad the movie, the studios can drag up a few favorable quotes. Indeed, as illustrated by an infamous ruse perpetuated by Sony, every once in a while the quotes and critics' names are complete fabrications. Sony's advertising executives created a fictitious critic called David Manning to pump up their films. He was billed as a reviewer for the nonexistent *Ridgefield Press* in Connecticut. Bogus quotes in advertisements were attributed to Manning for a number of films including *Hollow Man*, *Vertical Limit*, and Rob Schneider's *The Animal*. With Rotten Tomatoes, viewers are given a representative cross section of dozens of reviews.

TRANSPARENCY AND PRICE

You've done your research at manufacturers' Web sites, consulted services such as Epinions.com, and chosen the CD player or camcorder that you want. The next question: Who to buy it from? A host of online companies strive to empower consumers by scouring the Internet for the best prices on goods and services. Companies like BizRate.com, MySimon.com, Dealtime.com, and PriceGrabber.com offer advice on where to get the best value, which in many cases is not the same thing as the cheapest deal. As we saw with camera stores, any scoundrel can build a Web site and claim to offer great products at unbelievably low prices. "The lowest-price guy is often the one with the less-than-ethical business practices," says Chuck Davis, chief executive for BizRate.[4]

To make its service more accurate and useful, BizRate now offers four additional metrics to separate good from not-so-good online merchants: On-Time Delivery, Did Products Meet Your Expectations, Customer Support, and the bottom-line question, Would You Shop Here Again? Most price comparison sites offer similar ratings.

Online comparison shopping sites such as BizRate compile comprehensive ratings from shoppers on a scale that was unimaginable prior to the Internet. In January 2003, BizRate released a list of the sites that offered the best customer service during the 2002 holiday season. The list was based on critiques offered by more than 1.5 million online shoppers from November 25 to December 25, 2002. BizRate is unique not only by surveying customers at the time of purchase but by following up with email a short time after customers are scheduled to receive the product to see if they are still satisfied.

Price comparison sites save legwork and give consumers confidence they are making a smart decision. Seeing how popular price comparison sites have become, some innovative online vendors now offer their competitors' prices on their own site rather than relying on third-party Web sites to validate their claims of good value. Progressive, an auto insurance company, gives online quotes to customers who provide details about their age, marital status, car type, and so on. Progressive also calculates what its competitors charge, the basis of insurance company rating data that companies file with state governments. Progressive says it strives to make the comparison as accurate as possible, since it is confident its product will consistently offer top value. Sometimes it loses to lower-priced competitors. But some customers pay its higher rate because they conclude that it is a different kind of company, worthy of their trust and business. Open enterprises create trusting relationships, in part because they exhibit transparency.

Online purchasers are not the only ones who use online price comparison sites; the main users are people who plan to buy in a physical store. They go online to find out what prices are reasonable at their local merchant or to confirm whether an advertised supersale in their local newspaper is really a bargain. Price comparison sites can give the buyer a real sense of confidence, and soon this boon will be available over wireless devices as you shop in any store. In 2002, Pricegrabber.com teamed up with AT&T Wireless to make its ratings available anytime, anywhere. Tens of millions of people wouldn't think about buying a car until they know what their local dealers paid for it, and soon that information will be readily available on handheld devices.

PRICE DISCOVERY: THE RISE OF THE AGORA

Transparency not only enables buyers to know more about sellers and their goods and services, to find the best deal, or even to aggregate their purchasing power, it is also starting to change the way prices are determined. In *Digital Capital* we discussed how new communications media, especially the Internet, facilitate *price discovery*, whereby buyers and sellers cooperate and compete to arrive at a mutually acceptable deal.[5] Our discussion was not restricted to online transactions but rather embraced business models that may transcend the physical and digital worlds.

We called these "agoras," after the Greek word for marketplace. In ancient Greece, an agora was originally a gathering place for assemblies; it later evolved to become the marketplace at a city's center. Today the term applies to markets where buyers and sellers meet to freely negotiate and, by doing so, "discover" a price for goods. Agoras are enabled by and in turn facilitate transparency; they work best when buyers and sellers know more about each other and the goods and services to be transacted. As such they have the power to increase *liquidity:* the ease of converting assets into cash. Agoras achieve liquidity by *matching* buyers and sellers and enabling them to discover a mutually acceptable price.

Agoras historically served a special distribution function for goods of uncertain or volatile value. These were typically unique, distressed, or perishable items and commodities for which supply and demand fluctuated continually. Unsuited to traditional fixed-price models (there is no list price), the value of these goods had to be resolved—or discovered—through direct negotiation between producers and consumers.[6] With the exception of commodity exchanges and stock markets, most traditional agoras have been limited by time and space—by the transaction costs incurred in negotiating the price, that is, the time and effort entailed in doing so. In an Industrial Age economy of scarcity, buyers and sellers often preferred the predictability of fixed prices. Pre-Internet, large-scale auctions or exchanges were impractical. Success required a critical mass of buyers and sellers who wished to exchange the same good during the same time period and use the same mechanism to communicate and conduct price discovery. The only working examples were commodity and stock exchanges or limited auction events. But today the scope of variable pricing is expanding dramatically. Because of transparency, negotiated transactions between buyers and sellers are challenging pricing habits and value allocation models in one industry after another.

Usually one company (or a consortium) acts as a market maker and sets broad rules. It governs the nature of the playing field, its boundaries, player eligibility, and the processes of competition. After that, participants make their own decisions without interference.

Because of their multifaceted and dynamic nature, agoras present nearly unlimited opportunities for innovation in price discovery. Some agora operators, like Onsale.com or uBid.com, simply bring auctions to traditional retail goods. Fxall.com describes itself as a multibank portal, but it really provides the beginnings of an open market for foreign exchange and now accounts for $9 billion in trading daily.

Author and consultant Mohan Sahwney argues that openness can strengthen relationships rather than commoditize them—but only if you, as a seller, focus on value rather than just the lowest price. He says, "Transparency is only the enemy of profit if customers are ignorant about the value you provide." He encourages you to consider whether you are better or worse off with an informed customer. You need to understand what customers really value; you may conclude that price is only one of several important variables. One strategy is to develop flexible market offerings that allow customers to choose the services they value and to pay for only those they use. Then, "communicate your value proposition," to ensure that nonprice variables are fully quantified.

Unfortunately, not all agoras are based on the notion of increased customer knowledge. Priceline.com deliberately keeps the customer in the dark as to price and product. Users submit bids on what they are willing to pay for a three-star hotel in downtown Chicago, for example. Priceline's computers then look for a match. If the buyer's bid is high enough, Priceline confirms the booking. But the customer will never know if he could have bid lower or what other hotels were vying for his business. Alternately, if the bid is too low, the customer is not allowed to rebid. This prevents customers from trying to discern the floor price. Not all consumers tolerate Priceline's strategy of opacity. At www.biddingfortravel.com, Priceline customers come together to swap intelligence (when we checked it out in March 2003, posters reported booking four-star hotels in Manhattan for $75).

The world champion of agoras is, of course, eBay. Profitable almost from the day it was conceived, eBay is the heart of a nearly perfect business web: its customers, whether sellers or buyers, take on most of the work, cost, and risk. They carry the inventory, do their own marketing, and arrange for shipping. It costs eBay next to nothing to add customers, and the company's fees are 85 percent prepaid by credit card.

The source of eBay's success is a transparency tool: its reputation management system. Many companies would do well to learn from it.

It's a simple idea. Every time you buy something, eBay invites you to rate the seller: Was its sales pitch truthful; did it meet its commitments; did it go the extra step to make you happy? You also get to score its performance on a scale of -1–0–+1. In a remarkable example of an online community at work, about half the people who buy or sell on eBay reportedly take a moment to provide such feedback.

Some eBay members now have thousands, even tens of thousands, of individual feedback items—available for anyone to read.

Imagine if General Motors or Wal-Mart had something like this. Would it help or hurt? Harvard political scientist Richard Zeckhauser and colleagues performed an experiment in which they auctioned several lots of vintage Valentine postcards on eBay. One seller had an excellent, well-established feedback record. Another, using a new made-up identity, had little or no track record. After 200 postcard sales, the established identity had brought in 7.6 percent more sales dollars, on average. Earned reputation is hard to isolate in the real world (where well-known brands and personal contact introduce a variety of biases), so this 7.6 percent advantage is a striking little data point.

"Real" companies can learn from eBay, and some are doing so. A growing number of big firms have mini-sites on eBay to auction overstock and surplus merchandise. Dell and IBM, for example, each auction off-lease computers on a branded eBay "store." They submit to the disciplines of the rating system, with the attendant plaudits and pain. This is great for consumers. Not only can they get a deal, but they can also find out how other buyers rated the corporate seller. But can they also get this at the seller's own online store?

Surprisingly, some companies have learned their customer feedback lessons well, and even improved on them. For example, Dell and Apple host a wide variety of customer conversations on their own Web sites, with free speech as far as the eye can see. At Dell, customers debate whether it's okay to say nasty things about the company on its own site. The discussion quickly turns into a heated battle on the relative merits of Dell and Toshiba laptops (replete with full color logos of the competition posted by Toshiba boosters). Meanwhile, over at Apple, someone complains about the earphones on her new iPod while another seeks help to eliminate scratching sounds when the machine plays MP3s. Does such freewheeling discussion help companies?

We've said there are lots of sites, like Epinions.com, where customers can go to review products. Isn't it better to host such activity on your own Web site, observe the action, and be seen to care about the firm's customers? You might learn something, too. For example,

Dell claims that revamped laptop models announced in March 2003 respond to customer demands from its online forum.

Of course, inviting customers to self-organize on your own Web site is not without risks. What if they gang up on you? The answer is, as long as you meet their expectations, show goodwill, and avoid Firestone tire–type disasters, this should just be a good mechanism for keeping you on your toes and staying in touch. Indeed, the Zeckhauser study found that negative ratings had no impact on willingness to buy. In fact, transparent customer feedback forums can actually help push up prices. As they used to say in Hollywood, I don't care what you say about me, just spell my name right.

TRANSPARENCY AND CUSTOMER VALUES

Blood diamonds, also known as conflict diamonds, are a textbook example of an industry's turning a blind eye to atrocities in its own backyard—only to be exposed by transparency. Repeatedly, armed factions in different African countries have seized diamond mines in order to convert the gems into cash for weapons and ammunition. Though conflict diamonds account for only 4 percent of the global diamond supply, they are responsible for enormous pain and suffering, with more than 650,000 deaths in the Angolan diamond-funded civil war alone.

What a difference a little transparency can make. As recently as 1996 the De Beers annual report blithely described how its record purchases of Angolan diamonds ensured global price stability.[7] Most readers were not aware that the firm's money funded weapons and ammunition purchases. But as media reports and nongovernmental organizations began to educate consumers about the issue, De Beers had a dramatic change of heart. In a June 2000 public letter to colleagues in the world diamond industry, De Beers chairman Nicky Oppenheimer wrote, "You will be aware that the role of diamonds as a source of funding for rebel armies and warlords in several African states has become a major political and media issue. We are sure that you share our deep concern that the role, appeal and value of diamonds as a symbol of beauty and love should not be sullied by this connection with the atrocities of war."[8]

Nevertheless, because of its previous behavior, De Beers was subsequently barred from handling Angolan diamonds by the Angolan government. In a bid to reenter the market, De Beers insists it has mended its ways. Says De Beers managing director Gary Ralfe, "That was part of the old De Beers. It is not part of the new De Beers. We are not in the business of mopping up diamonds on the outside market."

The challenge to advocacy groups is to stop the trade in conflict diamonds but not jeopardize the employment of thousands of Africans in the legitimate diamond trade. Rather than call for a boycott, nongovernmental organizations demand a transparent diamond supply chain that can give consumers confidence that their purchases are not subsidizing war. They also want consumers to make clear to the diamond producing companies that blood diamonds is an issue the end buyers take seriously.

The industry's solution—the so-called Kimberly Process—was endorsed by governments of almost 40 countries. In it, every producing nation monitors and certifies that diamonds are from approved mines. Countries that buy diamonds have a similar system to ensure that only certified products are imported. Conflict diamonds are banned.

The Kimberly Process depends on transparency. Nongovernmental organizations want independent inspectors to audit and verify systems put in place rather than simply relying on the companies involved. They fear the temptation for individuals or corporations to act as a backdoor conduit for the conflict diamonds will be too strong to resist. The industry is currently scrambling to prove the system effective.[9]

Consumers across the world are increasingly punishing and rewarding companies because of their perceived corporate social performance. According to Environics International, the proportion of Americans that reported having punished a company for being socially irresponsible equaled 58 percent in 2002, an increase of 15 points from 2001. Furthermore, strong majorities in most countries believe that their actions as consumers can influence corporate behavior: 78 percent of Americans believe that they as consumers can make a difference in how responsibly a company behaves.

Among U.S. consumers with access to the Internet, 17 percent say they have recently searched for information on corporate social behavior online.[10] Young adults 18 to 24 with Internet access are more likely to have looked for such information online, with over one in four reporting doing so.

A recent study by the London-based New Economics Foundation (NEF) in partnership with the Co-operative Bank found that the value of ethical consumer purchases for fuel, housing, personal goods, transport, and subscriptions is small but growing rapidly, by 18.2 percent between 1999 and 2000—from £4.8 billion to £5.7 billion. Ethical purchasing is now growing at six times the rate of the overall market reaching a market share of 1.6 percent. Total ethical purchasing with banking and investments amounts to £13.4 billion in 2000, a growth of 19 percent from the previous year.[11]

VALUES IN LUMBER?

In this new environment, seemingly straightforward businesses become sudden lightning rods for political activism. Home Depot became a retail giant by selling hammers, nails, and lumber at deep discount prices. Then—wham—the Rainforest Action Network appeared. The Network wants to reduce the chopping of rain forest trees for the North American market. Rather than appeal to governments, the Network organizes customer product boycotts. As the largest retailer of old growth lumber—it sells more than $5 billion of lumber, plywood, doors, and windows each year—Home Depot was a prime target.

The Rainforest Action Network has 30,000 members and 150 grassroots groups in more than 60 countries. It uses the Internet for public education and to forge alliances with indigenous groups, human rights and environmental organizations, small businesses, and local politicians. When locked in battle with Home Depot, the Action Network's Web sites provided statistics about rain forest depletion, documentation about Home Depot's company activities, lists of actions and protests across North America, and information about other organizations working on the campaign. "Our highly effective activist network has used a variety of tactics such as hanging banners, blockades of buildings and meetings, street theater, protests, and stopping logging trucks and ships. These actions not only call attention to the plight of the world's forests but also help to stop the machine of destruction in its tracks." [12] The Network even posted "talking points" to activists for media interviews.

After two years of being hammered with bad PR and increasing resistance to new store locations, Home Depot surrendered. The company announced in 1999 it would phase out old growth lumber from its product lines by the end of 2002. On January 2, 2003, the Rainforest Action Network issued a press release assessing Home Depot's efforts. "The progress Home Depot has made removing products from endangered forests from its shelves is impressive. The company has succeeded in establishing meaningful 'chain of custody' to track the origin of nearly all its wood products. Home Depot's sale of wood products that are environmentally certified by the Forest Stewardship Council has dramatically increased. . . . Home Depot, however, has yet to take the final and most important step in its commitment—to use its power as the market leader to drive change within the forest products industry. Home Depot continues to do business with the worst actors in the logging industry." [13]

For its part, Home Depot says its customers appreciated the progress it has made to responsible forestry. "When someone purchases a piece of wood from The Home Depot, we would like them to think of that as them placing an order for another tree to be planted somewhere in the world," said Ron Jarvis, Home Depot's vice president of merchandising.[14] The company insists it has fulfilled the promises it made in 1999. "In our mind and the minds of most people we talk to we've gone a lot further than most people thought we would," Jarvis said. A spokesperson for the Action Network said it was possible the group would resume its protests.

"All of these companies are on a sort of a new road, so to speak, to providing wood products that give consumers the confidence that the wood they buy is coming from well-managed forests," said Roger Dower, president of the U.S. branch of the Forest Stewardship Council. Certification by the Forest Stewardship Council involves guidelines on environmental standards, biological diversity, and cutting in a manner designed to ensure that a forest continues to thrive. "They are ahead of the pack in terms of moving along that road," Dower said of Home Depot. "Is there further to go? I suppose there will always be further to go." [15]

PRODUCT COCREATION

In the transparent world customers can find out, inform others, and even self-organize. Whether it's teenagers sharing MP3 music, buyers' clubs aggregating purchasing power, geeks developing Linux software, or lonely singles creating a club to meet each other instead of going to the classified ads, customers can organize themselves more easily than ever before. This poses disaster or boon, depending on whether firms see transparency as threat or opportunity. Self-organizing systems have enormous implications for businesses. Smart managers are asking, "Is there a chance our customers could work together via the Internet to build a product that competes with us? How do we prevent this, and harness the energies and ideas of our customers to cocreate our product or service?"

This phenomenon has racked the music industry as much as any other. Rather than purchase CDs from stores, consumers construct their own music "playlists" of digital music downloaded from the Net. Cooperation among consumers—by sharing their digital music files with others via the Internet—creates an alternative to the industry.

The recording industry is a textbook example of how leaders of the old paradigm are often the last to embrace the new. Open enterprises, rather than viewing customer self-organization as a threat, should treat it as an opportunity to involve customers deeply in their operations. In doing so, firms harness the genius of customers for value creation as well as create superior customer experiences and strong, enduring customer relationships. To date, examples of this are few and far between.

As mentioned earlier, the toy company Lego chose the transparency route, bringing its customers into its design process. Best known for making little interlocking plastic bricks, Lego now makes high-tech toys for children and adults alike. One of its new product lines, Mindstorms, combines hundreds of Lego bricks with gears, motors, light and touch sensors, and a microprocessor, called the RCX, that allows users to build their own robots.

Lego and the MIT Media Lab wrote the original software for the RCX. But soon after the software release, a Stanford student reverse engineered it and posted it on the Internet. Since the RCX software was proprietary, Lego faced a decision: It could behave like the recording industry and take legal action against the Stanford student for attacking its intellectual property. Or it could sit back, smile, and see what happened. After initially leaning in the wrong direction, Lego chose to do the latter. The company has had reason to congratulate itself ever since.

After the Stanford student posted the RCX code online, an Illinois man posted software designs, and a German student did the same. Then others began to download the software and tinker with it. Soon amateur programmers were using Mindstorms to make devices ranging from photocopiers and slot machines to a dog named Grrr. (A remarkable creature, Grrr can distinguish colors and respond to voice commands.) Today Lego uses mindstorms.lego.com to encourage tinkering with the RCX software. The Web site offers a free, downloadable software-development kit; Lego's customers in turn use the site to post descriptions of their Mindstorms creations—and the software code, programming instructions, and Lego parts that the devices require. Lego might as well have made its customers part of its design department.

The company benefits hugely from the work of this volunteer business web. Each time a customer develops and posts a new application for Mindstorms, the toy becomes more valuable. A direct upshot of this customer involvement is a greatly expanded consumer market for Lego. Originally a children's toy, Lego Mindstorms now has broad appeal, particularly for university students and business professionals. Says Soren Lund, a director at Lego in Denmark, "It has kept the product vibrant and alive, even today," four years after it was first released. "I still get amazed when I see what's going on out there."[16]

Soon, more sophisticated collaboration and knowledge-management tools will be available, and far more complicated projects will be possible. It's easy to imagine any digitized content being developed this way—for example, a textbook.

The model could be transferred to many other sectors. Volunteer engineers could cooperate on the Net to provide design input into a new generation automobile. A car company such as GM could harness the creativity of its own customers to codesign a car. It could build an online collaboration arena that presents 3D visual prototypes. Partici-

pants could include style-conscious customers, fleet buyers, knowledgeable service technicians, supply chain partners, dealers, car buffs,
and industrial designers. These participants would be motivated to
provide their advice freely because they love cars, enjoy interacting
with other members of the online community, and gain pleasure from
influencing the design of a future car. When GM adopted an idea, it
could publicize the news to the community, enhancing the contributor's reputation. The manufacturer could return the favor by providing buyer rebates based on the quality and quantity of contributions.

CORPORATE INTEGRITY AND THE BRAND

Investor Warren Buffett says, "If you lose dollars for the firm by bad
decisions, I will be very understanding. If you lose reputation for the
firm, I will be ruthless."

For a growing class of products and companies, integrity—honesty,
reliability, consideration, and transparency—are the foundation of
brand architecture. Most brands have included some but not all of
these values in the past. Coke presents itself as reliable—delivering the
same taste worldwide. It communicates consideration—quality control, flavor, convenience, safety, philanthropic benevolence, even the
promise of lifestyle improvements—"Things go better with Coke."

But values like honesty and transparency were never really necessary for Coke's branding. In fact, the brand has always boasted of opacity, at least in the formulation of its secret ingredients (in that case
appropriate). Internationally in recent years, Coke has faced the murders of union organizers and the clear use of terror against workers in
its bottling plants in Colombia. Coke insists that it supports human
rights and that bottlers are independent of the Coca-Cola Company.
Reports of these crimes led the International Labor Rights Fund and
the United Steelworkers of America to launch a historic lawsuit in
Miami on behalf of the Colombian union against Coca-Cola and its
Colombian bottler.

Opponents of Coke's strategy of indifference with respect to its
suppliers say that "global corporations, such as the Coca-Cola Company, have a responsibility to ensure that the rights and safety of all
workers who produce, package/bottle or distribute their products are

protected. Just as they have a responsibility to ensure that the prod-ucts they sell are safe, Coca Cola has a responsibility to ensure that the conditions under which their products are produced are safe."[17] Crit-ics allege that "the real thing" is Coke's unfair labor practices.

Adding honesty and transparency to the formula creates a higher hurdle and more complex brand architecture. Today Coke must endeavor to behave and present itself as a leader in corporate citizen-ship and a company with great integrity. It has launched programs on the environment (water and natural resources, climate change, envi-ronmental education, and waste management). It has invested consid-erably in fighting AIDS through employee programs and bottling partners. Over the past few years it has invested tens of millions of dollars in educational programs in the many communities in which it operates. It has, however, had little success convincing critics that it has taken adequate steps to improve labor practices in its bottling plants, or even to accept responsibility for this challenge. Coke lives in a house of glass and consumers, especially in certain important mar-kets (youth, developing countries), can be expected to shift loyalties as Coke's brand architecture is undermined.

Some companies bake accountability into their brands to gain con-sumer support, even from the most surprising places. In 2001, animal rights group People for the Ethical Treatment of Animals (PETA) organized nearly a thousand demonstrations at Burger King restau-rants throughout North America, criticizing the fast-food giant for its suppliers' cruel treatment of animals. A year later, PETA's Web site glitzily urged supporters to put down their protest signs and chow down at Burger King. Why? In June 2001, following PETA's six-month campaign, the fast-food giant had agreed to hold suppliers account-able for upgraded standards of animal welfare. And Burger King also became the first fast-food restaurant to add a veggie burger (already available in Europe and Canada) to all its U.S. sites. Burger King is becoming an open enterprise—a company that serves meat to millions but is also accountable to animal lovers.

Royal Dutch Shell faced what we call a trust crisis that damaged its brand when it tried to sink an obsolete North Shore drilling rig called the Brent Spar in deep ocean waters. Public pressure forced Shell to reverse its decision and pay to have the rig dismantled on shore. The

Shell brand has always stood for reliability (good quality, consistent fuel products) and consideration (convenient locations, competitive prices.) Today, Shell places integrity at the center of its brand. Shell is now asking consumers to trust it not only to provide good gas but also to steward the environment and be socially responsible. It positions itself as an honest, transparent corporate citizen. Some critics allege that this is pure window dressing and that Shell's commitment to advertising how well it behaves is greater than its commitment to behaving well. But there is no comparison between the genuine shift in thinking and behavior at Shell and the thinking at other companies such as Exxon that have just begun to make the turn.

Clarica Life Insurance boasts it is "one of the fastest growing life insurance companies in the United States." From humble roots as the Midwest Mutual Life Insurance Company, founded in Fargo, North Dakota, in 1930, it grew slowly until relatively recently when it seems to have found the keys to success. Today the company is licensed in 48 states and the District of Columbia, has more than 6,000 agents, and serves over 225,000 policyholders. In May 2000 Clarica was sold to Sun Life Financial for $6.8 billion. Of that, the Clarica brand was valued at $700 million.

How could a brand have such a huge relative value? According to former Clarica strategist Hubert Saint-Onge the brand was based on values deeply held by every Clarica employee. The brand defined the Clarica corporate character, how employees worked with one another, and ultimately how they interacted with the external world and built relationships with customers. Says Saint-Onge, "If you want an authentic brand in financial services, the person that provides the service is the service. How you align that person to the values of the corporation is critical."

BRANDING CUSTOMER CANDOR

Openness is central to the Progressive Corporation brand and to its success in the marketplace. Its CEO Glenn Renwick explains that the information asymmetries in the auto insurance industry have been an impediment to trust. "The auto insurance field hasn't always been understood by consumers. You hold all the cards. Companies say here's my price and here are the contract terms. But customers are in the dark as to the rationale for prices and even what other companies are charging." Progressive has built a brand based on openness—giving all the information a customer needs to make a decision. "If you give consumers only one data point, then you're only as good as that one data point. If you give them Progressive's rate and put it in a context of what other firms are charging, you create something new. First is a shopping methodology that didn't really exist in auto insurance— where, say, like buying a DVD, customers can window-shop. Second you build a relationship. You may lose that transaction but candor opens the door to a relationship."

Credit rating is another tricky issue in auto insurance. "People are uneasy about it, because we seem to be asking them how much money they have," says Renwick. So Progressive decided to be open—explaining to prospects exactly how their credit rating score affects price and how by correcting errors or improving their credit rating they can lower the cost of insurance. Customers are very appreciative. Says Renwick, "Transparency has become part of our brand."

Telephone companies have a reputation for opacity. Telephone bills are obscure. The companies' bureaucracies are impenetrable when you have a problem. It is therefore shocking to see British Telecom (BT) as a world leader in the transparency revolution.

The past 20 years have been exciting times for BT. In 1984 the company was transformed from a government monopoly to a private sector corporation. Despite the enormous shock to the corporate culture, BT pulled off the transformation with finesse. For its first 15 years in the private sector, life was good. Dividends per share consistently rose, peaking in fiscal year 1999–2000. Then, as with many other telecommunications companies in the world, profits plunged after a disastrous investment in third-generation mobile phone licenses. In a bid to restore profits and investor confidence, BT management announced a host of initiatives built around a renewed top priority: customer satisfaction. Ben Verwaayen, the CEO, pledged "to outperform competitors consistently and reduce the number of dissatisfied customers by 25 per cent each year."

Reducing dissatisfied customers by 25 percent a year is an enormous undertaking. Company research shows that customers expect continuous improvement in customer care and quality of service. In other words, with escalating expectations, BT must continually improve its product simply to maintain levels of satisfaction. To increase them is something else again.

BT calls its plan "customer candor." Step one is to deliver a superior product. BT's market research makes clear that superior service does not require the cheapest price. Customers want to know they are being dealt with honestly and considerately.

The company strives to keep customers informed when problems occur. It gives customers a clear commitment when a job starts and updates them until the job is completed satisfactorily. Customers can track repair work via SMS messaging on their cellular phones. If service is interrupted for an extended period and the customer doesn't have a cellular phone as backup, the company provides one. The company pledges to do business in a way that:

- Maximizes the benefits of information and communications technology for individuals

- Contributes to the communities in which it operates

- Minimizes any adverse impact that it might have on the environment

The company sets out a statement of business practice, *The Way We Work*, which it makes widely available. It defines the business principles that apply worldwide, to all employees, agents, contractors, and others when representing BT. The statement also sets out specific aspirations and commitments that apply in the company's relations with customers, employees, shareholders, partners, and suppliers and in the communities in which it operates.

In the area of the environment, for example, the company has scores of programs that demonstrate its commitment to ecosensitivity, including details such as prohibiting advertising on pay phones that are located in areas of outstanding natural beauty, national parks, open countryside, or World Heritage sites. With respect to supplier relationships, the company pledges to ensure that all dealings with suppliers—

from selection and consultation to recognition and payment—are conducted in accordance with the principles of fair and ethical trading. The company's supply chain initiative, "Sourcing with Human Dignity," relies on standards based on the UN Universal Declaration of Human Rights and International Labor Organization conventions. "We intend to gain the support of our direct suppliers to promote these standards throughout our supply base."

Recent research shows that U.K. residents have a large and growing belief that companies should behave in a socially responsible manner. The research also shows that the customers most interested in socially responsible behavior tend to be the most affluent. These customers are demanding, and most likely to leave the company if dissatisfied. BT's conclusion is that corporate social responsibility (CSR) contributes solidly to the bottom line.[18]

THE NEW RISK OF GLOBAL BRANDS

In a world of diverse local values, evidence is mounting that global brands may not always thrive.

For the first time, there is considerable hand-wringing among marketing executives about global branding. Anticorporate activist Naomi Klein argued in her best seller, *No Logo*, that corporations like Nike, Shell, Wal-Mart, and McDonald's have become metaphors for a global economic system gone awry. For adherents to her view, these brands have become mistrust marks and targets for attack. She predicts that outrage against these brands will change the way the companies present themselves.

Some brand experts are working to determine whether the global qualities of their brand are positive or negative. Others are trying to measure the impact of corporate values on a global brand. According to Research International Observer (RIO), today's global consumers will adhere to their favorite brands and turn a blind eye to the company's political and ethical malpractices.[19] Most consumers in the 40 countries they studied love U.S. brands even though they may dislike U.S. policies. But even this study argues against homogeneous global brands or a "one-size-fits-all" approach. Says RIO global director Malcolm Baker, "Brands are [becoming] driven by a need for reconnection with local roots and a form of in-your-face authenticity that seeks to deny marketing construction. . . . Consumers want to find the brand and not the other way around."

Yet a low profile is not always the best policy. Monsanto, bruised and battered after its disastrous attempt to introduce genetically modified foods to Europe, is a telling example. In the United States the company had happy customers and a strong brand, but when it attempted to extend this to Europe, it landed in a firestorm of protest. Europeans had huge sensitivities to genetically modified foods, not shared by Americans. Monsanto had an active stakeholder web and didn't know it.

In explaining why the company was so out of touch with European public sentiment, its former president and CEO Hendrik A. Verfaillie said, "We didn't understand that when it comes to a serious public concern, that the more you stand to make a profit in the marketplace, the less credibility you have in the marketplace of ideas. When we tried to explain the benefits, the science and the safety, we did not understand that our tone—our very approach—was seen as arrogant. We were still in the 'trust me' mode when the expectation was 'show me.' "

Monsanto epitomized the wrong attitude to the brand for any company in an increasingly transparent society. Monsanto management felt that as a research leader, the company was in the best position to judge whether its products were safe. Knowing the subject to be controversial, the company decided to keep a low profile and attract as little scrutiny as possible. Fueling this point of view is the subject's aching complexity. There are no simple answers to the questions surrounding genetically modified organisms. Indeed, it's even hard to find agreement on the questions to ask. Nevertheless the company should have recognized the enormous contribution it could make to the debate and participated fully.

Monsanto is not the only company to suffer enormous losses and damage to its brand due to underestimating the public appetite for "good" values and responsible behavior. Unlike BP and Shell, Exxon-Mobil, until recently, chose to ignore growing public concern about the oil industry and the environment. Supporters praised its singular focus on shareholder value, arguing that it shows how so-called responsible behavior of its competitors does not contribute to and possibly undermines shareholder value.

Yet a poll conducted by MORI Social Research for Greenpeace in November 2002 revealed that 1 million U.K. motorists say they're boycotting Exxon because of its stance on global warming.

Another report released in May 2002 asserted that ExxonMobil's attitude toward climate change is fraught with "unnecessary risks and missed opportunities" that could threaten more than $100 billion in long-term shareholder value. The report, entitled "Risking Shareholder Value? ExxonMobil and Climate Change: An Investigation of Unnecessary Risks and Missed Opportunities," was commissioned by shareholder activist Robert Monks, the Coalition for Environmentally Responsible Economies (CERES), and Campaign ExxonMobil.

The report concludes: "While ExxonMobil continues to gain respect in many quarters for its financials, it also has marched into a potential minefield of reputational risk, future shareholder losses, exposure to litigation, and policy costs on the issue of climate change. . . . We find real and increasingly serious risks to shareholders have arisen from the way ExxonMobil has stood out from the crowd and let itself become the obvious chief 'climate change villain.' "

Commenting on the report's findings, Monks said, "This report suggests that ExxonMobil has little to fear, and much to gain, from a significantly more constructive approach to climate change. This is a respectful request to ExxonMobil. You say that you are right about climate change and yet the way in which you speak seems to create needless confrontation. You say that you have contingency plans in the event that you are proven wrong in five or ten years and yet you do not share them with the world. We know of the efforts by comparable companies to reduce carbon emissions; from you we have not only silence, but also rejection. You decline to engage in dialogue with other interested constituencies—that is to say, all the rest of us. This study is an effort to begin that dialogue."

Exxon may be starting to shift its view, but the evidence is scanty. In November 2002 it contributed $100 million toward a ten-year $225 million program at Stanford University for research into technologies that would help reduce greenhouse gas emissions. General Electric will contribute $50 million. ExxonMobil explained its contribution by saying new techniques for producing energy while reducing emissions of heat-trapping greenhouse gases were "vital to meeting energy needs in the industrialized and developing world."

So far many global companies that have suffered a values crisis that damaged their brands are having trouble fighting back. McDonald's has stuck its toe into the globalization debate to defend itself. In April 2002 the company published its first corporate social responsibility status report using some guidelines from the Global Reporting Initiative. The Initiative brings together a group of companies, governments, nongovernmental organizations, unions, accountants, and academics to develop standardized measurements of corporate social, environmental, and financial performance.

Pulling together its report was a complex and costly exercise that took almost two years, but McDonald's says it was worth it, since it hopes the report will temper its critics.

However, so far it has mainly drawn fire. Paul Hawken, author of *The Ecology of Commerce* and *Natural Capitalism* and founder of the Sausalito-based Natural Capital Institute, unleashed a withering critique of the McDonald's report, calling it the "low-water mark for the concept of sustainability and the promise of corporate social responsibility. It is a mélange of homilies, generalities, and soft assurances that do not provide hard metrics of the company, its activities, or its impacts on society and the environment."

Hawken cuts McDonald's no slack. "An honest report would . . . detail the externalities borne by other people, places, and generations: The draining of aquifers, the contaminated waterways, the strip-mined soils, the dangerous abattoirs where migrant workers are employed, the inhumane, injury-prone dead-end jobs preparing chicken carcasses for Chicken McNuggets, the global greenhouse methane gas emitted by the millions of hamburger cows in feedlots."

Hawken posted on the Web a list of 47 issues that McDonald's sidestepped in its corporate self-portrait. Example: "One fourth of the cows slaughtered are worn-out dairy cattle, animals most likely to be riddled with diseases, cancers, and antibiotic residues. McDonald's relies heavily on old dairy cows because they are lower in fat, cheaper, and allow them to say all their meat is raised in the U.S."

Despite McDonald's best efforts and no matter how many reports it issues, Hawken's list of 47 issues won't go away. It sits there like a PR nightmare, waiting to churn the stomach of its next visitor. Hawken represents a point of view shared by many critics. To silence them, McDonald's will have to revamp its business model or show why its overall contribution to society is positive. Ignoring the issue accomplishes nothing.

In the transparent world, corporations need a new ethos. The truth will out—even if the truth is never as extreme as the critics allege. McDonald's can't brush aside criticism of the fast-food industry by busily noting how many pounds of cardboard each franchise recycles every week. In the eyes of extreme critics, serving "billions and billions" of burgers is an egregious abuse of natural resources, and the company has to engage in that debate.

The value of the Internet is not to construct warring Web sites, each lobbing assertions at the others. It is a tool for dialogue. If McDonald's believes its use of resources and business practices are defensible, it should not shy away from the serious issues that accompany the fast-food industry.

THE DARK SIDE: PRIVACY

Transparency has a dark side. Not only are corporations becoming increasingly transparent to customers, customers are becoming increasingly transparent to corporations. As the Net becomes the basis for commerce, work, entertainment, health care, learning, and much human discourse, each of us is leaving a trail of digital crumbs as we spend a growing portion of our day touching networks.

The books, music, and stocks you buy online, groceries scanned at the supermarket or bought online, your child's research for a school project, the card reader at the parking lot, your car's conversations with a database via satellite, the online publications you read, the shirt you purchase in a department store with your store card, the prescription drugs you buy—and the hundreds of other network transactions in a typical day—point to the problem. Computers can inexpensively link and cross-reference such databases to slice, dice, and recompile information about individuals in hundreds of different ways.

In the past we only worried about Big Brother governments assembling detailed dossiers about us. But now the threat also stems from individual corporations and their data: Little Brother.[20] Intense competition is making marketing departments look for any edge they can get. Companies can't afford to squander marketing dollars on people who have no intention of ever buying their product.

That means companies want to know more and more about what makes each of us tick—our motivations, behavior, attitudes, and buying habits. The good news is that companies can give us highly customized services based on this intimate knowledge—and build trusting relationships. The bad news is that as these profiles are compiled, the net result is the potential for the destruction of everything that we've come to know as privacy.

To further complicate the issue, each of us has a different (often inconsistent) sense of what constitutes privacy and permissible encroachments. While some demand the right to remain anonymous, others clamor, for example, to exchange every detail of their online behavior for free gift certificates or air miles. Of course that's their choice. Privacy is all about the freedom to choose.

In January 2003, the California Department of Motor Vehicles (DMV) revoked Allstate Insurance Company's electronic access to confidential driver license and vehicle registration information, because the government said the company had failed to adhere to state laws and regulations concerning access to those records.

Allstate, the eighth-largest car insurer in California, had—and other insurance companies have—online access to DMV records to help investigate insurance claims and to set rates on the basis of a person's driving record. The department stated the reason it revoked Allstate's online access to data was because the company engaged in continuous and systemwide violations of the security provisions governing the data.

A DMV audit at seven of Allstate's California claims offices found that company employees routinely violated the confidentiality requirements of the company's contract with the government. In one case, an Allstate employee released a confidential home address that enabled a road-rage driver to send a written threat to another driver. The threatened driver complained to the DMV, which investigated. While it could not identify the person who leaked the address, the

DMV did find 131 other violations of confidentiality rules, including the staff's making up fake car-claim numbers to get into friends' or family members' DMV records. "The violations were so egregious here, without an ironclad agreement in our hands that it wouldn't happen again . . . we had to pull the plug," DMV director Steven Gourley told a local newspaper.[21]

Allstate not only violated privacy rules but also resisted the DMV's attempts to investigate and fix the problem. "There was such a lax culture at Allstate that they didn't even know it was regulated," Gourley said. "Sometimes they wouldn't let us in (to investigate) and in other cases they threw us out." Allstate spokesperson Mike Trevino called the actions by an undisclosed number of Allstate claims employees a "breach of internal policy" that Allstate "regrets." He added that Allstate had taken "decisive action" to make sure such breaches don't recur, but couldn't immediately say what those actions were.[22]

Almost always corporate breaches of customer privacy have a well-meaning intention, but the Allstate incident shows how companies can be breathtakingly cavalier about privacy concerns. Companies need to understand the principles that must be respected in good corporate privacy policies:

Consent. People must agree to having information about them compiled.

Limiting collection. The collection of such information must be limited to what is needed.

Identifying purpose. The purposes for which personal information is collected must be made clear.

Limiting use, disclosure, and retention. Unless authorized by the individual, information must not be used for purposes other than those for which it was collected. And the information must be kept on file only as long as necessary.

It would be a big mistake for companies to conclude that corporate transparency should be applied to individuals—that customers should get used to being naked. Customers will want to be clothed for the foreseeable future and firms need to respect their privacy. If corporate transparency is critical for trust, then so is individual privacy. When it comes to customers, privacy is good business.

CHAPTER 7

COMMUNITIES

"Community" is a rich, multifaceted idea, referring to a collection or system rather than individuals in precise roles (like customers or shareholders). Employees seek security, good pay, and job satisfaction. Customers expect value for money. Suppliers hope for long-term relationships and fair dealings. Shareholders want the stock to rise. But what do communities want?

When Starbucks opens a new store, it may change the character of a neighborhood. When it buys more Fair Trade coffee, it may change the social, political, economic and environmental dynamics of a town in El Salvador. When it puts Wi-Fi into a cafe, it may become a hub for a local business community—or a peace demonstration. With each such small change there will be community winners and losers—each affected far more broadly than the value of their financial transactions with the company.

Communities are multilayered and diverse. You are a member of many—each with unique interests that sometimes compete. There are your nuclear and extended families, your local neighborhood, town, and so on, up to and including the global "community" of living organisms. You may be in a variety of interest groups—a gay singles support group, an informal golf league, a business lobby, an international church-based environmental NGO, maybe a political party. Though these groups sometimes have conflicting objectives, this hodgepodge is a reflection of your personality and needs. Businesses face the same complexities and trade-offs, sometimes writ very large. A business could, with the same action, support the goals and values of one of your communities and offend those of another.

The 6 billion people of the world's communities have a stake in the actions of corporations like never before. Since the collapse of communism in 1989, market capitalism has continually consolidated its position at national, regional, and global levels. Trade, financial flows, and corporate forms have shifted in scale and volume from the local and national to the regional and global.

At the same time, governments have lost ground to multinational corporations. Companies are getting bigger faster than governments. In 1990, the value added by the world's 100 largest multinationals was 3.5 percent of the world gross domestic product; ten years later it was 4.3 percent. In 2000, 29 of the world's 100 largest economic entities were multinational companies, not countries—an increase from 24 in 1990. The two largest companies by value added were Exxon (number 45) and General Motors (47). They were comparable in size to Chile and Pakistan, more than half as big as Israel, Ireland, and Malaysia (among others), and bigger than such countries as Peru, New Zealand, the Czech Republic, the United Arab Emirates, Hungary, Kuwait, the Dominican Republic, and Guatemala.[1]

Meanwhile, many governments have willingly ceded power to free markets. They have privatized state-owned industries like telecommunications and airlines, while outsourcing the delivery of public services to the private sector. They have heeded demands for deregulation and self-regulation in industries from financial services to food to environmental protection and health care. Pressure to keep taxes and deficits low—whether from within (wealthy citizens and corporations) or without (competition from low-tax zones or demands from international financial agencies)—has placed pressure on public services and their capacity to regulate business activities.

The result is that corporations are more visible than ever before, more likely to attract criticism (and praise), and more likely to be "in charge" of solving the world's problems. The problems are big:

• Ethnic, religious, and national conflicts, along with terrorism, increased through the past decade and show no sign of abating. Global wealth is rising, but the income gap grows ever wider—both among countries and within countries. Over 4.5 billion people are poor (purchasing power income less than U.S.$3,470 per year). In India, over 80 percent of the population lives on under $2 per day, while in the United States income disparity and poverty are among the worst of the world's rich countries. Although the world can produce enough food for everyone, 800 million people are malnourished. World life expectancy has risen dramatically, while HIV/AIDS is producing a holocaust in Africa, with millions dying in China and India also. The world's worst killer is tobacco: responsible for one in ten adult deaths today, expected to be one in six by 2030. Seventy percent of these deaths will be in low- and middle-income countries. One of every five adults—880 million people—is functionally illiterate.

- The world's capacity to innovate and produce continues to increase but at the expense of the environment. World energy production rose 42 percent between 1980 and 2000 and will grow 150 to 230 percent by 2050, increasing global warming. Polluting emissions, such as sulfur and sulfur oxide, are rising worldwide; improvements in the developed world may be overshadowed by growing waste in the developing world. Estimates are that 2 to 6 percent of disease in OECD countries is a result of environmental degradation: air pollution and chemicals. Efficient production and recycling have dramatically improved the performance of many rich country economies, moderating and even reducing the use of physical materials. But the challenge only increases. Agriculture is putting pressure on water supplies, fish stocks, forests, and grasslands. Over 1 billion people lack access to safe water, and over 2.5 billion don't have clean sanitation facilities; by 2050, 7 billion people may suffer from lack of water. The current addition of 60 million new urban citizens per year is equivalent to adding the urban population of Paris, Beijing, or Cairo every other month. About 50 percent of the world's citizens have never used a telephone, only 7 percent have access to a personal computer, and only 4 percent have access to the Internet.

The digital divide has a corollary: a *transparency divide*. Where people and communities have limited or no access to the tools of transparency—a free press, the Internet, or even telephone service—they miss out on vital information that affects their self-interest. They have limited ability to inform others or to organize in defense of their own interests, especially when compared with companies, governments, and organizations that have abundant use of such tools. Naturally, in such communities, corruption and discrimination tend to run rampant.

At eSeva walk-in centers in the state of Andhra Pradesh, India, clerks use the Internet to help citizens pay utility bills, register births and deaths, and conduct many other dealings with the government. Customers, spared several visits to government offices, are enthusiastic. Chandrababu Naidu, the chief minister of Andhra Pradesh, says the main goals are "transparency, accountability, and speediness," and to "reduce the interface" between government and citizenry. Translation: computers rarely collect bribes. They also reduce corruption by, for example, making tender documents more readily available to all bidders.[2]

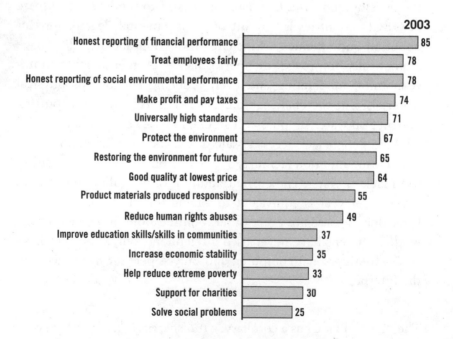

Figure 7.1 Corporations Held Completely Responsible For (U.S. Survey)
Source: Environics International

Who is responsible for all this? Governments, yes, but people also increasingly look to corporations. According to data from Environics International's 2003 CSR Monitor (Figure 7.1), majorities of U.S. respondents hold corporations "responsible for" specific outcomes like honest reporting of social and environmental performance, protecting the environment, restoring the environment for the future, producing product materials responsibly, and reducing human rights abuses. Interestingly, fewer respondents expect corporations to support charities than to achieve these more operationally demanding sustainability outcomes.

To corporate leaders who demur that such social and environmental outcomes are the province of government rather than business, we say, "Be careful what you wish for, because you just might get it." Business lobbies have asked governments to cut back their social investments and to let companies do the right thing and regulate themselves. This survey seems to say that Americans now take this "offer" seriously.

Mistrust runs high. Environics found that six in ten Americans said that their trust in American companies had decreased over the previous year, significantly more than in other countries surveyed.[3]

WHITHER SOCIAL CAPITAL?

In *Bowling Alone*, Harvard professor Robert Putnam builds a well-documented case that social capital has declined in the United States, a view that has become the conventional wisdom.

> During the first two-thirds of the [twentieth] century Americans took a more and more active role in the social and political life of their communities—in churches and union halls, in bowling alleys and clubrooms, around committee tables and card tables and dinner tables. Year by year we gave more generously to charity, we pitched in more often on community projects, and (insofar as we can still find reliable evidence) we behaved in an increasingly trustworthy way toward one another. Then, mysteriously and more or less simultaneously, we began to do all those things less often.[4]

Putnam tracks many declines:

- In voting, political or community group membership, attendance at political rallies and speeches, signing petitions

- Membership and attendance of chapter-based organizations (such as B'nai Brith, Knights of Columbus, Parent-Teacher Association), though self-help support groups are on the increase

- Church attendance (with the exception of evangelical conservatives)

- Membership in unions and national professional associations

- Home entertaining and visiting, card playing, informal socializing, and—yes, league bowling (though casinos, video games, and spectator sports are up)

- Philanthropy and participation in community projects (though youth volunteering is up)

- Perceptions of others' honesty and morality, observance of road stop signs

While acknowledging the growth of new forms of social mobilization, such as the "explosive growth of national environmental organizations," Putnam argues that membership in such groups for most people is not active participation. It entails little more than signing up and writing a check. Statewide referenda have also skyrocketed, but mostly driven by professional firms and special interests; surveys indicate a very low level of voter sophistication on the issues at hand. Putnam expresses some hope for the Internet and other new communications media as mechanisms for reengagement, but doubts they will make any more impact than the telephone.

Here, perhaps, he is wrong. A Harvard colleague of Putnam's, Pippa Norris, in a comparably documented book, *Democratic Phoenix*, picks up the rise of the environmental movement to analyze it as a proxy for a broader change. She describes it as "the transformation from the politics of loyalties [to traditional political parties, clubs, and churches] to the politics of choice [of values-aligned issues and interests]." Norris says that today's social movements and international advocacy networks are far more amorphous and tricky to gauge. The capacity for social movements concerned about issues such as globalization, human rights, debt relief, and world trade to cross national borders may signal the emergence of a global civic society. Networked agencies are characterized by direct-action strategies and Internet communications, loose coalitions, relatively flat organizational structures, and more informal modes of belonging focused on shared concerns about diverse issues and identity politics. Traditional hierarchical and bureaucratic organizations persist, but social movements may be emerging as the most popular avenue for informal political mobilization, protest, and expression.[5]

Norris documents the continuing growth of such movements with a history of the growing geographic breadth, diversity of issues addressed, and numeric size of protest demonstrations from the 1950s through the 1990s. Her book was published too early to take note of the largest global protest ever (as of this writing, anyway): the 10 million people or more—mostly in Europe, but 350,000 plus in the United States—who rallied on February 15, 2003, against war in Iraq. Indeed, as Norris suggests, not only have the modes of organization changed (from traditional hierarchies to amorphous networks and NGOs—what we call stakeholder webs) but so have their methods (from traditional politics to demonstrations, Internet-based forced transparency, direct engagement with firms and government agencies, and direct action to improve conditions in communities). Indeed, their targets have changed too: where once political participation, via political parties and community groups, almost exclusively targeted governments and politicians, today's activists also target, expose, and engage with companies, international agencies, business associations, and, for that matter, NGOs.

Norris found that people who support environmental activism are less likely than the average to vote but more likely to support protests such as demonstrations, petitions, and boycotts. They are also more likely to engage in mainstream civics, like sports and arts clubs, professional associations, and unions. All this comes together most especially in Scandinavia, Australia, New Zealand, Germany, and the United States (Norris's data do not include the United Kingdom, France, or Canada).

Why is this happening? With the decline in the power and function of states, the world's diverse networks of communities have increasingly concluded that, for their interests to be served, they must deal directly with corporations and international institutions. Call them what you will—civil society groups or NGOs—they've been on an explosive rise just about everywhere. The Union of International Organizations has been tracking the development of nongovernmental networks, especially nonprofit and voluntary associations, since 1907. It is now tracking over 45,000 such groups, compared with fewer than 10,000 pre-1980. NGOs receive over $150 billion in annual donations, about 80 percent from individuals and the rest from bequests, foundations, and corporations.[6]

NGOs are visible at the barricades exposing companies to new scrutiny, demanding accountability and changes in values and behavior. But these high-profile actions are the tip of the iceberg. Partnership is really the norm as NGOs provide advice and expertise, help strengthen community relationships, and participate as trustworthy third parties to monitor firm behavior. Where such relationships work well, real-life outcomes are substantially improved, while everyone gains market credibility and brand strength.

THE NEW CIVIL SOCIETY AND
THE POWER OF TRANSPARENCY

NGOs have racked up some impressive victories:

- The Campaign for Nuclear Disarmament, launched in the United Kingdom during the 1950s, was the springboard for a global movement whose efforts culminated in the ratification of the 1996 Comprehensive Test Ban Treaty by 136 countries.

- A broad coalition of environmental NGOs from Greenpeace to the Sierra Club was a prime mover in the drafting of the 1992 Kyoto Accord. Members of this coalition spent the next decade campaigning for ratification by individual countries and gaining commitments to change products, services, and industrial processes from carbon-intensive businesses and industries.

- The World Social Forum, the annual meeting of thousands of NGOs and political groups from around the world in Porto Alegre, Brazil, coincides with the World Economic Forum, the premier conference of world business and political leaders in Davos, Switzerland. Increasingly, Davos pays homage to Porto Alegre, vying to attract leading NGO speakers and attendees. In 2003, Brazil's newly elected president, Luis Inacio Lula da Silva spoke at both, by request bringing the World Social Forum message to the World Economic Forum.

- Countless companies, as we describe throughout this book, have changed their products and services, altered labor and employment practices, and even redefined core business strategies in response to NGO recommendations or action campaigns. Some, like McDonald's and Nike, paid a big price for their inability to visibly meet NGO and civil society demands and expectations.

NGOs at first glance are a peculiarly modern phenomenon, but their antecedents include millennium-old religious communities. Little more than a handful existed half a century ago; today, there are tens of thousands. Each typically focuses on a single issue or set of issues, most often side effects of today's global economy. Information—hence transparency—is particularly critical to NGOs. They lack the financial clout that other stakeholders enjoy. Mostly all they can do is learn, inform, volunteer, persuade, organize, and demonstrate. In extreme cases they will try to convince others who do have economic power to use it—consumer boycotts, for example. NGOs engage in several forms of action, all in the context of stakeholder webs that they build, lead, or join:

- Conduct research, produce and publish information.

- Work closely with business and political leaders to inform, educate, and advise them.

- Campaign for the support of community members, employees, shareholders, or other stakeholders. Once mobilized, such support can influence the decisions and actions of businesspeople and politicians.

- Conduct targeted, issue-oriented campaigns using a variety of tactics ranging from information dissemination to civil disobedience.

- Address problems directly. Some NGOs, like ActionAid, put workers in the field to tackle social or environmental problems. Increasingly, companies partner with—and subsidize—such activities as partners of NGOs. TakingITGlobal, founded by Canadian net generation entrepreneurs Michael Furdyk and Jennifer Corriero, uses digital technologies to help young people in more than sixty countries launch social, political, and creative networks.

- Perform specialized services such as auditing firms' corporate responsibility reports.

- Engage with other organizations to build networks of NGOs, common approaches, toolkits, and so forth.

Sometimes, NGOs, like any other organizations, lose track of their mission and turn into self-perpetuating, even corrupt institutions. And many NGOs lack the transparency that they demand of their targets. But overall, the record of NGOs is good, even exemplary. Top NGO brands outrank many consumer brands. Companies must make deliberate choices about which NGOs to work with, but ignoring them is not an option. Best to engage with them, since NGOs and other civil society groups can mobilize a-webs to support—or challenge—a corporation's very license to operate.

THE CHIQUITA STORY

Can a leopard change its spots? Maybe not. But a banana can. Consider Chiquita.

Bananas are the most popular fruit in the world: North Americans eat half a pound per person per week. Chiquita Brands International (which also sells other fresh fruit and Stokely canned vegetables), with $2.2 billion in revenues, is the world's largest producer. Most of its employees and production come from Central American countries like Costa Rica, Guatemala, Panama, Nicaragua, and Colombia. Carmen Miranda, the 1940s Latin American singer and movie star, inspired the company's ubiquitous "Miss Chiquita Banana" character and the popular "Chiquita Banana Song." The company has several historic firsts. In 1904, it perfected the first unbroken string of wireless communications from the United States to Latin America, permitting its transport vessels to communicate with company locations. In 1910, the United Fruit Company (as it was called until 1989) initiated banana research in Latin America to develop new disease-resistant varieties. In 1963 it was the first produce supplier to put a brand sticker on its products. And in 1992 Chiquita began work with the environmental NGO Rainforest Alliance on the Better Banana Project.

All this belies the slithery past of "the Octopus," as the company used to be called. In its new spirit of transparency, Chiquita now admits responsibility for past transgressions and attitudes. Founded in 1899, the United Fruit Company (as the company was originally called) routinely used armed force to keep employees in line. Its name is linked forever to the pejorative term *banana republic*, which describes a Central American country whose dictator is on the company payroll.[7]

United Fruit was directly involved in various U.S. military interventions and coups d'etat, including the notorious CIA-supported overthrow of Guatemala's democratically elected government in 1954—when U.S. Secretary of State John Foster Dulles was a company shareholder. Twenty-one years later, company president Eli Black jumped to his death from his Manhattan office window; an SEC investigation revealed that he had bribed the president of Honduras with $1.25 million (with another $1.25 million promised) for a reduction in export taxes and had also paid off various European officials to the tune of $750,000.

In the early 1990s, Chiquita had visions of a big banana market in postcommunist eastern Europe. It invested massively in ships and facilities, incurring a long-term debt of $1 billion. But rather than bound into an expanding market, the company slipped. The market failed to materialize. A global supply glut and depressed prices ensued. CEO Carl Lindner blamed the company's subsequent poor results on bad weather and crop disease.[8]

Then in 1993 the European Union decided to strengthen its preferential treatment for banana imports from former colonies in Africa (like the Ivory Coast) and the Caribbean (like Jamaica). While Dole had made investments in such countries and was more widely diversified, Chiquita was again caught flat-footed.

Carl Lindner, also the company's chairman and largest investor, decided to tackle the problem. As he moved in on the White House and the U.S. Congress, he gained a reputation as a pioneer of soft political contributions. Between 1993 and 1999 gifts from Lindner, members of his family, his companies, and their executives exceeded $5 million.[9] Lindner received several invitations to the Bill Clinton White House, including an overnight stay in the Lincoln bedroom. Politicians from the president on down—Republicans and Democrats—intervened aggressively on Chiquita's behalf. The U.S. government brought the banana case several times to the World Trade Organization. It ruled in favor of the U.S. complaint, but Europe didn't budge. So in 1999 the United States imposed punitive tariffs on nine types of European goods, severely hurting thousands of small U.S. importers in the process. In 2001, Europe gave in. But through the decade Chiquita lost many hundreds of millions of dollars.

A watershed event occurred on May 3, 1998, when the *Cincinnati Enquirer* ran a 20-page expose of the locally headquartered company. Spearheaded by investigative reporter Mike Gallagher, the article painted a detailed portrait of a company engaged in life-threatening labor and environmental practices, financial folly, political corruption, and borderline criminal mismanagement. Drawing on a year's in-depth research—including Chiquita's own internal voice mail messages, which were improperly accessed by Gallagher—and displayed on the Internet for the world to see, the series showed how transparency can devastate a company in the information age.

The article's introduction listed the following charges:[10]

- Chiquita secretly controls dozens of supposedly independent banana companies. It does so through elaborate business structures designed to avoid restrictions on land ownership and national security laws in Central American countries. The structures also are aimed at limiting unions on its farms.

- Chiquita and its subsidiaries are engaged in pesticide practices that threaten the health of workers and nearby residents, despite an agreement with an environmental group to adhere to certain safety standards.

- Regardless of that environmental agreement, Chiquita subsidiaries use pesticides in Central America that are not allowed to be used in either the United States or Canada or in one or more of the 15 countries in the European Union.

- A worker on a Chiquita subsidiary farm died late in 1997 after exposure to toxic chemicals in a banana field, according to a local coroner's report.

- Hundreds of people in a Costa Rican barrio have been exposed to a toxic chemical emitting from the factory of a Chiquita subsidiary.

- Employees of Chiquita and a subsidiary were involved in a bribery scheme in Colombia that has come to the attention of the U.S. Securities and Exchange Commission. Two employees have been forced to resign.

- Chiquita fruit-transport ships have been used to smuggle cocaine into Europe. Authorities seized more than a ton of cocaine (worth up to $33 million in its pure form) from seven Chiquita ships in 1997. Although the company was unaware and did not approve of the illegal shipments, problems were traced to lax security on its Colombian docks.

- Security guards have used brute force to enforce their authority on plantations operated or controlled by Chiquita. In an internationally controversial case, Chiquita called in the Honduran military to enforce a court order to evict residents of a farm village; the village was bulldozed and villagers run out at gunpoint. On a palm plantation controlled by a Chiquita subsidiary in Honduras, a man was shot to death and another man injured by guards using an illegal automatic weapon. An agent of a competitor has filed a federal lawsuit claiming that armed men led by Chiquita officials tried to kidnap him in Honduras.

The article also described former CEO Carl Lindner's campaign-contribution spree. Chiquita's recently appointed CEO, veteran company employee Stephen Warshaw, reacted to the report with anger. Although the *Enquirer* had first said that a company employee had provided voice mail messages to reporter Mike Gallagher, it turned out that he had misled the paper and had personally hacked into Chiquita's system to retrieve the messages. This became the basis for a legal offensive by the company. The newspaper issued a front page apology and, to the dismay of free speech advocates, disavowed the entire story. It removed the article from its Web site, fired Gallagher, and agreed to pay Chiquita $14 million in damages. Gallagher pled guilty to unlawful interception of communications and unauthorized access to computer systems. He was sentenced in 1999 to five years' probation. On the surface, Chiquita seemed to have won. Yet the newspaper's disavowal did not convince anyone that the charges in the article were false. As several observers pointed out, the company never rebutted them. And though the newspaper purged it, the article is available on other Web sites.

Chiquita killed the messenger but not the message. That message wasn't lost on the company's broader stakeholder web. Its employees didn't need anyone to tell them what parts of it were true and what parts false, exaggerated, or out of context. Shareholders, bondholders, suppliers, and retailers were concerned. Government agencies, the media, trade unions, and NGOs also began to pay new heed to the company.

The *Enquirer* shed light on issues that persist in many parts of the banana industry. In rich countries, minimum labor standards protect all employees—unionized or not. But in many banana-growing countries, rights and wages are reserved for those with money and power. In Ecuador as recently as 2002, security guards threatened striking workers seeking union recognition at a Dole supplier, while 350 company thugs, some armed, assaulted striking workers at a Noboa plantation (which produces Bonita brand bananas) on two separate occasions. Noboa fired hundreds of employees, only to be forced to reinstate them and recognize the union after its owner lost the election for the Ecuadorian presidency. In Colombia in 2002, guerrillas assassinated seven banana trade unionists (as well as two by-

standers).[11] In Guatemala in 2001, 22 men were convicted of perpe-
trating violence against striking workers at a Del Monte plantation. In
such an industry culture, and in the absence of a company code of
conduct with teeth, you would expect some Chiquita managers to
have behaved badly.

Chiquita's management group was at a fork in the road. It was not,
of course, entirely blameworthy. Chiquita had engaged with NGO
Rainforest Alliance in the Better Banana Project as early as 1992. It
had by far the largest unionization rate (70 percent) in its industry,
and decent relations with many unions. But it was far from being
entirely clean.

Jeffrey Zalla, now Chiquita's corporate responsibility officer, was
deeply involved with these questions at the time. As he puts it, "Hell
be damned was not the culture, but it wasn't engaged with the external stakeholder community, nor was it mindful of the standards
expected of respected global businesses. The dominant feature of the
company was that it was insular. It didn't communicate well, and was
too reactive. This is because it was frequently under attack; it had a
history and was the focal point of an international trade war. There
were commercial interests in bringing criticism to the company. So
the company was generally closed and defensive."

The company faced a billion dollars in debt, years of losses, a six-
year-and-counting trade war, and a confused workforce.

The company's CEO Stephen Warshaw initiated a period of reflection. Says Zalla, "Managers felt—we believe we do the right things.
How did people reach these conclusions about us? Have we done
enough to share a common set of values and educate people to live
these values? It became an issue of governance and process, standards,
and living the values. Social responsibility became a vehicle to establish clear values, disciplines, and accountabilities across the company.
He said don't talk to me about sustainability or CSR—talk about
codes of conduct. I want people to be accountable, no excuses. They
behave that way or they're out of here."

Warshaw's initial working group consisted of himself, Zalla, and the
VP of human resources. During the summer of 1998 they met with
several people in the field of corporate responsibility. Zalla singles out
the guidance of Robert Dunn, CEO of Business for Social Responsibil-

ity (BSR). "He provided insight on what it means to be an ethical leader and have high standards." In October 1998, Zalla formed a corporate responsibility committee. Its first project was to redefine the company's core values.

Today's responsible Chiquita is based on a five-part chain: values, standards, compliance, transparency, and engagement.

The **values** are a simple, easily communicated set of principles, e.g. "we treat people fairly and respectfully." Simple as they are, everything else depends on them. And creating them was not so simple. "We grossly underestimated the effort it takes to bring about this kind of culture change," says Zalla. "It took us 10 months. Steve Warshaw complained that we were too process oriented, it doesn't need to take this much time. But we ended up having a process of discussion and debate at three levels of the organization. We ended up with three values statements.

"There was enormous commonality on many issues: open, honest and straightforward communication, as well as ethical and legal action. But only the employees suggested that we recognize the importance of family in their lives. This was a vital process to gain alignment: now there's no lingering debate about it. If any employee sees the company not living up to the values, it's their job to challenge them. This turned out to be a hugely important investment in time."

Standards translate the values into rules for everyday life. Chiquita's own code of conduct protects freedom of association, nondiscrimination, and sets maximum hours of work. It based the code of conduct on two tough—and continually evolving—international standards. Social Accountability 8000 (based on UN, International Labor Organization, and ISO norms) is Chiquita's core labor standard and the Better Banana Project (from the Rainforest Alliance) sets rules for environmental and labor practices.

All employees—especially managers—are accountable for **compliance** with the values and standards. Managers have been trained on the relationship between values, standards, business performance, and continuous improvement. They are evaluated on compliance; their compensation, in part, depends on it. The company produced a comic book style Spanish-language version of its values and code of conduct for plantation workers. It trained them too. Compliance is rigorously assessed—not just internally—but by several sets of professionally qualified independent external auditors. In addition, employees are surveyed (also by external auditors, to encourage them to speak openly) for their own assessment of management compliance.

Chiquita's **transparency** is profound. Many companies expect employees to conduct open, honest, and straightforward communications, internally and externally. At Chiquita, this is a breakthrough concept. Rather than just call on employees to always tell the truth (often a feat in itself), Chiquita hangs dirty linen for all the world to see. By the time this book hits the stores, the company will have published its third corporate responsibility report. Each edition clearly presents and explains the results of its external audits and employee surveys; it sets specific objectives for the next year and reports on previous goals.

These reports, and more, are publicly available on Chiquita's Web site. The 2001 report reveals, for example, that the company's Costa Rican division "remains over-reliant on the use of agrichemicals for pest control," while "several female workers alleged sexual harassment" in Guatemala. (The reports contain more good news than bad; we sample the bad to illustrate our point.)

The old Chiquita made its own rules. The new one recognizes that trust depends on reciprocity and **engagement** with its stakeholder web. Zalla is proudest of a 2001 accord with the trade union movement—the first of its kind by a multinational corporation to cover workers in developing countries. Some six weeks before the May 1998 *Enquirer* story, 350 armed riot police had come to arrest 62 union supporters at a Guatemala plantation owned by Cobigua, a Chiquita-exclusive supplier. This resulted in a mass walkout, hundreds of firings, and a protracted dispute filled with "dirty tricks." Cobigua was a separate company and Chiquita disavowed responsibility.

In July 1998 the union (Colsiba) tendered an olive branch, formally proposing a get-together. Chiquita failed to respond. On September 10, 60 U.S. religious, human rights, and labor organizations published a letter chiding the company. The coalition organized press releases in Europe and Central America. The company agreed to meet, the first small step on a careful and deliberate path of consultation and collaboration that ultimately led to a ground-breaking agreement on labor and union rights in June 2001. As often happens in these situations, an independent NGO (U.S. Labor in the Americas Project and its leader Stephen Coats) played a role as convener, facilitator—and publicist. Also, once the IUF, a major international union body, came into the picture, the process, says Zalla, "gathered speed and focus."

Not a union contract, the deal is a framework for freedom of association and minimum labor standards in the company's banana operations. It bears signatures from Chiquita, two trade unions (Colsiba and the IUF), and the International Labor Organization (a UN agency). Its engagement is much more than skin deep, providing for a joint company-union committee which meets at least twice a year to oversee the agreement's application and address areas of concern.

Zalla makes two key points about this accord. First, it is based on ILO standards—such as freedom of association, collective bargaining, and fundamental human rights. "It was a lot easier to do since we had already adopted the core ILO conventions under SA8000 a year earlier." Second, the agreement includes an extraordinary commitment to fair dealing, continuous improvement, and mutual benefit. Both sides promise to abstain from nasty tactics (such as public anticompany campaigns or antiunion retaliation) until agreed negotiation timetables have been exhausted. For its part, the union agrees that effective labor-management relations depend on Chiquita's commercial success and sustainability.

As the open Chiquita value chain evolved, the company passed through bankruptcy (November 2001 though March 2002). The result: The company stayed in business and its bondholders ended up as majority owners. Through this process, the company worked hard to achieve "a fair balance among the concerns of the many stakeholder groups impacted by the process."[12] Transparency—open, honest, and straightforward communication—was central to crossing this chasm successfully.

Most broadly, there has been a dramatic change in the company's public reputation. Chiquita has won several awards and is widely cited as a leader in corporate responsibility—a sea change for a company that only a few years earlier was being dragged through the mud. But this is just the foundation: each of Chiquita's stakeholders delivered a meaningful return on the company's investment in values and accountability.

Employees kept their jobs. More to the point, they didn't quit: during the bankruptcy the company ran business as usual and experienced average employee turnover. Zalla insisted on developing the first corporate responsibility report during the bankruptcy; it was published in June 2002. Consultant Neil Smith, whom Zalla credits for guiding the company through its values process, worried that publication would make the company a target for critics. But Zalla insisted—rightly—that making the report's commitments public would strengthen their internal credibility and impact.

The company also used transparent processes to address the interests of other key stakeholders. In the end, bondholders traded $960 million of old company debt for 95.5 percent of the post–bankrupt company's shares and $250 million of new debt. Business partners remained on the company's side: Chiquita kept them informed throughout the process, paid its suppliers, and retained its customers. Previous shareholders had to content themselves with 2 percent of the company's new common stock, plus some warrants. But all the big ones stuck around. As Chiquita points out, this was a good deal compared to the typical Chapter 11 restructuring (where shareholders often end up with nothing).

Zalla lists other tangible benefits of the engaged, accountable, and transparent Chiquita. Environmental care has reduced spending on agricultural chemicals by $4.8 million. Recycling cut costs by $3 million. In 2002 improved labor standards saved the Costa Rican operation $500,000 in worker compensation costs.

Zalla insists that the big benefits—like crossing the bankruptcy chasm—are hardest to measure. Labor disputes and strikes have become fewer and shorter. A strike in Panama lasted 58 days and cost the company $21 million; in the old Chiquita, Zalla believes, it would have been far worse. The labor relations issues in Panama proved intractable, so the company decided to divest its operation. Zalla credibly argues that a transparent, engaged approach to this bad situation meant a less costly and painful outcome for all the players.

Cost and risk management are good, but what's the upside? In Europe, where Chiquita is number one, integrity sells bananas. Chiquita sold 54 percent of its 2002 volume to retailers who engaged with it on social responsibility issues. Some were diligent: they audited Chiquita's production facilities or had it complete a detailed questionnaire. The United States is a different story. Few U.S. consumers today make buying decisions on the basis of social responsibility, and only 7 percent of the company's volume goes through retailers who make it an issue. Zalla would like to see some external support—whether from government or from the social investment community—for retailers and produce managers who want to raise the ante.

At the end of the day, says Zalla, "We don't have as elegant or compelling a business case on paper as I would like. This effort was undertaken on the basis of values. You don't put a value on honesty: many companies have fallen apart because of a lack of integrity."

It's often said that trust takes years to build and can be destroyed in seconds. Chiquita's story is the flip side: where mistrust is entrenched, a genuine turnaround can work wonders quickly. The speed of this change also entails risk: Will it last long enough to become deeply rooted, or will short-term expedient strategies regain dominance? Nevertheless, Chiquita's new approach to transparency and accountability to community and environmental stakeholders is about as good as it gets today: not perfect, but a benchmark. It is also a compelling tale of redemption. Chiquita's conversion simply and poignantly illustrates the value of integrity, engagement, and accountability for all stakeholders.

Is Chiquita an anomaly, an outlier? Few companies have the history and reputation of a United Fruit, let alone a comparable record of mismanagement and near collapse. Chiquita had no choice but to clean up its act. Yet lots of stable and successful companies have similar (some equally dramatic) stories about a scary crisis that drove a business case for social and environmental accountability.

- Royal Dutch/Shell chairman Sir Philip Watts has said that "sustainable development—integrating economic, social, and environmental considerations in all our activities—has become central to how we do business." Shell did not adopt these principles lightly; they came after "bitter experiences" during the mid-1990s: human rights fiascos in Nigeria (including the assassination of Ken Saro-Wiwa) and the Brent Spar environmental boycott led by Greenpeace in the North Sea. After these events, Shell added two new components to its corporate values: the UN Universal Declaration of Human Rights and the principles of sustainable development. It also made itself accountable—warts and all—with the externally audited *Shell Report* on its social and environmental performance; its sixth was published in early 2003.

Shell supports the Kyoto protocol, which calls on developed countries to cut emissions of greenhouse gases by an average 5.2 percent from 1990 to 2010. Though its business grew 30 percent, Shell achieved a 10 percent emissions reduction in 2002—double the Kyoto target, years early. This conservation program helped achieve companywide cost reduction goals of 3 percent per year. Sustainability converges with Shell's business scenarios; it is preparing for the day when noncarbon fuels like electric fuel cells and hydrogen become a significant part of the market. One controversial measure of Shell's transparency is that it reports annually on any breaches of its strict antibribery policy. Bribery is a big issue in all extraction industries, which operate in many countries where the rule of law is weak.

- Citibank, the world's largest financial company, was—along with other banks like Morgan Stanley—already under scrutiny for financing of socially and environmentally damaging projects like China's Three Gorges Dam. It was also being blamed for predatory consumer loan practices by some U.S. subsidiaries. Then in 2002 its complicity in the Enron disaster and its conflicts of interest that cost investors millions of dollars turned scrutiny into crisis. Shareholders punished the company hard; at time of writing, its shares, though improved over their 2002 collapse, were still tottering well below typical historic values. The company made a variety of changes in corporate and business governance, including the formulation of policies to assess the social and environmental risks of any new financings. In an October 2002 presentation, the SVP of global community relations Pamela Flaherty pointed out that, in a decentralized business like Citi, sustainability principles start out at the corporate level. "Bringing sustainability into mainstream business is a challenge." The jury is out on whether and when Citi will articulate a business case or, for that matter, a consistent program with clear accountabilities. Presumably, anything the company can do to restore trust would help its share price.

Others have decided there's a business case even in the absence of crisis. Or maybe their crisis was indirect, lost in the swirls of history. Hewlett-Packard and Johnson & Johnson attribute their ingrained ethics and social responsibility to founding fathers who lived through the Great Depression.

Robert W. Johnson's 1935 pamphlet urged his fellow industrialists to adopt a "new industrial philosophy" entailing responsibility to customers, employees, the community, and stockholders. He believed that the corporate scandals that had led to the Depression might cause society to challenge business's license to operate. The payoff? Johnson & Johnson enjoys an enviable business performance record and, according to a Harris survey sponsored by *The Wall Street Journal*, has held the highest corporate reputation in the United States four years running, from 1999 (the first year this survey was conducted) to 2002.[13]

Bill Hewlett and David Packard founded their company in a Palo Alto garage in 1939. Jerry Porras, coauthor with Jim Collins of *Built to Last: Successful Habits of Visionary Companies*, once asked Hewlett what he and Packard were thinking about when they started the company. Hewlett said, "Look, we were a couple of young guys, just out of Stanford. We thought we were pretty smart, and we thought we could contribute something."

The concept of contribution—and humility—has stayed with the firm. This evolved into a perspective known as the HP Way, one of Bill Hewlett's chief legacies: respect for the individual, contribution to the customer and the community, integrity, teamwork, and innovation. Hewlett-Packard was the source or an early adopter of progressive management strategies like flexible work hours, "management by walking around," and open doors and cubicles. Many charged that CEO Carly Fiorina would jettison these values with the contentious 2001 Compaq acquisition. But HP emerged as a resolute leader—though still feeling its way—in global social and environmental responsibility and disclosure. Hewlett-Packard too wants a payoff: the billions of impoverished people today who represent the information technology marketplace of the twenty-first century.

THE GLOBAL CHALLENGE

The issues in this area apply everywhere in the world, but their character in rich countries is quite different from that in emerging economies.

- At a macroeconomic level, rich countries consume the lion's share of the world's resources and generate the largest volumes of global pollution—in particular the greenhouse gases that cause global warming. These are also the countries where the rule of law is most universal; corruption is least prevalent; and nearly everyone, even the poorest, can get their minimal basic needs met. Notable exceptions notwithstanding, this macroeconomic environment delivers—or imposes—a high-standard playing field for all competitors. At a microeconomic level, laws and regulations require companies to meet standards related to employment, safe goods and services, commercial transactions, and so on.

- The operating environment for companies in emerging economies is much more diverse and complex. A few nations—like China and Singapore—have strong governments. Others—like Brazil—are weaker but feisty. All too many lack the clout, maturity, and resources to manage the complex legal, social, environmental, and economic systems required to harness and control the impacts of globalization.

In this broader domain, the case for the new integrity—and sustainability—is, as we have already discussed, founded in trust. But trust is insufficient for an all-situation business case, particularly for choices that enhance sustainability. In this area, where the central principle is aligning present solutions with future needs, businesses must frequently lead their customers, shareholders, and other stakeholders, rather than just hold their confidence.

THE SUSTAINABILITY PARADOX

Many companies point to tangible payoffs from a social and environmental strategy that is aligned with their business strategy. Nevertheless, the paradigmatic business case to prove it remains elusive, and for good reason. The payoffs from treating customers, employees, and shareholders well are often obvious. But the social and environmental payoffs? Why not be a free rider and let others save the world?

Open enterprises are in the minority: few enterprises genuinely apply honesty, accountability, consideration, and transparency as a way of doing business. Fewer still have recast their business strategies for global sustainability. Even fewer fully meet the expectations of civil society and other social and environmental stakeholders. BP, a high-profile responsible company, continues to seek drilling concessions in environmentally sensitive areas like Alaska and Russia; it evidently believes it has no choice, and who's to argue with its business logic? If the case for always "doing good" were blindingly obvious, many more would apply it.[14] This problem reminds us of a 20-plus-year debate in the information technology arena. Firms invest in IT on the presumption that it will pay off: cut costs and maybe help generate new sales. But the return on investment in IT was invisible for a very long time. Beginning in the mid-1970s, economists and business executives pointed out that, though capital costs on IT were visibly soaring and the benefits seemed intuitively obvious, no one could reliably identify—let alone measure—the payoff. This problem existed both in the overall economy and at the level of individual companies. Though IT spending soared, productivity growth remained stuck at a national rate of 1.5 percent a year. And where productivity growth accelerated, no one could prove the link to IT. This productivity paradox didn't stop companies from buying computers. In fact, during the 1980s they did so with abandon, as individual departments bought PCs, printers, and local area networks.

In 1995, along with the rise of the Internet, productivity growth suddenly took off. Rates of 2.5 percent persisted at least until 2002, well after the dot-com crash. Economists and pundits offered all sorts of explanations for this sudden surge. One was simply the Internet—the new wonder that seemed to be changing everything. Another was more prosaic: It wasn't the Internet at all, but after thirty years of spending, there was enough technology out there to make a difference. A third was more subtle: Companies had finally figured out how to change their way of doing business to capitalize on the technology. The clincher explanation built on this third idea. Research by the McKinsey Global Institute (an arm of the consulting firm) shows that only a handful of industries and a handful of companies in these industries got the lion's share of the IT productivity payoff. Three high-tech industries—semiconductor, computer assembly, and telecommunication—contributed 36 percent of U.S. compound productivity growth between 1993 and 2000. And only three nontech industries—retail, wholesale distribution, and securities trading—contributed another 40 percent. The 52 other sectors made do with the remaining 24 percent of growth. McKinsey confirmed this insight in studies of France and Germany. The conclusion: Only a handful of industries drive a country's productivity performance at any given time.

How did these high-powered industries in each country succeed? The research suggests their executives solved the productivity paradox by taking charge of IT investment for business, not nerdy, objectives.

Leaders, according to McKinsey, did three things right. First, they tailored their IT investments very specifically to their industry, indeed to their company's own unique ways of doing business. Second, they ensured that projects occurred in the right order, from foundational through everyday operational to futuristic—building capabilities over time. Third, their decision makers managed IT decisions like any other business decision. To these, we'd add a fourth factor: Change happened across an industry when a ferociously motivated industry leader moved in to change the rules at a time when enough competitors had the means and competitive know-how to follow suit.

Sustainable environmental and social practices are no more a silver bullet than IT. Every business case and plan must be tailored to a company's specifics. Then, the devil is in the detail of executive leadership and stepwise implementation.

Over 700 million cars crisscross our planet, with 150,000 added every day. Most car manufacturers have jumped on the environmental bandwagon. But some—particularly those based in Detroit—have done so reluctantly, while building and selling ever more monstrous and inefficient SUVs. This problem is not easily solved: many consumers are indeed hooked on big cars. In 2002, customers lined up to buy GM's entire initial 20,000 vehicle run of the 4-ton, $55,000, 10-mile-per-gallon Hummer 2. In fact, Hummer dealer waiting list slots sold on eBay for $7,000 or more.[15]

Predictably, when President Bush in his 2003 State of the Union address proposed funds to develop hydrogen technologies and an incremental 7 percent cut in fuel economy standards for SUVs and light trucks by 2007, General Motors objected with forebodings of doom: an industrywide loss of 105,000 jobs, reduced safety because of lighter vehicles, a cost increase of $275 per vehicle, and a revenue loss to GM of $1.1 billion.[16] This is a lose-lose response. If GM is right, it's a sad commentary on the technological and adaptive capabilities of the U.S. auto industry; if wrong, it is obstinately so.

Toyota adopted a very different stance. The company immediately supported the Bush administration's proposed 7 percent fuel efficiency improvement as a good idea to achieve "desirable" results.[17] Why? Rather than a threat, Toyota sees the fuel technology revolution as an opportunity to strengthen its competitive position as an efficiency-driven price-performance leader with an ever-growing share of the automotive market. We could tell a similar story about Honda.

Toyota wants to establish market leadership in next-generation fuel-efficient automotive technology, in much the way that it changed the rules of the automotive industry through the quality revolution of the 1970s. In aid of this strategy the company is improving the internal combustion engine, developing a hybrid gas-electric engine, and looking forward to a future of hydrogen power.

As James Olson, its SVP of external and regulatory affairs for North America, says, "We can put three chickens in today's pot, two in the hybrid pot, and one in the fuel cell pot. All we need to do as we move forward is change the power source."

The proof is in the pudding. The Japanese were first to market in the United States with hybrids that consumers would actually buy—a specially fitted Honda Civic and Toyota's Prius. These are arguably successful experiments for a niche ecoconscious market, but chances are that by the time you read this, Toyota's hybrid Lexus SUV will be in its showrooms. Says Olson, "The Prius is not just driven by ethics, we are also fiercely competitive. The auto industry needs to be quick at getting clean and efficient—lead the parade to define and control solutions to its advantage. We also need to stay ahead of government intervention."

According to a study by the Union of Concerned Scientists, Honda and Toyota already outperform the Big 3 in emissions of global-warming gases and smog-forming pollutants. Is this because the Big 3 sell a lot of inherently "dirty" trucks? Say the scientists, "Nissan and Ford are ranked above GM [and DaimlerChrysler] in our analysis—despite the fact that they sell more trucks than cars—because their trucks have lower smog-forming emissions. High truck sales do not have to be an environmental liability."[18]

The Japanese also lead Detroit in making their manufacturing and their suppliers resource and pollution efficient, though the entire industry is now moving with dispatch on this issue. Perhaps Toyota is still spurred by the scary crises that surrounded its birth as a corporation: Japan's defeat in World War II and the need to rebuild the country's industrial capabilities. Perhaps it's the fierce culture of waste elimination that is at the center of *kaizen*. Now, car manufacturers around the world invest heavily in eco-efficiency and disclose like mad through their respective sustainability reports and Web sites. They all agree that waste-reducing manufacturing cuts costs. As for fuel-efficient cars, the tipping point is moving in from the horizon; this industry with serious excess capacity problems will increasingly be forced, pure and simple, to respond to—and lead—its customers.

The point is, the Toyotas and Hondas of the world are in the process of seizing a new kind of market advantage. Only this time, it's because they have internalized the convergence between the new integrity and sustainable competitive advantage. Rather than bluster that energy efficiency threatens jobs and profits, Toyota squares the circle. Eliminating all forms of waste—in human effort, in materials, in energy costs, and in negative externalities—not only contributes to short-term cost savings but is a central expression of the fanatical commitment to quality that is pivotal to the company's long-term success. This in turn leads to a substantial cost advantage, which translates into profitability and growth that relentlessly outpace the North American competition.

All this links into a game plan for sustainable shareholder value.

Toyota president Cho Fujio commented in early 2002, "We are determined to make 'long-term rewards for shareholders' a priority. I think it is best to proceed without too much concern for American-style corporate governance and becoming obsessed with 'superficial structures' such as short-term figures."[19] Perhaps the paradigmatic business case has been available all along; we just need to take a decades-long view to see it.

CHAPTER 8

THE OWNERS OF THE FIRM

From its early days in the nineteenth century, the New York Stock Exchange was the financial center of U.S. capitalism. Backroom deals, gambling, fraud, and self-dealing were rampant. Exchange members enjoyed lower trading rates than nonmembers. Share prices were rarely made known to the public or the press. Until Dow-Jones founded *The Wall Street Journal* in 1889—where the Dow-Jones Index ran on a daily basis from 1896—most financial newspapers were paid mouthpieces for stock promoters. This practice ended only after the 1929 crash.

Transparency would only happen as a result of aggressive state intervention. No one knew how much financier J. P. Morgan was at the center of the banking and commercial world until a 1912 congressional investigation revealed that he and a dozen partners held 72 interlocking directorships in 47 major corporations. In total, the officers of the Morgan and just three other banks held 341 directorships in 112 corporations, with resources of $22 billion (which exceeded the assessed value of all property in the 22 states and territories west of the Mississippi). In congressional testimony Morgan denied knowledge of his own connections and dealings. Until that moment of transparency and even afterward, Morgan and his partners denied the existence of a money trust.[1]

It took the worst business collapse in modern history—the Great Depression—to force transparency into the broader financial marketplace. The Securities Act of 1933 was the first piece of national securities legislation passed by Congress.[2] During the previous two decades, some twenty states had passed a patchwork of so-called blue-sky laws to regulate the issuance of securities, but these were rife with loopholes. U.S. financial markets, in both banking and securities, operated pretty much free of regulation and visibility until Franklin Roosevelt stepped in.

The act required sellers to register new securities and supporting information with the Federal Trade Commission. Issuers of foreign bonds (also the subject of various fraudulent schemes) were required to do the same.

Next, the Securities Exchange Act of 1934 created the Securities and Exchange Commission. For the first time, investment bankers were accountable to a government agency. Again, transparency was central. Any company or investment banker who made a false filing with the SEC would face prosecution. All publicly traded companies would henceforth be required to register and provide quarterly and annual financial reports. To gain the right to register newly issued shares of other companies, investment banks would also have to provide financial information about themselves. This was revolutionary, since most companies—from the house of Morgan on down—had never published annual reports.

The underlying structural issue was the separation of ownership from control. This began with the capitalization of railways in the nineteenth century and became dominant across most industries by the 1920s. Adolf A. Berle and Gardiner C. Means first analyzed this change in 1933.[3] As joint stock companies grew and investors traded shares with one another, the stock market took on a life of its own. Thousands, then hundreds of thousands of individuals bought shares. By and large, no individual owned even 1 percent of any one company. As a result, shareholders as a class became weak, while managers inside the firm took control. Berle and Means explained the resulting risk for shareholders: "The controlling group . . . can serve their own pockets better by profiting at the expense of the company than by making profits for it."[4]

This core problem has played out ever since. In theory, the managers of the booming 1950s and 1960s cared about shareholders; after all, they measured their success in rising share prices. But the practicalities of shareholder accountability were absent. Peter Drucker, in 1974, worried that boards have become "a fiction." They are "either simply management committees [i.e., controlled by inside directors], or they are ineffectual."[5] He listed three causes which ring true today: the dispersion of share ownership (the fundamental cause), the separation of ownership and control (the result), and the fact that top management doesn't want a truly effective board:

> An effective board asks inconvenient questions. An effective board demands top-management performance and removes top executives who do not perform adequately—this is its duty. An effective board insists on being informed before the event—this is its legal responsibility. An effective board will not unquestioningly accept the recommendations of top management but will want to know why. . . . An effective board, in other words, insists on being effective. And this, to most top managements, appears to be a restraint, a limitation, an interference with "management prerogatives," and altogether a threat.[6]

Shareholders who took issue with any of this could only "vote with their feet" and sell their shares. Management tightly choreographed annual meetings and shareholder ballots. The typical shareholder didn't care, since he (typically male at the time) was but one of millions of unrelated small-holding speculators. He didn't want to be bothered about corporate governance. As long as his shares went up, he was happy. Opacity was A-OK.

In the 1970s, U.S. management practices were shaken by stagflation and the stunning rise of Japanese competitors (despite books on the "Japanese way," it was impossible for Western firms to emulate Japan's complex webs of interrelationships, not least because of their opacity). Their credibility again falling into disarray, U.S. firms paid dearly for their lack of transparency and accountability in the corporate raids of the 1980s and the business reengineering craze at the turn to the 1990s. Driving these events were two additional structural shifts. First was a new industrial revolution: a demanding, innovation-centric economy made possible by information and communications technologies. Second was the rise of investor capitalism: shareholders, including institutional investors and market players (such as the corporate raiders of the 1980s and the venture capitalists of the 1990s), challenged the separation of ownership and control.

The merger and acquisition (M&A) boom of the 1980s was a forced shakeout of the excess capacity and bureaucratic inefficiencies of managerial capitalism. There were 35,000 M&A transactions between 1976 and 1990, with a total value of $2.6 trillion (1992 dollars).[7] Many described the boom—along with some huge payouts that went with it—as a greedy maneuver by corporate barbarians who sucked innovation and investment out of the economy, degraded the country's competitiveness, and destroyed the lives of hundreds of thousands of terminated employees. Critics attacked exotic techniques such as leveraged buyouts and junk bonds, which eliminated size as a barrier against takeover and let nonestablishment foxes into the corporate chicken coop. Certainly, corporate raiders made tons of money while loyal employees lost jobs, paying dearly for a situation few of them created.

But underlying all the fire and fury, investors were finally doing more than voting with their feet. Corporate raiders and institutional investors reasserted the right of shareholders to have a say in the fate of the firm. Business visibility increased dramatically, as players' failings, inefficiencies, maneuvers, and self-dealings were scrutinized as never before.

Eventually a new consensus urged that the continuous bloodletting had to stop. It was, as some put it mildly, "too disruptive." By the early 1990s the M&A boom was over. The corporate and fiduciary communities reached a new consensus: accountability to investors, and particularly long-term investors like pension funds, would be better served through ongoing oversight by management and directors within the firm and by institutional investors outside the firm. Corporate governance activities rather than battles over corporate control would become the norm. Then, in the exuberance of the dot-com boom, the expected oversight failed to happen. Result: the 2002 corporate governance crisis.

The Internet bubble lubricated the governance crisis, most visibly in the case of Enron, by diverting attention from old-fashioned standards of profitability and governance amid hype about "new rules for a new economy." But crooked dealings at accounting firms, multibillion-dollar write-downs at over 150 companies, and conflicts of interest at securities firms can't be blamed on the Internet.

In April 2003, ten Wall Street firms agreed to split penalties totaling $1.4 billion, a relatively painless outcome considering how they vaporized the integrity of core processes at the heart of market capitalism.

For corrupt practices like publishing falsely favorable analyst reports, sending clients advance copies of analyst reports, and using shares of hot initial public offerings to virtually bribe CEOs of client firms, the brokerages avoided admissions of guilt while their executives escaped criminal prosecution. Some 40 percent of the fines were mitigated by tax deductibility or insurance. And, as *The Economist* observed, the entire amount is equivalent to a few days' collective profits and a tiny percentage of what the firms earned during the boom.[8] The two entities that should have been policing these firms—the New York Stock Exchange and the National Association of Securities Dealers—also escaped censure. Investors' civil suits were bound to follow.

Ultimately, the bubble merely exacerbated the perennial problem—that is, the separation of ownership from control. When there is personal gain at stake, too many corporate executives tune their values to rationalize malfeasance.

Transparency proved to be a constructive force. Whistleblowers came forward against Enron, Andersen, WorldCom, and others. The media delivered the story. Institutional investors like CalPERS pressured Congress to act and tightened up their own operating guidelines. Investors pulled out of the market; this resulted in a massive value collapse and sent a clear signal that visible change was a matter of urgency. Many companies began to rethink and revise their governance.

The history of the past century shows that the transparency-driven surge of powerful market forces is not sufficient to change corporate behavior. As a matter of economic necessity, many firms may embrace norms of candor and integrity that exceed minimum legal requirements. But free riders will take advantage of the system as long as the legal umbrella protects them; and many, as we've seen, are quite willing to break the law.

Thus, free markets need strong governments. Public interests are greater than the sum of private interests. And open market economies depend on clear rules, rigorously enforced.

WHO OWNS THE CORPORATION?

The last few decades have produced five dramatic changes in corporate ownership.

First, stock ownership has become the dominant form of liquid wealth (equities, bonds, and cash), which itself is growing rapidly. The world's trove of liquid financial assets grew sevenfold between 1980 and 2000—from $11 trillion to $78 trillion. Of this, equities grew from 25 percent of the pot to 40 percent.[9] Since the 2001 market crash, many investors have shifted some of their holdings to bonds and other less risky assets. However, this is a small blip in a big-picture trend. The historic shift to equities means that a greater proportion of society is betting on corporate ownership to build wealth.

Second, stock is owned increasingly by institutions. In capitalism's earlier days, tycoons in silk hats owned firms. As recently as the early 1970s, a relatively small number of individuals still owned almost 80 percent of U.S. equities. Today institutions are the primary owners of the corporation. Pension funds, mutual funds, insurance companies, other institutional investors, and a broad range of individuals own or manage most public equity. In 1987 institutions held an average of 47 percent of the total stock in the largest 1,000 U.S. corporations. That figure had soared to 60 percent by 1997 and by 2003 it had risen to 64 percent. In 1987 only 4 of the largest 1,000 companies had institutional ownership in excess of 90 percent. Today there are over 60 such companies. In 1987, 45 percent of companies had institutional ownership of 50 percent or more, but today the number is greater than 66 percent.[10] Today there are more mutual funds than publicly traded companies.[11]

Third, pension funds, which invest pension savings on behalf of

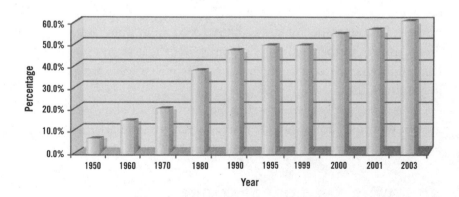

Figure 8.1 Institutional Investor Holdings of
Total Outstanding Equity, 1950–2003

Sources: The Conference Board, CIBC World Markets

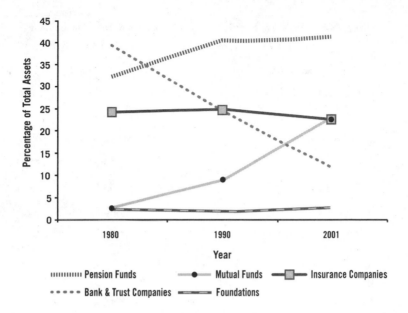

Figure 8.2 Percentage of Institutional Assets by Category, 1980–2001
Source: The Conference Board

employees of corporations, government agencies, or other organizations and which are to be withdrawn on retirement, are the largest
group of institutional investors. Pension funds grew from 32.5 percent
of all institutional assets ($868 billion) in 1980 to 41.5 percent ($7.87
trillion) in 2001. During that period, mutual funds also grew dramatically while assets owned by banks and trust companies declined from
39.9 to 2.7 percent. Internationally, pension funds own over $12 tril-
lion in assets.[12] (See Figure 8.2.)

Pension funds own 13 percent of Microsoft (about the same as Bill
Gates), 17 percent of IBM, 18 percent of GE, 19 percent of Exxon, 20
percent of AT&T, and 45 percent of British Telecom.[13]

Many pension funds are huge. The GE fund has $59 billion in
assets, Texas Teachers Retirement $70 billion, General Motors $87 billion, New York State Common Retirement Fund $100 billion, Califor-
nia Public Employees Retirement $133 billion, and the Stitching
Pensionenfonds ABP (Netherlands) $160 billion.[14]

Pension funds are now the principal owners of the U.S. economy.

Many pension funds say they lack the expertise or resources to
manage their own investments, so they hire others to make their day-

	Percentage of Total Shares Held by Institutional Investors
1. General Electric Co.	51.1
2. Microsoft Corp.	41.8
3. Pfizer Inc.	59.8
4. ExxonMobil Corp.	49.0
5. Citigroup Inc.	69.7
6. Wal-Mart Stores Inc.	33.8
7. Intel Corp.	46.2
8. American International Group Inc.	56.8
9. Merck & Co. Inc.	56.3
10. IBM Corp.	47.4
11. Cisco Systems Inc.	56.9
12. SBC Communications Inc.	45.1
13. Johnson & Johnson	56.7
14. Verizon Communications Inc.	43.5
15. Coca Cola Inc.	52.9
16. Bristol-Myers Squibb	60.5
17. Philip Morris Cos. Inc.	59.6
18. Oracle Corp.	42.4
19. Home Depot Inc.	56.7
20. Time Warner Inc.	67.7
21. Procter & Gamble Co.	48.8
22. Eli Lily & Co.	65.9
23. EMC Corp.	64.9
24. AT&T Corp.	41.7
25. Wells Fargo & Co.	60.0
Total all companies	63.4

Figure 8.3 Concentration of Institutional Investor Holdings of the 25 Largest Corporations (ranked according to market capitalization)
Source: Conference Board

to-day investment decisions—assigning substantial amounts of their assets to other fiduciaries, such as money managers, insurance companies, and banks. In 2001, pension funds held 41.5 percent of total institutional investor assets, but managed only 21.1 percent—about half.[15] This passive approach undermines their influence to make companies transparent and accountable to shareholders.

Fourth, the number of Americans owning stock has soared during the past four decades. Today more than half of all U.S. households own company shares or units of mutual funds.[16] Direct and indirect stock holdings as a share of family assets has jumped from 34 percent in 1992 to more than 56 percent today.[17] Many millions of U.S. families have a big stake in the stock market and how it performs, even though the average *direct* holdings per family amount to only $6,000. The same household *indirectly* owns about $77,000 of stock through pension funds alone.[18]

This "pension fund revolution," as Peter Drucker aptly called it in 1976 has today given upward of 100 million Americans a personal interest in the stock market and the performance of corporations worldwide.[19] Their increased dependence on capital markets has affected other aspects of their lives, notably, their retirement planning, job satisfaction, and productivity in the workplace. They think of themselves as investors. If they own stock or options in the company they work for, they are better motivated to do a good job and they tend to identify more strongly with their company.[20] And in light of the post–technology meltdown many of them paid close attention to the impact of the bear market on the erosion of wealth in their retirement portfolios.

An additional trend is causing pension holders to care—the historic shift toward defined contribution plans, where the individual takes a higher risk and has a higher upside or downside. Defined benefit plans, as the name implies, specify the level of benefits to be received by the employee on retirement. Defined contribution plans, again like the name, specify the level of contribution but not the amount of benefit payments. Thus they offer less security with greater potential upside reward and greater downside risk. The number of employees in these plans now exceeds the number in defined benefit plans by ten to one.[21]

Fifth, notwithstanding the broader distribution of share ownership, there is no universal democratization of wealth in the United States as some have suggested. According to one authoritative investigation, over the last decade the share of all wealth held by the top 1 percent rose by 5 percentage points, while the share held by the bottom 40 percent showed an absolute decline.[22]

The greatest change, however, is not that the top quintile is getting marginally more of the pie but that there is a superrich elite that is getting richer faster than the regular rich (and everyone else). Within the top 20 percent of moneymakers, the biggest beneficiaries were the top 5 percent. According to an extensive study by Thomas Piketty and Emmanuel Saez, in 1970 the top 0.01 percent of taxpayers had 0.7 percent of total income; that is, they earned 70 times as much as the average. But in 1998 the top 0.01 percent received more than 3 percent of all income. That meant that the 13,000 richest families in the United States had almost as much income as the 20 million poorest households; those 13,000 families had incomes 300 times that of average families.[23]

This change has led many, such as liberal critic Paul Krugman, to conclude that there is a crisis of inequality in the United States:

> This [really rich getting even richer] transformation has happened very quickly, and it is still going on. You might think that 1987, the year Tom Wolfe published his novel *The Bonfire of the Vanities* and Oliver Stone released his movie *Wall Street*, marked the high tide of America's new money culture. But in 1987 the top 0.01 percent earned only about 40 percent of what they do today, and top executives less than a fifth as much. The America of *Wall Street* and *The Bonfire of the Vanities* was positively egalitarian compared with the country we live in today.[24]

This situation makes the country vulnerable to increased conflict between two classes of shareholders—those who own massive wealth and those who own a little—exacerbating demands for transparency and accountability.

These five trends have set the stage for a new wave of transparency. The 2001 stock market collapse and the crisis in corporate governance have hurt funds' ability to meet their liabilities and created a crisis of trust. Some funds have been pushing on these issues for years. They gained an opening thanks to the crisis. Moreover, a greater proportion of the population than ever before wants to know more about companies because they are shareholders. Many invest through so-called socially responsible investing (SRI) funds, which are much more active than the typical mutual fund.

In theory, business operation is the job of corporate executives, while ensuring transparency and accountability to shareholders is the job of the board. In practice, however, too many boards are simply extensions of management. Result: Investors "own," managers "control," and there is no substantive communication between the two. If investors are unhappy, their only effective option is to vote with their feet and sell their shares.

WHAT DO SHAREHOLDERS KNOW?

Although there is still considerable opacity in capital markets, the Internet gives shareholders unprecedented access to information and lets them share this information with one another. Unfortunately, much of this information is neither readily available to the average person nor particularly trustworthy or useful. Savvy observers in Enron chat groups nailed the company's weaknesses long before it collapsed. James Felton, associate professor of finance at Central Michigan University, and Jongchai Kim, assistant professor of finance at Xavier University of Louisiana, examined hundreds of thousands of anonymous listings on the Enron message boards on Yahoo! (YHOO) Finance. The two discovered damning and surprisingly detailed allegations about Enron's finances apparently posted by frustrated company insiders.

On March 1, 2000, when Enron was trading at $68, a posting by "arthur86plz" warned, "Dig deep behind the Enron financials and you'll see a growing mountain of off-balance sheet debt which will eventually swallow this company. There is a reason why they layer so many subsidiaries and affiliates. Be careful." Earlier, on June 17, 1998, "JanisJoplin298" wrote that Enron's financial structure was deceptively complex. Enron "could just as easily bring greater shareholder value by simplifying its capital structure and clearly articulating its deals."

Felton and Kim conclude that far from being useless sources of misinformation, "Stock message boards contain better information than is widely believed."[25] This may be true, but how do individual shareholders sort out the wheat from the chaff—in this case tens of thousands of breathlessly positive opinions about Enron?

The problem is that chat rooms are just another side of shareholder opacity. Most shareholders, especially the hundred million or so small shareholders operating in the marketplace through retirement and mutual funds, don't even know what companies their fiduciaries have invested in. Economists call this a "cascading agency problem" where, in this case, the individual shareholder is several times removed from the action—invested through pension funds that invest through money managers who in turn depend on company boards of directors to oversee the CEO and his or her subordinates. They may learn of individual holdings at the end of the quarter, year, or not at all.

Further, few individual retail shareholders have time, competency, or attention to track corporate performance. Even if they did, they are not privy to the real story. None of the 2001–02 scandals started with shareholder-originated information.

Finally, many pension and mutual funds are indexed to the S&P 500 or other major indices. As a result their shareholders have even less of a stake in the success of any one company. Instead they put their faith in the economy and stock market as a whole.

It is institutions, not individuals, that have (or should have) the tools, resources, access, and clout in the battle that has evolved between the forces of transparency and the forces of opacity. However, passive funds, in particular those that rely on indexing, don't take advantage of this power. Fortunately, a new breed of active investor is working hard to understand what's really happening with the companies it invests in. In doing so, it is setting the table for corporate accountability to shareholders.

Consider the Ontario Teachers Pension Plan, a $50 billion dollar fund responsible for the retirement income of 154,000 schoolteachers, 83,000 retired teachers, and 92,000 former teachers. Teachers is a success story with an annual rate of return of 11.7 percent since 1990.

Unlike many other funds, Teachers uses its own staff of 200

to research companies and make most investment decisions. Bob Bertram, executive vice president of investments, says that much more information is publicly available than ever before. But to him, incremental knowledge comes from dedicated people talking to management and boards of companies. Teachers's analysts have a deep understanding of a company's products, business strategy, human resources, marketing plans, financial assets, and competitors, to name a few. But they know more. "Sure we know lots of factual information. But by spending time with management we know about their thinking processes. We have intimate knowledge about the people making decisions. We understand a lot about their culture and what makes them tick."

This level of scrutiny brings its own moral hazard: insider information. "If we get material information about a company that's not public we'll shut down trading in the company until the information is released," says Bertram. "It's not a problem."

Teachers, however, is among a minority of fiduciaries. Such funds need intensive research to understand the companies they invest in, yet almost none have adequate research staff. A combination of bad behavior and cheap online trading has destroyed the margins that fund Wall Street brokers' research. Even if trading volumes return to normal, it will be tough to find a business model that can support smart and trustworthy research. Ironically, this problem is a result of transparency—the transparency that cheap networks bring to the buying and selling of shares.

A study by consulting firm Shelley Taylor & Associates shows that many companies resist the thirst for reliable information about them.[26] The study, in its tenth year, examined information on operations, results, and corporate governance contained in Web sites and annual reports of 50 of the largest global corporations. A minority of companies provided shareholders with information on topics like challenges and risks, new product pipeline, management background, board policy for evaluating the CEO, and objectives. The researchers found steep declines in companies' willingness to discuss "bad news" compared with two years earlier. "People just don't want to be held accountable," Taylor said.

Some public companies are considering going private to avoid the public eye. Currently, public markets are in a dead zone, yet U.S. private equity markets are booming. Especially in the midcap range, companies are looking to go private to escape the costs, regulations, and scrutiny of the new environment. Their managers don't like being under the microscope. Of course, they can run but they can't hide. While going private means a company can sidestep shareholder scrutiny, this doesn't diminish the growing scrutiny from the other members of the firm's stakeholder web.

Opacity hurts market value and makes it tough to raise money. "Equity capital is expensive because investors are dubious about the transparency of companies," says PricewaterhouseCoopers partner Joel Kurtzman. "Capital markets are down because of concerns about transparency—more than a trillion dollars of lost shareholder value. Take a great company like GE. Its share price is less than half of what it was, largely because many shareholders lost faith in the company to be open, honest and act in shareholders' interests."

Lawyers are the front-line soldiers in the battle between shareholder openness and management opacity. Transparency champion Robert Monks notes that in the 70 years since the 1933 SEC legislation, "The bar has essentially created language and sets of understandings around transparency and reporting that are so misleading they are Orwellian." Pointing to the disclosure of Jack Welch's elaborate compensation plan, revealed only through his divorce proceedings, Monks says, "Everybody runs around nodding their heads and saying my God isn't it wonderful that we have got all of this disclosure and then we find out that, hey, we don't know anything." This has created a "vast world of apparent transparency" for shareholders that is misleading and dangerous. (Monks quips that if all CEOs were forced to go through a divorce proceeding, shareholders might find out the truth about their compensation.)

But to move forward, we should probably reject Shakespeare's advice to kill all the lawyers. On the side of transparency is a tiny but growing battalion of barristers who have taken to the courts to defend shareholders. Government lawyers are newly active, as are the lawyers hired by various shareholders rights groups, institutional shareholders, NGOs, and sundry other civil society organizations. Monks himself has left the public policy arena to rehang his shingle as a lawyer and undertake a campaign for open enterprises.

Shareholders are getting active for transparency. But this is the tip of the iceberg. Shareholders are organizing to hold firms accountable in many more ways.

Institutional Catch-22: Why We're Passive Investors

Boards are supposed to represent shareholders. Institutional investors own the lion's share of equities. But most institutions are passive investors, and they refuse to get involved in governance at all, let alone to sit on boards. The result is that most stockholders are effectively disenfranchised. Depending on whom you talk to, there are different reasons for this.

Many institutions select the stocks in their portfolios on the basis of a predetermined formula rather than on an assessment of an individual corporation's prospects. The word *index* comes from broad-based indices such as the S&P 500 or the Dow-Jones Index that some funds attempt to mirror. The institution, be it a mutual fund or a pension fund, figures that if it matches the index's performance, it is doing satisfactorily. Indexed funds have generally performed as well as actively managed funds.

- Active involvement in corporations could create a marketing problem for institutional investors. This doesn't apply to pension funds, but it does apply to private sector funds like Fidelity. Pension funds place hundreds of millions—even billions—with private sector funds that theoretically have the knowledge to manage these investments well. But companies like Fidelity also manage pensions (such as 401(k) plans) for corporations—the same corporations in which they may be investing on behalf of, say, New York City's employee pension fund. In other words, they face a very real conflict of interest. How can a Fidelity be expected to take on a shareholder battle with the management of an Enron or a General Motors if Fidelity is also hoping to renew its 401(k) contract for the company's employees—awarded at the discretion of management?

- It's a lot of work to be actively involved in companies. A typical pension fund might invest in more than 3,000 companies, yet only have a staff of 60. One manager told us, "It's tough enough just to track these firms let alone be active in their governance."

- Funds that churn their portfolios (buy and sell stocks frequently) avoid close connections with individual companies. To sit on a board, they say, would qualify them as insiders—restricting their ability to buy and sell that company's stock because of the blackout periods insiders face. A cop-out, says Monks: "They don't give a damn. There are a thousand ways around that problem. In reality, they are making a ton of money without doing anything. They want to do as little as possible and avoid angering prospective or current corporate clients."

The Old SEC View:
Keep Shareholders in the Dark and Asleep

From the day it was founded in 1934, the Securities and Exchange Commission dismissed the notion that shareholders had a right to know and influence a company's behavior. But following court battles, intense public pressure, and fiascos like Enron and WorldCom, in September 2002 the SEC finally seemed to accept the idea that shareholder activism is a good influence in the market.

Time will tell how genuine the SEC's conversion really is. For the first seven decades of its existence, the basic principle underlying the SEC's approach was that a corporation's management should be left alone to manage the corporation. If a shareholder didn't like what the company was doing, the solution was simple: sell the shares. If many people followed this path, the company's share price would fall and presumably management would mend its ways. This was the SEC vision of corporate democracy.

A major component of shareholder activism is the ability of crusading shareholders to propose resolutions for adoption at a company's annual general meeting. In 1942 the SEC promulgated Rule 14a-8 of the Securities Exchange Act, commonly known as the shareholder proposal rule. The rule permitted shareholders with "properly framed" proposals to have the proposal distributed, at the company's expense, along with the company's proxy material that went to shareholders before an annual general meeting.[27] The SEC specified that the only permitted resolution topics were those that dealt with "a proper subject for security holders." Even then, under state law most resolutions aren't binding on a company because the board of director's authority is seen as paramount. This has proved particularly contentious where boards have adopted antitakeover poison pills when shareholders, particularly institutional investors, don't agree with the board's decision. The question of the balance of authority among shareholders, the board of directors, and corporate management is one that shareholders want clarified by the courts. Shareholders are frustrated by too many boards that believe majority rule may be a fine way to run a country but it's too radical a notion for corporations.

What constitutes a "proper subject" for shareholder resolutions in the SEC's eyes became clear in 1951. Greyhound refused to distribute in its proxy materials a resolution calling for the company to stop racially segregating passengers on its buses. The SEC agreed with Greyhound and ruled the resolution improper. Lest there be any misunderstanding and to protect other companies from being pestered with such requests, in 1952 the SEC amended Rule 14a-8 to exclude any resolution in which "it clearly appears that the proposal is submitted . . . primarily for the purpose of promoting general economic, political, racial, religious, social or similar causes."[28]

This was a profound shackling of shareholder rights. If a part owner of a company can't raise with his co-owners the company's approach to political or social issues, then who can? From the SEC's point of view, the answer seemed to be nobody.

This disconnect prompted Adolf A. Berle to observe in 1954:

> In effect, when an individual invests capital in the large corporation, he grants to the corporate management all power to use that capital to create, produce, and develop, and he abandons all control over the product. . . . He is an almost completely inactive recipient. He can spend his dividends or sell his shares for cash, taking care of his needs for consumption and enjoyment. But he must look elsewhere for opportunity to produce or create."[29]

The SEC's philosophy remained unchallenged until 1969, the height of the Vietnam War. The Medical Committee on Human Rights, a group of young doctors, asked Dow Chemical to circulate a resolution to shareholders instructing the company to stop making napalm, a horrific chemical weapon used by U.S. forces. Dow refused, the SEC supported the company, and the committee took the SEC to court. In the summer of 1970 the U.S. Circuit Court of Appeals for the District of Columbia ruled in the committee's favor. The decision strongly endorsed the idea that shareholders have a right to review corporate decisions with political implications.

The Dow decision coincided with similar action against General Motors. A group of public interest lawyers formed Campaign GM and submitted a number of proxy resolutions concerning the automaker's corporate citizenship. Campaign GM was able to generate tremendous media interest, and the SEC ultimately decided that two of the resolutions should be voted on at the annual general meeting.[30] Shareholder activism had arrived.

This immediately turned up the heat on pension funds, universities, foundations, and other large shareholders. Students at Harvard, for example, pushed the university administration to sell its shares in Gulf Oil because the company supported the repressive regime in Angola. When Harvard president Derek Bok refused to meet the demands, students occupied his office. After the sit-in, Bok's special assistant, Stephen Farber, went to Angola to gather information that would help Harvard decide on future actions as a responsible Gulf shareholder. Soon after, Harvard launched its Investor Responsibility Research Center to investigate similar questions.

The momentum grew. In 1972, Yale published a report arguing that the university should consider and support reasonable shareholder resolutions. The Ford Foundation commissioned a report that concluded that it was inappropriate for an institution like Ford not to vote proxies on the new social policy resolutions.

But while shareholders mobilized, the SEC was not to be outdone. Having tried and failed to ban shareholder resolutions on social or political issues, the SEC moved to prohibit resolutions "relating to the conduct of the ordinary business operations of the issuer."

The idea is to prevent shareholders cluttering up the annual general meeting agenda with votes on mundane day-to-day issues of running the company. If management wanted to introduce a new product or hire a director of marketing, these were issues for management to decide, not the shareholder. Seems simple enough, but management seeking to avoid shareholder scrutiny and votes became increasingly aggressive in its definition of "ordinary business," well beyond what advocates of shareholders' rights viewed as appropriate.

Questions such as child labor in the supply chain, environmental policies, or workplace diversity are central to a company's reputation and therefore financial future. These could be critical to whether the company prospers, and it is grossly misleading to simply dismiss them as "ordinary business." In the early 1990s, Citicorp and Bank America used the "ordinary business" provision to dismiss resolutions concerning writedowns of Third World debt, and DuPont brushed aside a resolution to phase out chlorofluorocarbons—a highly contentious topic.[31] Cracker Barrel Old Country Stores, a Tennessee-based restaurant chain, claimed that its firing of 11 gay and lesbian workers was also ordinary business, despite criticisms that discrimination hardly qualifies as such.[32]

In September 2002, Harvey Pitt, then chairman of the SEC, endorsed shareholder resolutions, saying they "give shareholders a chance to inform management how they feel regarding major issues confronting corporations." Pitt announced that he had asked the commission's director of corporation finance "to consider a proposal to eliminate the 'ordinary business exception' from the list of reasons that companies can exclude otherwise validly promulgated shareholder proposals. It is my hope that we can (make) shareholder suffrage a reality."[33]

Shareholder advocates want more. They want shareholder resolutions to be binding. The Interfaith Center on Corporate Responsibility (ICCR) is a 30-year-old association of 275 Protestant, Roman Catholic, and Jewish institutional investors with combined portfolios worth an estimated $110 billion. Its members include religious denominations and communities, pension funds, hospital corporations, foundations, dioceses, and publishers. Each year ICCR-member institutional investors press hundreds of corporations to improve their social and environmental performances. "We use the shareholder resolution as a means of transparency," says ICCR executive director Sister Patricia Wolf. "Most of our resolutions ask for a report. That report we use as a vehicle to gain information about the company and then engage that company in direct dialogue. The resolutions also serve to educate the pub-lic." Wolf says nonbinding resolutions achieve some change, but she wants true shareholder democracy. "I would love to see the company have to adopt a position if it got more than 50 percent of the vote."

A key issue for shareholder activists, as the Fidelity story in chapter 1 shows, is whether mutual funds should be compelled to disclose how they vote on proxy resolutions. Until recently mutual funds were not required to disclose this information, and only a small number of funds volunteered the data. Activists viewed this as a major impedi-ment to corporate transparency and accountability, but most mutual funds prefer the existing opaque system. "The purpose of disclosure is to provide meaningful information that investors can use to make sound investing decisions," says Chris Wloszczyna, a spokesperson for the Investment Company Institute, which lobbies on behalf of the mutual fund industry. "That includes information on fees, risk, invest-ment strategy. But you have to draw the line somewhere, and proxy votes just aren't meaningful.[34]

"We've long believed in quiet diplomacy [with companies], and think that's worked well for our shareholders," Fidelity spokesperson Vincent Loporchio said. "If that information, released publicly, were to have a negative impact on the stock, then that would have a nega-tive effect for our shareholders." David Weinstein, Fidelity's chief of administration, echoed this: "Shareholders hire us to manage their money and we can do the best job of that without disclosure of our proxy votes."

Despite these views, in early 2003 the SEC ruled that mutual funds would have to disclose. Outgoing SEC chairman Harvey Pitt had ear-lier justified the measure by saying voting disclosure "gives investors fundamental information about the practices of those who vote prox-ies on their behalf. They also would discourage or expose proxy voting conflicts of interest. The securities belong to fund investors, who are entitled to know how their property is being voted."[35]

WINNING BACK THE FRANCHISE

The 2001–02 corporate scandals may yet prove to be a milestone in the development of the U.S. economy. In response to criminal behavior, bad decisions, and egregious excesses on the front pages day after day, the number of shareholder resolutions for the 2000 companies monitored by the Investor Responsibility Research Center soared from 802 in all of 2002 to more than 850 in just the first two months of 2003. Most concerned corporate governance.

This is cause for hope. It suggests that more shareholders understand that the economy's welfare demands that they play a greater role in the system than simply providing capital. If the system is to function well, shareholders must exert constant vigilance over corporate conduct. If they don't, bad things happen.

To date, corporate managers have enjoyed free rein, with many boards' exercising no discipline whatsoever over their company's affairs. Often board members were drawn from management or were friends of the CEO. They fostered an illusion of corporate governance. Creative accounting became the order of the day. In 2002, more than 250 companies restated their earnings. Free of constraints, senior executive compensation packages soared to unjustifiable heights. In 1970, the average full-time worker earned $32,522, while the average compensation among the top 100 CEOs was $1.25 million, according to *Forbes* magazine's annual survey. In 1999, the average worker's pay had climbed only slightly, to $35,864. The average compensation of the 100 top CEOs had increased more than 2,800 percent, to $37.5 million.[36]

Much of the blame for corporate misdeeds belongs squarely on the shoulders of the major institutional investors. Rather than be active and diligent, they have been passive and negligent. As institutions grew to become the dominant holders of wealth, they assiduously shirked the attendant responsibilities. In *Fair Shares—The Future of Shareholder Power and Responsibility*, Jonathan Charkham and Anne Simpson persuasively argue that large shareholders must acknowledge and exercise their responsibilities to ensure our economic system's proper functioning:

> It is because the good working of the market-based system demands it for economic, social and political reasons. The economic reason is that there needs to be a mechanism for controlling boards that do not work well so as to prevent unnecessary waste of resources; the social reason

is that listed companies are a crucial and integral part of the fabric of a modern society and their success reduces alienation; the political reason is that the limited liability company has achieved its far-sighted originators' aims beyond their wildest dreams, of producing concentrations of power and resources, and that those who exercise these powers must be effectively accountable for the way they do.[37]

The need for active shareholders shouldn't be confused with the idea of shareholder activism we discussed earlier. Active shareholders ensure good corporate governance and independent board members to help guarantee that shareholders' interests are fully represented at the board level. But as we've seen, in its clumsy (and misguided) effort to keep companies from being entangled in social or political issues, the SEC doggedly disabused shareholders of any notion they had a role to play in corporate conduct.

Many institutional investors were utterly content with the SEC's vision of shareholder impotence. They didn't want responsibility for corporate behavior. It would require judgment, effort, and time. Long-term investors, pension funds in particular, wanted to buy a stock and sit back and relax. But as the corporate scandals of 2001–02 showed, this is a prescription for management misbehavior. Increasingly institutional investors will understand the need for them to play an active role in the accountability webs of companies in their portfolios.

The few institutional investors who take a hands-on approach say their funds are better off for it. The State of Wisconsin Investment Board (SWIB) is the 10th largest pension fund in the United States and the 19th largest public or private pension fund in the world. Once it has invested in a company, it believes it has an ongoing fiduciary responsibility to help the company achieve maximum returns. Cynthia Rich is the fund's director of corporate governance, charged with the task of ensuring that healthy governance structures are in place for all the companies in which the fund has invested. In small-cap companies, SWIB is often the largest or second-largest shareholder. She told us she is vigilant that her goal of good governance doesn't evolve into "micromanaging," but that the fund does step in and, for example, assist with board member recruitment if that's what it feels is required. Its fiduciary responsibilities demand nothing less.

The Ontario Teachers Pension Plan discussed earlier has much the same philosophy. Bob Bertram argues the irrefutable logic of being an active investor applies to the managers of index funds. Just because they are forced to hold a stock doesn't mean they have to passively accept whatever management wants. Indeed, since they can't vote with their feet and sell the stock, the incentive—and fiduciary requirements—for them to become active is even stronger. "Voting shares for an index fund in my mind is much more important because your investment strategy doesn't give the option to walk away from a bad situation."

Bertram says the hands-on approach offers a number of other benefits, explaining why it has outperformed market benchmarks. "Active investing encourages developing better management skills because it gives us opportunities for adding. It has the added benefit of being a long-term-oriented strategy that in turn forces the organization to maximize the results over the long haul."

VALUES-BASED INVESTING

In 2002, many investors in mutual funds cut their losses and ran. According to Lipper, Inc., U.S. diversified equity funds posted outflows over the year of $10.5 billion. But one prominent group of mutual funds bucked the trend. So-called SRI funds enjoyed $1.5 billion in growth. The number of socially screened funds and their assets under management soared during the mid-1990s, particularly funds with an environmental emphasis. In a world of growing transparency, socially responsible investment funds are attracting new converts.

Most institutional investors view these funds as a sideshow or, worse, as dangerous to shareholders. They argue that their fiduciary duty is to maximize the performance of their fund, not improve society. But SRI funds are showing good financial results, initiating some serious head scratching. This is leading to a far-reaching shift in the criteria used by many investors to select firms, in turn driving changes in the firm itself.

At their simplest level, SRI mutual funds practice "negative" screening. They refuse to invest in companies operating in industries such as tobacco, gambling, firearms, or alcohol. More sophisticated funds also

practice "positive" screening, seeking firms with good employee relations, strong records of community involvement, excellent environmental impact policies and practices, respect for human rights, and
safe and useful products.[38]

Today hundreds of SRI funds compete for investor interest. The
largest SRI family is the Calvert Group. While small SRI funds have
existed for decades, Calvert gave a big boost to the concept in 1982
when it introduced both mutual and money market funds with social
screens. It was also the first mutual fund to oppose apartheid in South
Africa and was subsequently one of the first mutual funds to reinvest
in a free South Africa in 1994, following Nelson Mandela's election
victory.

Not only does Calvert demand transparency from companies in
which it invests, the company strives to be a model of transparency
itself. This is typical of the SRI industry. Web sites of SRI funds often
run on with lengthy explanations of their approach to hot public policy issues. The funds take pains to explain how they arrive at their
decisions. Regardless of a fund's sterling financial performance,
investors may shun a fund because its managers made the wrong call
when faced with a difficult decision. When a fund says it won't invest
in companies that produce tobacco, should it also reject retail chains
that sell the weed? Must a fund that shuns alcohol stay away from a
restaurant chain that sells wine?

The Calvert site maintains detailed issue briefs on topics of interest
to its investors. The list currently includes alcohol and gambling, animal welfare, board diversity, cocoa, community relations, environment, firearms, high technology, human rights, indigenous peoples'
rights, layoffs, nuclear power, proxy disclosure, tobacco, weapons,
women, workplace issues, and workplace violence.

Just as important as a fund's approach to an issue is what criteria it
uses to judge whether a company passes an investment screen. Many
companies claim to be pro-environment, for example, but few SRI
funds have the resources to independently scrutinize the environmental behavior of the companies in which they are interested. They rely
on third party assessments from organizations like World Wildlife
Fund or Sierra Club.

All this applies to the retail investor as well. With the Internet turning desktop computers into geysers of information, individual investors can learn almost as much as fund managers. The largest site for individual SRI investors, SocialFunds.com, features more than 10,000 pages of information on SRI mutual funds, community investments, corporate research, shareowner actions, and daily social investment news. Much of this information is derived from a company's growing accountability web. Environmental infractions can be unearthed from government reports and posted on the Web. Forums allow potential investors to exchange views and discuss ways to drill down on issues of potential concern. Notwithstanding corporate efforts for opacity, the individual investor has never been so well equipped to judge whether his investment will help him make money while advancing—and *through* advancing—broader societal goals.

Social Responsibility and Stock Performance

Many investment managers shun SRI funds because conventional wisdom holds that these companies underperform the market. In other words, a socially responsible investor forfeits profit to advance other societal goals. "I have big problems with a company that doesn't say its top priority is to shareholders," as one pension executive put it. The U.S. Department of Labor has dubbed SRI as inappropriate for Employee Retirement Income Security Act (ERISA) investments (its own pension fund), stating that the trustee's duty is to invest "solely . . . and for the exclusive benefit of" plan participants.

Mainstream fund managers feel SRI issues take them into the political arena, where they do not belong. They're money managers, not politicians. Public policy issues are prey to judgment and interpretation, requiring skills not normally within the money manager's ambit. Money managers, so the argument goes, rely on interpreting solid business issues, not divining capricious public sentiment. Shareholder value is created by maximizing profits. Profits are maximized by excluding extraneous factors like social responsibility. In fact, the more a firm can legally externalize costs to society—such as the costs of pollution—the better for its bottom line.

This sentiment is seemingly reinforced by financial theory, which predicts that returns on investment must be lower if constrained by SRI guidelines. By ruling out some firms for immoral products while favoring others for good behavior, SRI funds artificially reduce the number of companies eligible for investment. In a theoretically efficient market, SRI funds would suffer a diversification cost. Accordingly, SRI constraints are inconsistent with a goal of maximizing return.

However, if screening for corporate values and responsibility identifies companies that are more likely to meet or beat the market, then the foundation of conventional thinking begins to crumble. And as we discuss in a moment, that is exactly what many studies show. The implications are profound when coupled with the clear trend of investor sentiment. We see that SRI funds are increasingly popular even when investors as a whole are shunning the stock market. The growing number of shareholder resolutions show investors are concerned with corporate conduct and governance. As investors increasingly look for evidence of corporate integrity, they will rely on some of the SRI screening tools already in use. How well and fairly a company treats its employees is a good indicator of corporate values. So is a company's attitude to environmental issues. And increasingly, product, service, and operational strategies that incorporate sustainable social and environmental factors are more likely to result in growing sales and reduced costs. Companies that recognize these facts will prove increasingly attractive to capital. Corporations that fail these screens will be spurned. The upshot is that more and more companies will want to look SRI-friendly, whether or not they care to pass the screens of SRI funds.

In their comprehensive 1995 book *Corporate Responsibility and Financial Performance: The Paradox of Social Cost*, Moses Pava and Joshua Krausz analyzed 21 studies and concluded that SRI screening *enhances* investment performance rather than harming it.[39] In 2001 Joshua Daniel Margolis and James Patrick Walsh examined 95 studies on the relationship between a firm's social performance and financial performance. Among their findings was, when corporate social performance was treated as an independent variable, taken to predict or causally precede financial performance, it had a positive relationship with financial performance in 42 of the studies (53 percent), no relationship in 19 studies (24 percent), and a negative relationship in 16 (19 percent).[40]

A January 2003 study by the Social Investment Forum[41] assessed the performance of socially responsible mutual funds through the end of 2002 by using data from Lipper, Inc., and Morningstar, the top mutual fund–rating agencies in the United States. Morningstar's ratings compare each fund's historical returns to its measure of risk on the basis of historical volatility. Funds showing the highest return to risk ratios get Morningstar's coveted five stars; those with the lowest ratios get one star. The Lipper rating system gives an A or B rating to top-performing funds.

Major findings of the Forum's analysis include:

- Nearly two-thirds of social funds earn highest ratings. Of the 51 socially screened funds with a three-year performance record tracked by the Social Investment Forum, 33 (65 percent) received the highest marks from either Lipper or Morningstar. According to the Forum, 25 (49 percent) of the funds tracked received an A or B ranking from Lipper based on one- and/or three-year total returns within their investment categories. A total of 22 screened funds (43 percent) earned either four or five stars from Morningstar for at least three-year risk-adjusted performance.

- Nearly three out of four of the largest socially responsible funds get top ratings. Of the socially screened funds with more than $100 million in assets, 13 of 18 (72 percent) received top rankings from either or both Lipper and Morningstar.

- A socially responsible index outperforms the S&P 500 both during 2002 and on a total returns basis for ten years. For the ten-year period ended December 31, 2002, total returns for the Domini 400 Social Index (an index of 400 primarily large-capitalization U.S. corporations, roughly comparable to the S&P 500, selected on the basis of a wide range of social and environmental criteria) showed an annualized gain of 9.99 percent, while the S&P 500 rose 9.35 percent over the same period. In 2002 the Domini Index fell 20.10 percent, while the S&P fell a full 2 percent further, losing 22.09 percent.

Social Investment Forum president Tim Smith said, "We can say categorically that socially responsible funds can go toe to toe with the broad universe of mutual funds and, in fact, do better than other types of funds."

A 2003 study by GovernanceMetrics International, an independent corporate governance ratings agency in New York, found a tight correlation between corporate performance and good governance. The company pioneered the concept of governance ratings on the premise that: "Companies that emphasize corporate governance and transparency will, over time, generate superior returns and economic performance and lower their cost of capital. The opposite is also true: companies weak in corporate governance and transparency represent increased investment risks and result in a higher cost of capital."

GovernanceMetrics looks at 600 measures, such as labor and environmental practices, poison-pill tactics to stymie takeovers, and board independence. The company ranked Standard & Poor's 500 firms on governance and then compared the rankings to share performance over one-, three-, and five-year periods. Companies with high governance rankings significantly outperformed the S&P index, while those ranked lowest fared much worse. In the S&P 500, the average decline of a stock over the three years that ended March 20, 2003 was 2.3 percent. But the stocks of the five companies earning the firm's highest governance score rose 23.1 percent on average. The top 15 companies averaged total returns of 3.4 percent. Stocks of the poorest governed 50 firms fell 11.1 percent. Top-governed companies also outperformed their competition in measures such as return on assets, return on investment, and return on capital.[42]

Integrity Screening

How can this be? Why do companies that behave in a socially responsible manner perform better? Some management thinkers argue that social responsibility is not causally related to financial performance but rather that it simply correlates with other factors that are the real roots of success:

- Socially responsible behavior may simply be an indication of management competence.[43]

- Social responsibility could be a by-product of prosperity and financial success, not the cause. Firms that have done well have more money to invest in doing good.[44]

- SRI funds are more often actively managed. Active involvement by fiduciaries in investee companies has been shown to improve corporate performance.

- Innovative and growth-oriented managements may be more likely to have good employee relations, environmental programs, and corporate citizenship.[45]

Some research suggests that even when adjusting for such variables, funds that screen for social responsibility still perform better than the average. This is a highly disputed topic and much remains to be learned.[46] But there is an initial trend emerging with profound significance. Not all funds are alike. They screen for different factors. Funds that screen for social responsibility can be divided into two broad categories:

1. Some funds use screens that have no demonstrable relationship to factors that drive sustainable business performance, for example, abortion (for or against), gambling, or alcohol. Such funds may or may not perform better than the market. If they perform better, it is likely for indirect reasons like those cited above.

2. Others have screens that reflect the values of the new business integrity—honesty, accountability, consideration, and transparency. These include factors like consideration of the environment, employee development, enhancement of human rights, open relationships with business partners and communities, and candid financial disclosure. In such cases responsible behavior is a surrogate for the new business integrity.

Evidence is mounting that the second group tends to perform better, especially over the long term.

Companies that manage themselves according to principles of the new integrity are likely to be more efficient. They also avoid costly regulation. For example, Robert Repetto and Duncan Austin use discounted cash flow models and scenario analysis to show that the financial impact of future environmental regulation may be quite material (up to 11 percent of market value) for U.S. pulp and paper companies in coming years.[47]

Open enterprises are less likely to be investigated or sued. They save money through eco-efficiency. Codes and standards of conduct help ensure accountability and cost control. Integrity enables successful business processes, which require honesty, accountability, and transparency. Trust drops contracting, collaboration, and transaction costs. Supply chain transparency reduces inventory and other operational costs.

Benefits such as these fall directly to the bottom line and affect the performance of investee firms. Funds that screen for social responsibility may be implicitly screening out risk—avoiding investments in unsustainable businesses that externalize costs and expose themselves to the risk of lawsuits, scandals, or legal penalties.

The highly successful Calvert Social Equity fund favors companies that:

- Perform regular environmental audits of their facilities, especially those that publish reports describing the results of those audits

- Apply rigorous standards for reducing or preventing pollution and for responsible use of natural resources to all their facilities worldwide

- Utilize innovative pollution prevention or natural resource protection programs

- Undertake positive environmental actions, including participation in government, private sector, or company-specific programs

- Make senior managers accountable for environmental performance and have internal programs that reward employees for environmental improvement

- Actively hire and promote minorities and women, compensate their workers fairly, strive to achieve and maintain good labor-management relations, provide programs and benefits that support workers and their families, and provide a safe and healthy workplace

Internal policies, especially hiring and firing, are also key indicators. One study that evaluated the social records of companies, reported in the book *Built to Last* by James Collins and Jerry Porras, found that those companies that had good social records had superior employee relations and diversity records.[48]

The fact that firms of integrity can better build trust and orchestrate partners seems to pay off in share price. Better capability leads to innovation, product differentiation, and performance. Environmental standards not only reduce costs; they can result in growth and better shareholder value. One study showed that between 1994 and 1997, U.S. multinational corporations with high global environmental standards tended to have higher price-to-book ratios than companies adopting local environmental standards, even after adjusting for factors such as industry membership, R&D intensity, and advertising intensity.[49]

Corporate brands have equity value. Sandra Waddock and Sam Graves show a strong correlation between reputation rankings in *Fortune*'s most-admired list and ratings of corporate social responsibility.[50] Social screening may be a proxy for success screening.

All this means that fund managers, in order to meet their fiduciary obligation to their investors, should screen for business integrity and/or use the surrogate of social responsibility. In the age of openness this is possible, and the payoff for investors significant.

During the height of the dot-com excitement, we wrote: "In the future no one will speak of e-business—as all business will be e-business." We stand by this prediction. Similarly, we believe that in the future investors will not speak about socially responsible investment. Responsible investment and profitable investment will be synonymous. Of course, there will be some funds that for social, religious, or other reasons screen for factors completely unrelated to financial performance. But if SRI advocates continue to show, as they do now, that SRI funds outperform the market, then investment managers have a fiduciary duty to embrace SRI methods of operation.

This has profound implications for corporate management. Pension funds are an enormous block of capital that can't be ignored, and open enterprises will be at the front of the line of their investment candidates.

Investing When You Own the Economy

As institutional funds grow in size, they alter the nature of the economy because they fundamentally alter the nature of corporate ownership. James Hawley and Andrew Williams coined the phrase "fiduciary capitalism"[51] to describe this new era, coming on the heels of Alfred Dupont Chandler's managerial capitalism and the entrepreneurial corporate capitalism practiced before that. Hawley and Williams describe the phenomenon of "universal owners" who are now at the heart of the new economy. These institutional funds essentially hold a cross section of the economy, either because they are so big or because that is their asset allocation strategy. For universal owners, it no longer makes sense or is possible to pick winning and losing companies; their fundamental interest is in the health of the economy overall, which obviously includes its long-term sustainability. The only thing that can raise all the corporate boats is a rising economic tide, so responsible fund managers should not only ensure that corporations operate in peak form but that the economy does too.

The universal owner has a much different agenda than an investor simply playing the market. When you own all companies, you no longer assess an individual company in isolation. It makes more sense to consider a company's impact on the whole economy rather than on just its own bottom line. Irresponsible corporate behavior that captures short-term gain at the expense of heavy external costs shouldn't be tolerated by the prudent universal owner. It doesn't make fiduciary sense. Prudent universal owners only want companies that deliver a net positive return to the economy. This closely aligns their interests with SRI advocates.

CERES: STEPPING UP TO THE PLATE

The rising knowledge of the retail investor, the growth of SRI funds, the power of business integrity determining financial performance, and the long-term interests of the universal owner are complementary forces advancing the interest of the open enterprise.

A case in point is the Coalition for Environmentally Responsible Economies, or CERES. Headquartered in Boston, CERES comprises environmental, investor, and advocacy groups working with companies that have endorsed the CERES Principles, a rigorous code of environmental conduct. By endorsing the CERES Principles, a company does more than implement a blue box program. It says that environmental awareness will be imbued in every facet of its operation, even to the extent of being factored into the selection process for board members. It would have been inconceivable two decades ago that any major corporation would pledge to behave in such a manner. But open enterprises realize that satisfying such demands makes it easier to compete for capital and to thrive in general.

The basic idea is that negative externalities such as the destruction of the environment may not be as "external" as was previously believed. There are huge risks in externalizing environmental costs. Firms and fiduciaries alike need to step up to the plate and take action to mitigate these risks, for competitive advantage and for the economic well-being of all firms.

The CERES Principles were formulated in 1989 in the wake of the *Exxon Valdez* disaster. Initially big corporations showed no interest, and the CERES Principles were adopted mainly by companies that already had strong "green" reputations, such as Ben & Jerry's and The Body Shop. Yet, through the 1990s, the momentum for transparency grew. In 1993 Sunoco became the first Fortune 500 company to endorse the CERES Principles. Other companies like AMR, Bank of America, Bethlehem Steel, Coca-Cola, Ford Motor Company, General Motors, Green Mountain Power Corporation, and Polaroid followed. By the end of 2002, more than 50 firms endorsed the CERES Principles, including 13 members of the *Fortune* 500. According to CERES, more than 2,000 companies worldwide regularly publish environmental reports.

In 2002 CERES released a landmark study—*Value at Risk: Climate Change and the Future of Governance*—showing mounting evidence that failure to respond to the risks posed by climate change could result in multibillion dollar losses for U.S. businesses and investment portfolios and stating that this failure could represent a breach of fiduciary duty on the part of corporate directors and investment decision makers. The report is one of the first to make a direct link among climate change, fiduciary responsibility, and shareholder value. It was

CERES corporate endorsers commit to ten principles

1. PROTECTION OF THE BIOSPHERE

We will reduce and make continual progress toward eliminating the release of any substance that may cause environmental damage to the air, water, or the earth or its inhabitants. We will safeguard all habitats affected by our operations and will protect open spaces and wilderness, while preserving biodiversity.

2. SUSTAINABLE USE OF NATURAL RESOURCES

We will make sustainable use of renewable natural resources, such as water, soils and forests. We will conserve non-renewable natural resources through efficient use and careful planning.

3. REDUCTION AND DISPOSAL OF WASTES

We will reduce and where possible eliminate waste through source reduction and recycling. All waste will be handled and disposed of through safe and responsible methods.

4. ENERGY CONSERVATION

We will conserve energy and improve the energy efficiency of our internal operations and of the goods and services we sell. We will make every effort to use environmentally safe and sustainable energy sources.

5. RISK REDUCTION

We will strive to minimize the environmental, health and safety risks to our employees and the communities in which we operate through safe technologies, facilities and operating procedures, and by being prepared for emergencies.

6. SAFE PRODUCTS AND SERVICES

We will reduce and where possible eliminate the use, manufacture or sale of products and services that cause environmental damage or health or safety hazards. We will inform our customers of the environmental impacts of our products or services and try to correct unsafe use.

7. ENVIRONMENTAL RESTORATION

We will promptly and responsibly correct conditions we have caused that endanger health, safety or the environment. To the extent feasible, we will redress injuries we have caused to persons or damage we have caused to the environment and will restore the environment.

8. TRANSPARENCY I—INFORMING THE PUBLIC

We will inform in a timely manner everyone who may be affected by conditions caused by our company that might endanger health, safety or the environment. We will regularly seek advice and counsel through dialogue with persons in communities near our facilities. We will not take any action against employees for reporting dangerous incidents or conditions to management or to appropriate authorities.

9. TRANSPARENCY II—AUDITS AND REPORTS

We will conduct an annual self-evaluation of our progress in implementing these Principles. We will support the timely creation of generally accepted environmental audit procedures. We will annually complete the CERES Report, which will be made available to the public.

10. MANAGEMENT COMMITMENT

We will implement these Principles and sustain a process that ensures that the Board of Directors and Chief Executive Officer are fully informed about pertinent environmental issues and are fully responsible for environmental policy. In selecting our Board of Directors, we will consider demonstrated environmental commitment as a factor.

written for CERES by Innovest Strategic Value Advisors, an investment research and advisory firm.

James Martin, chairman of Innovest and former chief investment officer for TIAA-CREF, one of the largest pension funds in the United States, explained why environmentalism is now inextricably linked to investing. "The evidence is increasingly compelling that companies' performance on environmental issues does indeed affect their competitiveness, profitability, and share price performance," said Martin.

"Since climate change is arguably the world's most pressing environmental issue, it follows logically that companies' response to the threats and opportunities of climate change—or their lack of response—could have a material bearing on their financial performance and therefore on shareholder value." [52]

"Because climate change will have an impact on all economic sectors, climate risk is now embedded, to some degree, in every business and investment portfolio in the United States," said Robert Massie, former executive director of CERES. "The risks are two-fold: first, the economic/financial risk from the damages due to climate change itself, and second, exposure to the cost of greenhouse gas emissions from climate change regulation and potential litigation. This is another case of an off–balance sheet risk that is not being reported to shareholders." At the same time, Massie explained, "proactive action on climate change presents opportunities for new and expanded business activity, reduced costs, and increased shareholder value that will produce a net economic benefit." [53]

The report documents the risks of climate change for a wide array of industrial sectors. "One of our main conclusions is that climate risk is not limited to any one sector," Massie said. "It is now difficult to identify a sector of the economy that would not be affected in some way by climate change. The question is no longer whether any given portfolio contains climate risk, but how much." Sectors covered in the report include electric utilities, petroleum, gas, agriculture, manufacturing, tourism, water, forestry, electronics, building construction and real estate, and insurance.

Fiduciaries supporting CERES call for greater corporate candor, honesty, accountability and investor diligence. This is great news for firms with business integrity. Their efforts will be increasingly rewarded.

GOVERNANCE OF THE OPEN ENTERPRISE

If you took 99 percent of the boards and dissolved them, there wouldn't be a perceptible change in corporate governance or shareholder influence over companies.

—Roger Martin[54]

The rise of active shareholders who screen for integrity and demand openness has enormous implications for the way companies govern themselves. Discussions of corporate governance have focused on how to make a better board. Governance analyst Jeffrey Sonnenfeld, for example, has argued eloquently for boards that create a climate of openness and candor, foster open dissent among board members, use a fluid portfolio of roles where directors are not typecast, ensure individual accountability of board members, and evaluate performance of the board itself.[55]

When it comes to empowering shareholders, however, tougher rules are needed. The Sarbanes-Oxley Act of 2002, prompted by the Enron meltdown, is a step in the right direction, but it falls short in the critical reforms necessary for accountability. These include enhanced board independence, abolition of staggered boards, expensing of stock options, and increased disclosure on social and environmental issues.

Shareholders need to be able to meaningfully affect the composition of the board, something they currently can't do. Consider how difficult it is for shareholders to nominate a director. They must produce and distribute a proxy at their own expense, in some cases to tens of thousands of other shareholders. They must hire lawyers as the mailing has to be approved by the SEC and might be contested by the corporation's lawyers. One nomination for a large public company could easily cost more than $1.5 million. This is a lot of money even for a large pension or mutual fund, let alone an individual shareholder. As a result, management's slate of board nominees is always elected. These logistical and financial roadblocks facing a non-management-endorsed candidate make a mockery of any concept of shareholder democracy. Imagine a country where an election "challenger has to pay for his campaign out of his own pocket, while the incumbent uses the government's treasury," says Guy Adams, managing director of GWA Capital Partners, a Los Angeles–based money manager. "You'd say what a banana republic this is."[56]

Shareholder activists have proposed a host of reforms to give owners more say in board elections. At Verizon's April 2003 annual general meeting a resolution called for the board to nominate twice as many candidates as there were seats, thereby giving voters a choice. The resolution sponsor complained that the current system means that directors "answer only to fellow directors." Verizon's proxy statement rejected the proposal: "Nothing in law requires that an election provide a choice of candidates or that shareholders have a 'right' to nominate candidates." If there were competing candidates, Verizon added, "It would be difficult to predict which individuals would be elected."[57] Need we say more?

A similar proposal by the American Federation of State, County and Municipal Employees would have independent board candidates placed on the ballot if owners of at least 3 percent of a company's shares nominate that person. "This is an attempt to break up the system of coronation and make it a system, when shareholders want it, of a real election and a real choice," said Michael Zucker, the director for corporate affairs at AFSCME, which tried to get the idea on six corporate proxies this year, including that of Citigroup.[58]

Legislation that makes it easy for shareholders to put nominees on proxy statements would easily rectify the situation. For example, if a block of shareholders representing 10 to 15 percent of all stock were unhappy with management nominees, they could make a nomination to appear on the management proxy statement. Such a law should not permit takeovers or hogtie the company. But shareholders would be able to nominate a board minority. Says Damon Silvers, associate general counsel of the AFL-CIO, any new legislation should be a "vehicle for voice not for control." Corporations need to take the lead here. And smart ones know it is in their interest to do so—not just to avoid legislation but also to engage shareholders and other stakeholders for success.

A recent study found that investors pay more for well-governed companies.[59] McKinsey & Company surveyed more than 200 institutional investors who together manage approximately $3.25 trillion in assets. They found that three-quarters say board practices are at least as important to them as financial performance when they are considering evaluating companies for investment. Over 80 percent of investors say they would pay more for the shares of a well-governed company than for those of a poorly governed company.[60] The premium that investors say they would be willing to pay for a well-governed company varies from 18 percent in the United States to 27 percent in Venezuela.

Understanding this, open enterprises govern themselves differently from traditional corporations and invite shareholder engagement in a number of ways:

- They seek shareholder advice on board composition. Management meets with important institutional investors to discuss the board and listens to their suggestions on criteria for board members as well as specific nominations.

- Boards of open enterprises provide leadership on corporate values and on behalf of shareholders to enforce the elements of the new business integrity—honesty, accountability, consideration, and transparency. They periodically review whether the company behaves according to values. They ask "What's the right thing to do?" rather than "What's the expedient thing to do?" Boards do their own integrity screening on everything from the selection of a CEO to the development of business strategies.

- Boards in open enterprises understand that stakeholder value is part of shareholder value. At Johnson & Johnson the shareholder comes last after customers, employees, and society. Says CEO Bill Weldon, "This was General Johnson's great genius. He understood that by putting the shareholder last he was putting him first."

- Open enterprises also understand that the owners of wealth—the hundred million Americans who own stock—are stakeholders in the firm as customers, employees, partners, and members of society—raising their families, breathing the air, and hoping for a safe, peaceful, and prosperous world.

PROGRESSIVE: GETTING NAKED FOR FUN AND PROFIT

Progressive Insurance CEO Glenn Renwick is an inquisitive shareholder's dream come true. His philosophy is to tell shareholders as much as possible as clearly and frequently as possible. The company's 2002 annual report, entitled *Bare All*, features avant-garde photos of a naked man. Progressive is the only Fortune 500 company to report

operating results on a monthly basis. Some might argue that as an antidote for the short-term performance disease that has lately inflicted
the markets, companies should be reporting less often than the traditional quarterly statement, not more often. Renwick counters that a
steady stream of reliable information helps shareholders evaluate
whether the company is meeting long-term strategies. Says Renwick,
"Why give monthly information? Because we have it. I view it as the
owners' information. When you have information, you should disclose
it, good or bad, exactly as it is."

Renwick said the first time he sat down to write a press release to
explain why the company would not meet analysts' projections, he
was struck with a sense of absurdity. "Here I am trying to explain why
I'm not going to make a target that I didn't set in the first place." Progressive issues no guidance whatsoever. "I don't know what we will
make next month. And I think it is foolhardy in our business to give
guidance that people could or should rely on. More important, I view
my job primarily as a strategist. I should be evaluated long term on a
body of work and collection of results rather than a quarter by quarter
estimate."

This policy contributes to honesty and candor. The company has no
need to make any month look better or worse because it has created
expectations that it will simply tell it like it is. "We don't make predictions and create expectations so we have no problem sharing information. If it doesn't meet the expectation that someone else has created
that's not our concern. We're in it for the long term."

Renwick continually tries to come up with useful revealing information for the firm's monthly disclosure that would help anyone who
is interested in analyzing the company. This includes the number of
customer policies in force. "Some companies would want to keep that
a secret, but I can't imagine why."

Progressive, radically, is also candid with shareholders regarding the
amount of financial reserves it sets aside. "In our business, reserving is
the cookie jar relative to earnings management." Some suggest firms
use reserves in their quarterly statements to increase or lower revenues, and in doing so, to smooth out earnings to correspond to Street
estimates. "We've gone exactly the opposite way. We say we've got to
run our business every day trying to get as much right as possible. So

we'll be happy to tell you what our reserve adjustments are on a frequent basis." This way, reserves are set aside to meet business needs rather than to engineer financial results. "With such a personal management philosophy, it's easy to share reserve information with shareholders."

Renwick says it's "liberating" to run a company this way. "Once it's reported it's over. I don't worry every month about whether we're going to make our earnings numbers. They are what they are so I have no need to manipulate them. I'm in the mode of reporting reality as opposed to smoothing reality and that enables us to focus on long-term strategy."

On the surface being open pays off. It builds trust in management and contributes a brand of candor to the company's considerable success in the marketplace and solid performance for shareholders. (Its share price has increased from $10 to $60 over the last decade.) But transparency runs deeper; it's part of the company's corporate character. Says Renwick, "In insurance, the foundation of success is trust. To be trusted you need integrity and you need to be open. It's fun to manage in an environment where you are always sharing what you know. It's part of who we are."

PART III

Being Open

CHAPTER 9

HARNESSING THE POWER

In June 1998, Royal Caribbean Cruise Lines (RCCL), a Liberian corporation headquartered in Miami, pleaded guilty to conspiracy and obstruction of justice. The U.S. court forced the company to pay $9 million in fines after a Coast Guard investigation proved it had intentionally and repeatedly dumped massive volumes of waste oil into the ocean—fouling the same waters whose pristine purity it touted in tourist brochures.

RCCL had the capability to prevent this fiasco. It had installed special devices in its cruise ships to separate waste oil from water and then filter the water for safe disposal in the ocean while storing mucky used-up oil for legal disposal in port. But the cruise line's operations personnel had systematically bypassed the separation devices with homemade piping and poured the untreated oil-water mix directly into the ocean.

The company promised such actions would never happen again. Jack Williams, newly appointed president, issued a statement saying, "We deeply regret our role in polluting the marine environment and we are particularly sorry for the attempt to conceal that pollution. These acts were inexcusable, they were wrong, and we accept full responsibility for these violations."[1] But, astonishingly, only a month later another RCCL ship was found dumping oily waste overboard. Within a year the company again pleaded guilty, this time to 23 counts of illegally polluting the ocean and tampering with evidence on ships operating in the Caribbean, off the ports of New York and Miami, and in Alaskan waters. It paid another $18 million in fines. RCCL also admitted to regularly dumping other pollutants (including chemicals from photo processing, dry cleaning, and printing) into the sea. Williams blamed the problems on a "group of employees who knowingly violated environmental laws and our own company policy." He added, "The majority of these violations reflect a lapse in our enforcement efforts—not a lapse in our corporate conscience or our commitment to protecting the ocean."[2]

The court disagreed with its president's claim that the company's hands were clean and its employees were to blame. It found the violations "were so systemic, repetitive and longstanding that the criminal conduct amounted to a routine business practice for RCCL."

The firm's own compensation policies effectively led senior employees to pollute the ocean. Running the oil-water separators and disposing of oil waste in port cost ships hundreds of thousands of dollars a year. Ship's officers' bonuses depended on keeping costs down, so those who wanted to meet their performance targets, be seen to care about their jobs, and receive their year-end payouts had little choice but to dump oil into the ocean.

The RCCL story shows that it's one thing to adopt a set of values and quite another to build a company that lives by them. For the new integrity to take root requires leadership, stewardship, and specific work to ensure that values-driven outcomes are embedded in every employee's performance plan. The new integrity must be as much a part of the organization as human resources, finance, information technology, or sales and marketing. These corporate functions may seem natural today, but some had to fight their way to gain legitimacy, authority, accountabilities, resources, and seats at the executive table.

In this chapter we discuss the practical how-tos of giving the new integrity a meaningful seat, and in doing so build an open enterprise. Throughout, we will refer to a two-part, or "yin and yang," approach to values-based performance. The yin (the female principle in Chinese philosophy) is productive, sustainable stakeholder relationships; the yang is competitive, sustainable business practices. Integrity requires trust-based, engaged relationships—based on transparency—with a broad portfolio of stakeholders. It also means rethinking products, services, and business operations to maximize financial, social, and environmental objectives. Motivation, will, leadership, planning, and hard work will get you there.

MINIMAL VERSUS MAXIMAL TRANSPARENCY

Firms, or more specifically firms' various operations, work at any of three levels of transparency (drawn from work led by our colleague David Wheeler; see Figure 9.1).[3]

- Level 1 firms focus on *compliance*. They obey laws and follow customary norms of behavior in society. Such firms may maximize business performance, but they only minimize negative externalities when they must or when no effort is required. Compliance-focused firms view most transactions as win-lose-draw encounters in which their job is to seek the maximum advantage for the lowest possible cost. (Secret lawbreakers who pretend to be level 1 may really be level minus 1.)

- Level 2 firms comply with the law, but they go further when it comes to *relationship management*. They invest in strengthening relationships with close and important stakeholders, whether customers, employees, communities, or business partners. Eschewing the harsh win-loss mindset of level 1, relationship managers adopt a paternalistic "trust us, we know what's good for you" stance; they

Figure 9.1 Three Value Levels of the Firm[4]
Source: Wheeler, Colbert and Freeman

apply trade-off analysis to difficult decisions. They typically provide business partners with rewards for good behavior, engage in some philanthropy, and encourage "communications strategies" for all.

- *Level 3 open enterprises* see transparency, stakeholder relationships, and sustainability as sources of competitive advantage. They redefine their products, services, and business processes to strengthen long-term stakeholder relationships and to achieve alignment with changing social and environmental goals. They apply transparency and engagement to stakeholder encounters, conduct genuine dialogue in an atmosphere of equity, and hold themselves accountable for commitments. Faced with difficult decisions, they seek innovative solutions that maximize value for all parties.

No firm is exclusively at any one of these levels in all operations; many function vigorously in all three. In the mid-1990s Chiquita was at best merely legal in its labor relations and political contributions, while actively managing a relationship with the Rainforest Action Network on some environmental issues. When the company passed through Chapter 11 in 2001, it operated with creditors, shareholders, and employees somewhere between levels 2 and 3. Now it is an open enterprise when it manages to high levels of performance, transparency, and engagement on labor standards and environmental care.

In this chapter we treat the open enterprise as the target, and describe the features of such sustainably competitive firms.

WHAT ARE WE MANAGING HERE?

The new integrity needs to be managed from the top: board-level governance, officer-level leadership, and so on. A number of companies have already done this. Some have mandated a senior executive like the VP of corporate affairs, human resources, or strategy to be responsible for stakeholder/sustainability objectives. Others have gone so far as to create full-time positions such as corporate responsibility officer or VP of sustainability. Is this a passing fad like the "chief knowledge officers" who proliferated during the 1990s in response to theories of

organizational learning? Obviously, firms can and should exhibit
integrity without a full-time executive. But to move the broader issues
to the center of the corporate agenda requires at least a part-time, if
not a full-time, executive job assignment.

What is the case for a broader mandate, beyond basic integrity?
Consider where executive mandates come from. Every big company
has a chief financial officer and VP of human resources (HR); most
people roughly agree on the scope of these jobs. This is because we see
both money and people as key resources which need careful stewardship. The case for a CFO is easy: someone has to keep track of the cash
and comply with myriad regulations from paying taxes to shareholder
reporting. Finance pays for itself by minimizing taxes and getting managers to cut costs. Similarly, HR performs mundane administrative
tasks like hiring and benefits. HR delivers added value when it ensures
that you have the right people, that thorny personnel issues are solved,
and that performance management helps keep employees focused on
what counts.

Simply stated, corporate finance stewards a firm's money, while HR
stewards its people. What does "corporate integrity" steward? Can this
"what" be as intuitively and distinctively critical to firm performance
as money and people?

The case is becoming clear. Simply stated, the "corporate integrity"
function stewards two sets of strategic resources: stakeholder relationships (yin) and sustainable business practices (yang). Are these
resources intuitively distinctive and critical to business performance?
This has already happened in many firms.

> Executive vice president–stakeholder relations Lise Kingo is a member
> of the six person executive management committee at Novo Nordisk,
> a $3.5 billion Denmark-based pharmaceutical firm. Her mandate is (a)
> "stakeholder engagement" which "enables us to stay attuned to emerg-
> ing issues and concerns"; and (b) "the objective to balance social,
> environmental and economic concerns in every business decision"
> which "translates into both corporate and individual targets."[5] Kingo
> nets this all out as license to operate, "a key parameter for pharmaceu-
> tical companies these days, that's why trust and transparency are so
> important."

What about the job title? Many in current use seem vague (EVP corporate affairs) or narrow (EVP stakeholder relations). Coining the "chief financial officer" moniker, we propose a new formulation that may be more on target: Business Integrity Officer (BIO). The term connotes commitment to values and principles, effective risk management, and governance stature—all vital to this mandate. It also has an appealing acronym. The balance of this chapter describes the mechanics of the BIO mandate.

TEN CHARACTERISTICS OF THE OPEN ENTERPRISE

Open enterprises display similar qualities—ten sets of practices that, together, shine out. In each of these, the firm infuses the values of the new integrity: honesty, meeting commitments, caring, transparency, and the maximization of economic, social, and environmental value.

1. *Leadership.* This begins with the CEO and board and is visible to all.
2. *Governance and reporting.* Not a burden, good governance and transparency drive engagement, clarity, integrity, and focused performance.
3. *Strategy and entrepreneurship.* The new integrity has unique implications for each industry, company, and business activity. In open enterprises, all plans address new integrity criteria clearly and specifically—both in the way planning is conducted (stakeholder inclusion) and in its content.
4. *Corporate character.* This is about embedding the new integrity into the DNA of the firm through such programs as internal communications, performance management, and training.
5. *Brand and reputation.* The new integrity is not spin, but it must be communicated. Infusing the brand with the firm's lived values enhances its values for customers, shareholders, and others.
6. *Environmental engagement.* Critical to success in the stakeholder realm is a healthy, stable, and open operating environment: sustainable ecosystems, peace, order, and good public governance.

7. *Stakeholder engagement.* Open enterprises put resources and effort into reviewing, managing, recasting, and strengthening relationships with stakeholders, old and new.
8. *Products and services.* Sustainable innovation leads to long-term economic, social, and environmental performance.
9. *Operations.* Open enterprises lower risks and costs by applying new integrity thinking to everyday operations.
10. *Information technology.* Not just a driver of transparency, information technology is a powerful tool for enabling a firm's transparency, stakeholder engagement, and sustainability strategies.

We discuss each of these qualities in the sections that follow. For each, we provide a set of "outcomes," which when present, indicate that a company has achieved the hallmark practice. We also describe "strategies": actions that companies take to achieve the desired outcomes.

Note that while the list is in rough logical order, these practices do not occur in any particular sequence in the real world. Companies can—and do—start just about anywhere. All the practices happen in parallel over extended time. Each entails roadblocks, setbacks, confusion, and contradiction. Change is work.

Novo Nordisk: An Open Enterprise

Novo Nordisk,* a Danish pharmaceutical firm with 18,000 employees and operations in 68 countries, is the main case study in this chapter. Though it's not a household name, the company is an award-winning global leader in transparency and stakeholder-focused sustainable practices.

Novo was spurred into this terrain way back in 1970 when it was a

* We use the names "Novo" and Novo Nordisk" interchangably.

(continued on next page)

manufacturer of enzymes for laundry detergent. Ralph Nader led a campaign that claimed the enzymes gave skin infections to the company's factory workers. Sales fell by 50 percent. A year later the charges were proven unfounded, but Novo had learned the power of stakeholders driven by an emotional social and environmental issue. The scars are etched in the company's collective memory, and it made a commitment never to allow such an event to happen again.

In 1990 the company initiated a formal process of engagement on the hotly debated issues of genetic engineering with NGOs, employees, and other stakeholders. It engaged in "triple bottom line" accounting and reports—with external verification—in 1993. It added social and environmental criteria to business unit and employee key performance indicators and balanced scorecard programs.

Was there a cost? Perhaps, but the company's performance is robust. Despite 2002 troubles from a first-quarter earnings warning and a canceled drug trial, Novo is an upbeat company in a downtrodden sector. Between 1997 and 2002 its revenues grew from $2.5 to $3.5 billion while earnings per share nearly doubled from $.86 to $1.66. Novo's 2002 operating margin was 24 percent and its net was 16 percent. The share price has consistently outperformed the industry, for example, gaining 15 percent in the first three months of 2003 while the industry was flat.

Diabetes, the root cause of nearly one in ten deaths worldwide, drives 70 percent of the company's revenues. Insulin is the main diabetes drug; Novo has a 47 percent share of the global insulin market by volume and provides a variety of other diabetes-related products and services. It is also a player in hemostasis management, growth hormone therapy, and hormone replacement therapy.

The company's activities inevitably expose it to controversy.

- While diabetes is more or less under control in rich countries, it afflicts more than 100 million people in the developing world. The number will more than double in the next 25 years.
- Novo relies heavily on genetically modified microorganisms to produce drugs.
- It is an advocate of stem cell research.

- It tests drugs on rabbits, mice, rats, and other animals.
- Novo has supported industry efforts to protect pharmaceutical patents in developing countries.

Novo's people and public statements are bracingly candid. It doesn't flinch from describing mistakes and challenges. Novo Nordisk has walked the walk of transparency for some time. But, as it learned in 1998, no company, no matter how "good," can be complacent. Here's what happened.

In 2001 Novo Nordisk joined 38 companies in a lawsuit against the government of South Africa charging it with violating the World Trade Organization's Trade Related Intellectual Property agreement (TRIPS). South Africa had passed legislation giving itself the right to abrogate patent rights for any pharmaceutical product. Although Novo was not in the AIDS medication business (which was the main issue), it participated because it believed that TRIPS properly addressed the needs of developing countries.

The lawsuit backfired into a global public uproar against the pharmaceutical industry—a crisis driven by the antiglobalization movement, enabled by the Internet, and fanned by the media.

The crisis happened mere weeks after Lars Rebien Sørensen became CEO of Novo Nordisk. For employees who remembered the 1970 Ralph Nader campaign, it was the return of a surrealistic nightmare. On February 15, 2001, the headline on the country's leading liberal newspaper read, "Danish companies impede delivery of essential drugs." This kicked off a crisis that continued for two months. ATTAC, a new Danish antiglobalization group, led the charge. Newspapers ran heart-rending human interest stories about AIDS in Africa. A massive demonstration rattled the gates of the company's Copenhagen factory. The media picked up, and repeatedly ran, a defensive statement by the new CEO that "we are not a humanitarian organization." The firm later said that it was "the longest and most severe media storm our company has ever faced."[6]

Sørensen's response combined spirit with spunk—and engagement. He met the company's critics and went to the factory gates to "listen to

(continued on next page)

and talk to the demonstrators, to get the feel of the people's sentiments and arguments against globalization."[7] He defended the view that "we cannot give away our products, or give up our intellectual property," while acknowledging the need to slash patent drug prices in developing countries. Sørensen and his Novo colleagues pointed out that well over 90 percent of medication needs in developing countries could be met with cheap off-patent drugs (like aspirin and insulin), that the real challenges were alleviating poverty and improving access to health care services.

The drug companies and South Africa reached a settlement in April, whereby the cost of medications was reduced.

Novo Nordisk announced a plan to tackle poverty and access: the Leadership in Education and Access to Diabetes care (LEAD) initiative, "our response to ensuring better access to global health care." It included formation of the World Diabetes Foundation with a ten-year commitment and a $60 million endowment. The foundation is an arm's length organization with an independent board of directors. Its mandate is to advance national disease strategies, care capacity, and low prices—including practical matters like education, distribution of medicines, prevention, diagnosis, and treatment. Sørensen presented the idea to the firm's major insti- tutional investors and won their approval. "They, too, expect us to act on our responsibility as a global corporate citizen."[8]

You might say that facilitating more and better diagnoses is merely a cynical plan to sell more insulin. Our view is that there's nothing wrong with a strategy that invests in delivering better, more cost effective care in a way that is financially sustainable for the company that makes the investment.

The dispute with South Africa had a silver lining for Novo Nordisk. It fostered a new context: revitalized and more disciplined commitment to stakeholder engagement and the alignment of financial, social, and environmental outcomes.

Leadership

It is precisely because Novo's leadership was engaged with its stakeholders and had a strategic framework in place that Lars Sørensen responded vigorously to the South African drug patent controversy.

The organization swung into action, and stakeholders ended up trusting the company even more.

Novo has been applying new integrity leadership strategies (Figure 9.2) for many years. Its practices have evolved in fascinating ways. For simplicity we will just describe how the company applied these strategies in the past couple of years.

Novo publishes three annual reports to stakeholders. Although reports are but the tip of the iceberg in transparent communications (Novo makes the point that person-to-person communication is far more important), they set the tone and begin to define a public record. Novo's reports are clear, informative, and logical; they consistently anticipate and answer questions. The *Annual Review* is a compendium of information and marketing content including financials, activities and events, features, and news. The *Annual Financial Report* is the official set of audited accounts and notes, and the *Sustainability Report* (also audited by a major accounting firm) reviews "our strategies, activities and targets regarding social, environmental, ethical and socio-economic issues affecting our future performance." All shareholders receive the *Annual Review* by mail and may opt to receive the other two reports. All three, along with an archive of past reports, are on the company Web site.

Sørensen's letter to stakeholders mostly discusses traditional financial and business issues—especially important after a tough year (in which the company ultimately pulled through and met its targets). But Sørensen also describes Novo's focus on employee development,

Outcomes	Strategies
Top management commitment and focus	Visible CEO and board leadership
	Leadership by example
Organizational commitment and focus	Director and officer assignments
	Transparent processes and
Stakeholder belief the firm is serious	communications
	Corporate values, code of conduct
Core values and charter defined	Use of industry codes
	Engagement with corporate
	responsibility industry

Figure 9.2 Leadership

social responsibility, human rights, and environmental management. In the 2001 report—after a better financial year and on the rebound from the South Africa challenge—Sørensen forcefully displayed his personal commitment to stakeholders and sustainable business practices right from the opening paragraphs.

But effective CEO and board leadership requires more than words in a report or dialogue at a barricade: it must be systemic. EVP stakeholder relations Lise Kingo is one of only six members of the company's executive management committee. Hers is a full-time job, not an add-on for a senior marketing or human resources executive. The company first created this position in April 2002.

The company's 2002 *Sustainability Report* (which Kingo edits and produces) says. "A particular responsibility for keeping the company's actions attuned to stakeholders' demands lies with the Board of Directors, Executive Management and cross-organizational committees." Sustainability issues are on the board agenda twice a year. Three cross-functional committees (environment and bioethics, social and industrial relations, and health policy), each chaired by a member of executive management, identify issues, set policies, and devise strategies, targets, and action plans.

The underpinning of all this—the constitution, as it were—is the Novo Nordisk Way of Management, which includes a vision, charter, and policies—what we think of as corporate values and code of conduct. Some aspects of these are homegrown: "We will be the world's leading diabetes care company. Our aspiration is to defeat diabetes. . . ." Novo has also adopted several industry codes, such as the International Chamber of Commerce's Business Charter for Sustainable Development and the UN Global Compact.

In 2002 company executives spoke at and participated in industry conferences, from the World Economic Forum to the Johannesburg summit on sustainable development (where it cohosted a workshop), as well as many lower-profile events. In 2001 Novo became a cofounder and main sponsor of Bridging Europe, a grassroots initiative for rethinking the continent's political institutions. It also cofounded the Nordic Partnership with 17 other companies and the World Wildlife Fund, aiming to bring sustainability into core company operations on the basis of a solid business case and stakeholder engagement.

In addition, Novo works with socially responsible investment organizations and tries to push SRI up the agenda of the mainstream financial community.

Hewlett-Packard senior vice president for corporate affairs Debra Dunn is another active and effective business integrity officer. Dunn reports to CEO Carly Fiorina and is a member of HP's executive committee. She displays infectious enthusiasm and determination to change the way corporations behave in the world. Dunn is responsible for worldwide functions including social and environmental responsibility, e-inclusion (HP's program for bridging the digital divide), emerging markets offerings, government affairs, public affairs, and philanthropy. She focuses heavily on the digital divide where she seeks to apply HP's resources to provide solutions that can become deeply rooted. Some of Dunn's work is intensely local (Andhra Pradesh, Dublin, and East Palo Alto), while in other cases she engages in global diplomacy (the creation of a UN-sponsored microfinance program). Internally, Dunn is a key player in the development of HP's overall strategic plan, employee communications around stakeholders and sustainability, and addressing breaches of corporate ethics.

Governance and Reporting

In the aftermath of 2002, most observers agree that directors and officers must be independent, governance must meet or exceed legal and industry standards, executive compensation policy needs a rewrite, and a portfolio of good governance processes is essential, including objective performance assessments of boards and directors (Figure 9.3). Rather than march this well-trodden ground, we take a tour of another core transparency topic: formal stakeholder and sustainability reporting, of which Novo happens to be a leading practitioner.

Every publicly traded company—and every manager whose variable compensation depends on company performance—understands that reporting is a two-way street. Yes, the stated reason to publish regular, detailed financials is accountability to shareholders, regulators, and the public. But financial reporting is also part of a feedback loop that changes behavior inside the firm. It helps employees understand they are all in the same rowboat and makes them use common formats to describe results. Published results also benchmark performance

Outcomes	Strategies
Business integrity	Director/officer independence
	Meet/exceed legal requirements &
Executive flexibility and performance	pertinent industry standards
	Good governance processes
Perceived accountability to stakeholders	Transparent reporting, independently
	audited
Access to capital	Full-cost accounting
	Credible executive compensation model
	and process
	Shareholder/stakeholder rights

Figure 9.3 Governance and Reporting

against the competition and the economy. They help employees, customers, and partners evaluate the firm's financial dependability. Financial reports affect (for better or worse) how employees do their jobs, especially when bonuses are at stake.

Hundreds of businesses also report regularly on social and environmental performance. As with financial reporting, so with social and environmental reporting: the internal feedback loop is a key part of its value. At Chiquita, as we've described, reporting was a key driver of change and employee commitment at a time of crisis. At Novo, which embeds stakeholder/sustainability targets in employee job targets, the annual sustainability report sums up the last year's accomplishments, sets targets for the next, and describes a current agenda of dilemmas that challenge the business. (For example, "How can we respect others' cultural beliefs and positions on a sensitive issue such as stem cell research, and yet maintain a competitive edge in the quest to defeat diabetes?"[9])

Many social and environmental reports are selective and self-serving sales pitches: they tout a company's purported contributions to employee health and safety or philanthropy, with no external assurance of these claims. Few reports, by contrast, rigorously describe financial, social, environmental, and corporate governance performance; like financial reports, the best of them are designed and inde-

Novo Nordisk's Unique Governance Structure

Novo Nordisk ownership is split between A shares and B shares. A shares are held by Novo A/S, a holding company that itself is wholly owned by the not-for-profit Novo Nordisk Foundation. Novo A/S owns 26.7 percent of Novo Nordisk shares; a multivoting mechanism gives it 69.8 percent of the votes.

Novo Nordisk B shares are publicly traded via the Copenhagen, London, and New York stock exchanges. They are the most actively traded of Danish company shares.

None of Novo Nordisk's nine directors are company executives. Three, in accordance with Danish law, are elected employees. Another three (including the board chairman and vice chairman) also sit on the board of its holding company, Novo A/S.

pendently audited in accordance with publicly available, credible standards.

One problem is that standards for social, environmental, and governance reporting are immature. Leading standards, and standard setters, have emerged only recently. The Netherlands-based Global Reporting Initiative (GRI) provides a widely accepted approach to the principles and specifics of economic, social, and environmental reporting within a context of stakeholder engagement.[10] By April 2003, over 200 companies in 24 countries (North American firms include AT&T, BC Hydro, Chiquita, Dow, Ford, HP, McDonald's, Nike, P&G, and Suncor) affirmed they used GRI guidelines. But a handful (e.g., Novo and Johnson & Johnson) claimed to have met the stricter criterion of reporting "in accordance with" the guide.

BearingPoint partner Eric Israel, a leader of its sustainability practice, comments that "the meaning of citizenship for one particular company can be completely different than for another. So how do you benchmark an organization and compare it to others in the same industry? Up to now, there's been no equivalent of generally accepted accounting principles (GAAP) for social responsibility. That's where GRI comes in."[11]

GRI provides a template for a stakeholder/sustainability report, including:

- Vision and strategy for sustainability, including a statement from the reporting organization's CEO

- Profile: overview of the reporting organization and scope of the report

- Governance structure, overarching policies, and management systems in place to implement the organization's vision for sustainable development and to manage its performance

- Economic, environmental, and social performance indicators

The indicators are the heart of a GRI compliant report.

- *Direct economic indicators* measure monetary flows between the organization and key stakeholders, as well as indicate how the organization affects stakeholder economic interests. These are conventional metrics, allocated by stakeholder. For example, net sales and geographic breakdown of markets are mapped to "customers"; cost of goods and services purchased to "suppliers"; payroll and benefits to "employees"; interest and dividends to "providers of capital"; and taxes, subsidies, and philanthropic donations to the "public sector."

- The GRI also suggests reporting on *indirect economic impacts*, namely the major externalities associated with an organization's products and services.

- *Environmental indicators* concern an organization's impacts on living and nonliving natural systems, including ecosystems, land, and water. These indicators are presented in both absolute figures and normalized measures (e.g., resource use per unit of output). The absolute figures provide a sense of scale or magnitude of impact, while normalized data illustrate efficiency and support comparisons from one organization to the next. Sample indicators are materials use, energy use, water, impacts on biodiversity, greenhouse gas emissions, rate of recycling, and incidences of fines for noncompliance with environmental regulations.

- *Social indicators* enjoy "less of a consensus than environmental performance management."[12] They draw on international standards from the United Nations and the International Labor Organization. The indicators include employment creation, union membership (a measurement whose value is hotly contested), injury rates, and training rates. Many GRI social indicators use qualitative measures such as an organization's systems, policies, and procedures. Qualitative indicators include informing, consulting, and negotiating with employees over operational changes such as restructuring; worker-management health and safety committees; human rights; community impact of operations; political contributions; customer health and safety; and product information and labeling.

In addition to its generic reporting guide, the GRI plans to produce sector- and issue-specific guidelines.

GRI only solves part of the problem. It mainly provides the "what" part of the new GAAP. The other issue is *how* to report, more precisely how to verify whether a report is credible, whether it meets the needs and expectations of stakeholders. The reporting problems of the 2002 corporate governance crisis were not caused by a dearth of indicators. Rather, it was due to problems with compliance, with the spirit of disclosure beyond compliance, and with the quality of the audits (and auditors) that theoretically provided assurance of the reports' quality.

To address this problem, in 2003 AccountAbility, a not-for-profit U.K.-based institute, released a new standard to guide and assess the work of "assurance providers" such as auditors and other third parties.[13] Among the members of AccountAbility are the Association of Chartered Certified Accountants (United Kingdom), Business for Social Responsibility (United States), Co-operative Bank (United Kingdom), Instituto Ethos (Brazil), KPMG, LeaRN (South Africa), New Economics Foundation (United Kingdom), Novo Nordisk, and PricewaterhouseCoopers. The AccountAbility framework, *AA1000 Assurance Standard*, defines five principles for sustainability reporting.[14]

- *Inclusivity.* An organization's commitment to (a) identify and understand its social, environmental, and economic performance and impact and the associated views of its stakeholders; (b) consider and coherently respond (whether negatively or positively) to the aspirations and needs of its stakeholders; and (c) provide an account to stakeholders for its decisions, actions, and impacts.

- *Materiality.* The assurance provider states whether the "reporting organization" (e.g., a company) has included the information that stakeholders need to make informed judgments, decisions, and actions. Information is material if its omission or misrepresentation could influence the decisions or actions of stakeholders.

- *Completeness.* The assurance provider evaluates the extent to which the reporting organization can identify and understand the material aspects of its own sustainability performance. Where the assurance provider finds gaps, it should encourage the reporting organization to fix or describe them; failing a fix, the assurance provider should describe them in its assurance report.

- *Responsiveness.* The assurance provider evaluates whether the reporting organization has responded to stakeholder concerns, policies, and relevant standards and has adequately communicated its responses in its sustainability report.

- *Evidence.* The assurance provider evaluates whether the reporting organization has provided adequate evidence to support the content of the report.

Such standards are still immature and evolving, and other players (like the International Standardization Organization) are in the game. For now, the GRI and AA1000 are your best bets, not only for reporting but for building structured models for transparency-driven stakeholder engagement.

Two other pieces still come up short. First, stakeholder/sustainability reporting lacks a standard format, or look and feel. We have nothing comparable to an income statement or balance sheet—a concise set of figures that nets out the overall situation in a company. Second, few countries require or regulate stakeholder/sustainability reporting.

Finally, voluntary reporting means that fewer companies report, and lack of regulation also means slack and disjointed reporting standards.

Regulation makes a difference, says a BearingPoint study. In Japan, which mandated environmental reporting and guidelines in 2001, 72 percent of the top 100 companies put audited environmental results into their 2002 financial reports. Following but well behind were the United Kingdom (49 percent) and the United States (36 percent). Germany and the Nordic countries were in the 25 to 35 percent range, while in Canada only 19 percent did the same.[15]

Novo Nordisk's *Sustainability Report* 2002 is explicitly "in accordance with" the GRI guidelines and AA1000, duly assured by accounting firm Deloitte & Touche. In early 2003 it was one of the few available textbook implementations of these standards, a model of stakeholder engagement, completeness, business reasoning, and inspiration. In addition to its downloadable report, Novo provides statistical and qualitative information on its Web site; there is also a detailed cross-map of its report to the GRI indicators. Nevertheless, there's room for improvement. Going back and forth from paper to various Web pages can be confusing. And, though Novo has been reporting for a decade, it provides comparative trend data for only a few indicators.

Strategy and Entrepreneurship

Peter Drucker said half a century ago that the purpose of a business is to create a customer. Customers are the first—though not the only—stakeholders for any business, and meeting their needs is the essence of strategy. Meeting the needs of growing numbers of desirable customers over the long haul is the essence of sustainable strategy. What is new, in the age of transparency, is that gaining the trust and commitment of its other stakeholders enables the firm to serve customers best (Figure 9.4).

As Toyota and Shell illustrate in their strategies for noncarbon fuels, such companies seek competitive advantage from stakeholder/sustainability strategies that focus on the customer. Where costs are inevitably associated with externalities, leading companies work with their industries to raise the civil foundation of sustainable business practice—again, with customers as the focus. The Kimberley Process

Outcomes	Strategies
Short- and long-term optimization of financial, social, environmental performance	Embed in all planning processes.
	Analyze industry/stakeholder/firm specific issue/risk/opportunities.
	Identify, analyze obstacles to change.
Competitive advantage	Apply creative, analytic, business-casing techniques to multiple time views
Raising industry civil foundation	(immediate, mid, long term).
	Engage existing/potential stakeholders in
Addressing obstacles to change	strategy development.
	Engage competitors, governments on raising standards.
	Develop timetable with milestones.

Figure 9.4 Strategy and Entrepreneurship

(Chapter 6) is one example: the diamond industry (prodded by consumers, governments, and NGOs) got together and agreed to eliminate the purchase of gems that financed vicious wars in central Africa.

Best-in-class companies don't just have a few great integrity programs. Their policies require all plans to address stakeholder/sustainability issues along with competitive, financial, human resource, information technology, and other core factors. They encourage and reward entrepreneurial stakeholder/sustainability initiatives. And they require planners to engage with stakeholders while making their plans—not after the fact.

Novo Nordisk describes its strategy framework for sustainability in three tiers (Figure 9.5).[16]

1. The corporate governance structure, which "defines our commitments" (described above under "leadership")
2. Stakeholder engagement, which "enables us to stay attuned to emerging issues and concerns"
3. Target setting and systematic follow-up procedures, which "help ensure continuous improvement and exchange of better practices in the organization"

Figure 9.5 From Strategic Objectives to Business Goals

In the areas of bioethics, environment, health and safety, and social responsibility, the strategic objectives are built into the annual balanced scorecard targets for relevant units. At production sites, for example, targets for reduction of water and energy use reflect the strategic objective to improve ecoproductivity. The people strategy, in turn, and its specific targets, applies to all organizational units.

Source: Novo Nordisk

In order to attune its strategies to stakeholder interests and sustainability objectives, Novo squarely tackles "strategic dilemmas." In 2002, these included:

- How to ensure diligent observance of risk management while nurturing a spirit of innovation and the pursuit of opportunities

- How to improve access to diabetes care by making profits more affordable in developing countries while sustaining a profitable business

- How to respect cultural beliefs and positions on questions like stem cell research while maintaining a competitive edge in the quest to defeat diabetes

- How to justify to shareholders that investing in nonmaterial assets such as environmental management is good business and preserves share prices

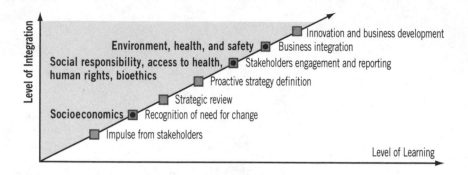

Figure 9.6 Novo Nordisk Learning Curve

The Novo Nordisk learning curve reflects the process of addressing issues, beginning with the initial impulse from stakeholders to framing our response and, as we learn, to fully integrating this response into business processes. For example, environment and health and safety issues are well integrated in the business, whereas assessing the socioeconomic impacts of our activities as part of decision making is an emerging issue with which we are still coming to grips. For each key issue, we have identified indicators that will help provide reliable and quantifiable data upon which stakeholders can base their assessment.

Source: Novo Nordisk

Lise Kingo describes the Novo Nordisk learning curve (Figure 9.6) as a formal process for moving issues from leading-edge to mainstream company practice. Kingo's 27-person stakeholder relations group incubates and manages an area until it becomes fully embedded in business processes across the company, at which point it lets go and moves on to newer topics.

> The stakeholder group is like a greenhouse. We spot new trends and figure out which will be more important for Novo Nordisk going forward; we spotted human rights five years ago.
>
> Through our engagements with stakeholders, politicians, or opinion leaders, we try to stay attuned to the emerging issues. When we sense that something is coming up that may affect our company's long-term business interests, we commission an external review to assess the extent to which it involves us and the state of our compliance. This usually takes a year. Out of this process we determined that we needed to do better on human rights and diversity, as well as access to health care. So we launched 2 projects, then a proactive strategy and a toolbox. Next we started to do stakeholder engagement and integrated

these initiatives into the company. Equal opportunities and access are still in stakeholder relations since they are still incubating, not yet fully in the line. Environment, health & safety on the other hand are more mature, and now managed mainly in the line.

Novo sets both corporate and individual targets that balance social, environmental, and economic goals. These goals, effectively the company's management framework, are built into corporate and business unit balanced scorecards, with measurable targets across a wide variety of domains. Examples of targets that the company set and achieved (or, for long-term targets, was on track to achieve) in 2002:

- Vice presidents to establish plans with targets for addressing equal opportunities issues

- 90 percent of suppliers evaluated on environment and social performance

- To develop a sustainable business model for helping people in poor countries gain access to diabetes care

- 80 percent of all employees to meet and dialogue with patients

- 90 percent of all managers with direct reports to establish one business goal on how they will develop their people

- By 2005, to increase annual ecoproductivity of water by 5 percent and of energy by 4 percent

- To contribute to the total removal of animal tests for biological product control by 2004

One example of Novo's approach is its strategy for sustainable diabetes care in developing countries. The business opportunity is significant, but so are the challenges. In China alone, where some 30 to 40 million people are estimated to have type 2 diabetes, the diagnosis rate is 10 to 15 percent, compared with 50 percent in Europe. This is an obstacle to the company's own market growth but also an obstacle to treatment for patients. Rather than simplistically peddle drugs, the company has adopted a holistic strategy in countries from China to Costa Rica. The goal is to create infrastructures capable of competently delivering diagnosis, care, medicine, and equipment. It has decided to knock down the key barrier—widespread ignorance regarding diabetes among sufferers and caregivers. Novo fosters national plans, strategies, and programs of awareness and education for patients and health professionals. These in turn require partnerships with local champions and seeding the political will of governments.

Novo framed the challenge as a dilemma. Insulin, the main drug for treating diabetes, is off-patent and cheap enough to price for the poor. But the company also has the world's best pipeline of new, advanced medications for the diabetes epidemic. The costs of R&D and production make these drugs affordable only in rich countries. Novo's LEAD initiative and World Diabetes Foundation will help raise diagnosis rates and get insulin to patients quickly (at little direct return to Novo), while paving the way toward a future in which some patients gain the means to seek more advanced treatments.

This is a classic alignment of doing well by doing good at the highest levels of business strategy. These initiatives place Novo at the center of future diabetes programs in the world's largest emerging markets. They illustrate how a firm does work—like patient education, that in rich countries would be paid and performed by government—leading to improved outcomes for a broad collection of stakeholders from patients (customers) to physicians (partners), communities, employees, governments, and shareholders.

Corporate Culture

If stakeholder/sustainability objectives are to be met, they must be lived every day in the organization—be embedded in its DNA. As Lise Kingo says, "Thousands of employees at Novo Nordisk have some sort of sustainability work, providing health and safety programs, access to diabetes care, and so on." Every employee must be aware, attuned, and motivated. This in turn requires consistent internal messages, exemplary programs, effective performance and compensation management, targeted education and training, and the use of technology to enable the entire system.

The balanced scorecard and annual sustainability report are the

Outcomes	Strategies
Values and code of conduct guide employee behavior.	Embed new integrity metrics in scorecards and performance management.
	Use reporting cycle to drive learning and improvement.
Plans, programs, processes, and daily interactions embed new integrity.	Promote purpose, values, business case, and game plan internally.
Improvement on new integrity outcomes and metrics is continuous.	Include education, training, and career development.
	Use new integrity knowledge management systems.
	Develop information and communications technology, tools, and infrastructures.

Figure 9.7 Corporate Culture

foundation of Novo's corporate culture programs (Figure 9.7). Using these tools, Novo communicates its strategies and programs, benchmarks its successes and failures, and structures performance and compensation management activities. Kingo's personal performance targets are identical to the enterprise-wide indicators listed in its sustainability report. They include tangible measures of living the company's values, access to health care in developing countries, employee safety and development, use of animals, eco-efficiency, and company financial results.

If your values are genuine, your employees will know. And if they are not, they will eventually figure it out. Novo describes the centrality of its employee programs to its entire strategy:

> More than any other stakeholder group, our employees are the essence of Novo Nordisk. We therefore consider it essential to monitor how Novo Nordisk employees worldwide think about the company, their job, and their opportunities to develop their skills and competencies.[17]

The company internally promotes and celebrates its many stakeholder/sustainability initiatives. In Novo's 2001 employee survey, 85 percent agreed that social and environmental performance are important to the company's future. The survey gave the company subpar grades on employee development metrics such as the presence of personal development plans, ability to stay up to date on work-related issues, and future resource requirement planning. As you might expect, Novo responded with an aggressive, metrics-driven, employee and career development program.

Novo organizes its programs for employees in a "people strategy" with five focus areas: winning culture, customer relations, attraction and development of the best people, developing people, and equal opportunities. Novo tries to make strategies for its employees and other stakeholders mutually reinforcing.

- Employees gain meaning, motivation, and ideas when they connect with the end users of their products. Meanwhile, research on the psychosocial aspects of living with diabetes shows that relationships are as central to successful care as products and services; providers who learn from this insight can gain a competitive advantage. Novo asked all its employees to meet with people with diabetes or other health care needs that it serves. In 2002, 80 percent had patient dialogues. Said a Novo regulatory affairs executive in India, "[The discussion] was very thought provoking. It made me feel that I should start contributing by whatever means possible."

- The company has a series of workplace equal opportunities programs based on the UN Universal Declaration of Human Rights. Novo decided in 2001 that in the age of globalization and talent wars, it needs access to an increasingly diverse labor force, "recognizing diversity as an opportunity rather than a problem." The company has its work cut out. In Denmark in 2002, where the vast majority of its employees live, only 5.9 percent were immigrants or descendants of immigrants from developing countries—below the modest national ratio of 7.6 percent. Of 198 top executives (vice presidents, senior scientists, and above) only 20 percent were women. The company is tackling this challenge with its usual array of actions—staff assignments, formal objectives and metrics, and a variety of proactive programs.

We've already mentioned some of Novo's tracking and reporting mechanisms—group and individual targets built into the balanced scorecard, and externally audited sustainability reports. Novo has another unique mechanism called "facilitations": arm's-length internal audits that review each dimension of the business on a four-year recurring cycle. The facilitation function resides with the Novo Group, a holding company that controls Novo Nordisk and several other firms. Facilitators interview employees on how they perceive the quality of their management and how it reflects the company's fundamental values and approach to business. Facilitators write up recommendations to management and follow up on the action points; in 2002, 95 percent of action points were fulfilled.

Organizations that wish to make their commitments stick invest to educate and train their employees. Novo has a big training program that provides the knowledge to identify bottom-up opportunities to reduce costs through environmental and materials management.

Other companies have embraced large-scale training on ethics and values, often under the rubric of "compliance." Kate Kozlowski, director of business ethics and compliance at Ford Motor Company, says that for a company such as hers, legal and ethical issues crop up everywhere. "Thousands of people work on compliance across the company, whether in building cars, providing credit and financing, car rentals, parts, services, and warranties. It's part of doing business. There's a compliance price tag in every part of the company." The only way to ensure predictable and consistent standards in a 300,000-person company like Ford is to provide a lot of training. "And now, it's not just compliance," says Kozlowski. "There's more pressure for training on ethics."

Ford sources online ethics and compliance training from a company called LRN. Many of the modules are off the shelf; others, which Ford developed with LRN, will then be sold to other car companies. Much of LRN's training uses the "dilemma" as a teaching construct: acting out the legal and ethical issues of making a tough decision. Kozlowski says, "We use online training to create awareness, but for the next level we use face to face education—for example, teaching senior managers the code of conduct, dealing with issues of globalization, or when we encounter a tough issue like Sarbanes-Oxley compliance. Sometimes the compliance and ethics group does the training; other times it's human resources."

Brand and Reputation

Marketing and business integrity have not always been comfortable bedfellows. Often enough, marketers have seen being "good" as an issue of message rather than substance or have sought to "leverage" philanthropy or limited stakeholder value while downplaying painful truths. As they say, "Let's put some lipstick on this pig."

The Marlboro Man is an apt symbol of this problem: he was the advertising personification of clean living and rugged American values. But he was a lie. David Millar, Jr., the original Marlboro Man, died of emphysema in 1987. After David McLean, another Marlboro Man, died of lung cancer, his widow sued the company for damages. Later on, Marlboro Man Wayne McLaren testified in favor of antismoking legislation before he died of lung cancer. In 2003 Marlboro's parent company, in a torrent of sparkly waterfall advertisements, changed its name from the tobacco-stained Philip Morris to the wholesome-sounding Altria Group. Now the company openly admits that its product kills customers and campaigns against smoking. Meanwhile it continues to advertise where it can legally do so while expanding into emerging economies. This is an extreme case. Let's face it, nobody in the business of cigarette manufacturing can be a truly open enterprise,

Outcomes	Strategies
Improved and sustained brand value	Review brand messages and marketing programs.
Growth and market share	Engage financial sector and key stake holders in change dialogue.
Customer loyalty	Strengthen transparency communications to all stakeholders.
Low cost of capital	Describe strengths, admit weaknesses, publish improvement benchmarks.
	Review crisis management programs.
	Monitor stakeholder issues.

Figure 9.8 Brand and Reputation

because the product causes harm. Marlboro's stakeholder-friendly message is impossible to reconcile with its behavior as a pusher of life-threatening substances that also add costs to overburdened health care systems around the world.

Cynicism regarding the branding of "doing good" is common, and not just among activist critics of "greenwashing" (i.e., whitewashing with an ecotint). The trade journal *Sporting Goods Business* wondered recently whether "cause marketing" makes any difference to the bottom line. An article discussed a Danskin cost-benefit calculation of contributions to the Susan B. Koman breast cancer foundation. "Danskin prefers this grassroots approach over extensive ad campaigns or celebrity/athlete sponsorships. 'We integrate event and cause marketing, and our efforts mean a lot to our customers, many of whom make buying decisions based on our partnership,' says Joyce Darkey, Danskin's SVP of marketing."[18]

Indeed, breast cancer is a coveted cause: it afflicts affluent target customer segments, the ethical dilemmas are few, and it is associated with wholesome sports events, like Run for the Cure, that use sponsors' products. Also, participation can be more cost-effective than organizing a marketing campaign for a company's own products (which requires hard work with ad agencies): pay the sponsor fee, send some volunteers, and everyone wins. The business case is easy and compelling, while the project matches the mandate and skills of the marketing department.

Such causes, while worthy of support, present few of the dilemmas or organizational demands of which Novo Nordisk speaks. Or that Nike, a fellow firm to Danskin in the sporting apparel business, took on when it decided to stick its neck out and respond to the challenges of working conditions in the industry supply chain. Companies like these have made deeper choices, as we have discussed. They have taken on the task of rethinking their entire mode of operations in line with a transparent stakeholder/sustainability agenda. What they increasingly conclude is that their brand message must convey the malleability and universalism of such engagement, warts and all (Figure 9.8). They are open and candid about the dilemmas they face, and describe their failings and limitations honestly. When a crisis happens, they respond quickly and take responsibility for their actions. So when you go to the Web site of Shell, Ford, and some other risk-accepting engaged corporations, you will find discussion forums that include comments from their harshest critics.

How should marketers rethink their role? Paul Taaffe, chairman and CEO of marketing consultant Hill & Knowlton, says that spin is dead, but its legacy means that the marketing function itself has a credibility problem. "Marketers seem to have figured out that transparency is the universal enabler of trust. But, ironically, they have been labeled as the most deceitful in the past, the part of the organization that doesn't need to tell the truth. This is thanks to situations like Nestlé and tobacco. There are still people in public relations who are spinners, but this is not sustainable. It hurts credibility over the long haul."

Taaffe argues that the inevitable but unpredictable crisis is the litmus test of a company's ability to respond. "The costs of a crisis increase substantially if you haven't identified where it will come from and how you will respond to it in advance. For example, after the Brent Spar incident with Greenpeace in the North Sea, Shell had trouble recruiting university graduates. And after a crisis, there is often a court case; it is less painful and costly when the company has responded quickly, behaved with integrity, and managed the issue. Shareholder, NGO, media activism mean that every company will have more crises every year, so this moves from being exceptional to being a normal part of business." The problem is, most companies don't train themselves for crisis through everyday transparent behavior, nor do they prepare in advance by defining crisis management processes and assignments.

Taaffe's pessimism notwithstanding, the "transparency virus" is spreading. Even some not particularly "sustainability" focused companies have learned the value of adding open dialogue to their brand messages. As we described in Chapter 6, computer companies Dell and Apple host a wide variety of customer conversations on their own Web sites. In some of these conversations visitors even defend a competitive product.

From a marketing perspective, the message is clear: You're going to be naked, so you'd better be buff.

Environmental Engagement

You can't have a successful company in a failed world. Conversely, you can't succeed if the world won't let you. Businesses have an economic interest in the well-being and support of both their sociopolitical and natural environments (Figure 9.9).

Most observers agree on the sociopolitical challenges, even if they disagree on the risks to the natural environment. Businesses do well when trust and social capital are high; where people obey the law voluntarily, not by compulsion; where corruption is minimal or absent; where citizens are educated and healthy and can make a decent living; and where life is safe and peaceful, not filled with fear. Most agree that these conditions are wanting in too many places.

Novo gets involved in reshaping the sociopolitical environment. The company sees "political indifference, especially among young people, as a huge challenge to democracy." Its Bridging Europe initiative with the World Economic Forum aims to involve young people in shaping a sustainable Europe through multistakeholder engagement. Activities include an interactive Web site involving 1,000 young Europeans from 33 countries, working papers, and international forums.

The vice president of corporate communications, John Iwata, reels off IBM's approaches, as a global corporation, to fostering supportive external environments. The company's national operations around the world are run as local businesses, with local executive teams, hiring,

Outcomes	Strategies
Peace, order, and good governance of external operating environments	Support good government, antibribery. Obey local laws.
License to operate	Have a local presence, local people, local partnerships. Support social diversity.
Preservation of global ecosystems	Combat global warming and threats to biodiversity. Identify and address stakeholder interests.

Figure 9.9 Environmental Engagement

and promotion. IBM's diversity programs are long standing and deeply rooted. The firm manages environmental matters, philanthropy, and volunteerism with as much discipline as other parts of its business.

None of this is simple. Local ownership and management don't always protect McDonald's restaurants from violent protests, or Coca-Cola from politically motivated competition. Such conflicts reinforce Novo's case for the business value of moving tolerance, trust, and democracy to an even higher level on a global scale.

Corruption is a core sociopolitical challenge, pervasive in many countries. Some firms, like IBM, Celestica, and Shell, will walk away from deals if they must bribe to get them. For a cash-rich company with nine- and ten-figure profits, this is a viable—even a competitive—strategy. For others that live closer to the line of survival, such choices can be difficult, even life threatening. However all too many companies with the economic wherewithal continue to fail on this important issue, as Transparency International points out. Most agree in principle on what is the right thing to do, even when they fail to practice it.

There is less agreement regarding the natural environment. Many argue that the risks of global warming and other threatened catastrophes are immaterial or that they pale against advancing technology and continual improvements in the standard of living. Though things may not be quite "good enough," they continue to get better, and we can trust in progress to prevent the risks from turning to disaster. Bjørn Lomborg, a young Danish political scientist, statistician and author of *The Skeptical Environmentalist*, is often cited for this viewpoint:

> Global warming, though its size and future projections are rather unrealistically pessimistic, is almost certainly taking place, but the typical cure of early and radical fossil fuel cutbacks is way worse than the original affliction, and moreover its total impact will not pose a devastating problem for our future. Nor will we lose 25–50 percent of all species in our lifetime—in fact we are losing probably 0.7 percent. Acid rain does not kill the forests, and the air and water around us are becoming less and less polluted.[19]

Many scientists see the world differently. The editor of *Scientific American* commented that Lomborg's book is "often marred by an incomplete use of the data or a misunderstanding of the underlying science. Even where his statistical analyses are valid, his interpretations are frequently off the mark—literally not seeing the state of the forests for the number of the trees, for example. And it is hard not to be struck by Lomborg's presumption that he has seen into the heart of the science more faithfully than have investigators who have devoted their lives to it; it is equally curious that he finds the same contrarian good news lurking in *every* diverse area of environmental science."[20]

Executives of oil companies like BP, Shell, and Suncor, for whom life would be simpler if they could agree with the likes of Lomborg, still say that global warming and the loss of biodiversity threaten the sustainability of their businesses. Novo Nordisk's view is:

> A company's ability to effectively manage environmental risk is under the lens of government authorities and environmental watchdog groups, as well as investors and the general public. We are well aware of the environmental risks associated with our operations and are proactive in assessing those risks and taking action to address them.[21]

Novo follows the precautionary principle in assessing environmental risks. A product of the 1992 Rio de Janeiro summit, the principle says that in the face of threats of serious or irreversible damage, lack of full scientific certainty should not be used as a reason to postpone cost-effective measures to prevent environmental degradation. Novo is directly affected by another environmental threat: loss of biodiversity. Pharmaceutical innovations continue to be mined from the world's shrinking store of natural life forms.

Novo explains its environmental methodology:

> In consultation with a range of stakeholders, we carefully consider the risks that may arise from current operations as well as from past and future actions. Insufficient risk management can damage a company's reputation and in worst cases its license to operate, while superior risk management opens the door to new business opportunities.[22]

One Novo environmental initiative addresses threats to animal and plant species that arise from disposal of one of its product lines, estrogenic hormones. A leading scientific hypothesis blames growing increases in reproductive disorders among males of various species around the world on estrogen-based female sex hormones in the environment. These hormones come from the urine of pregnant women, women using contraceptives or hormone therapy, and from the direct disposal of estrogen-like chemicals. Novo says that it disposes of estrogen production waste safely, so the main environmental impacts arise from patient use. The company has begun to tackle these issues. It has published—and shared with relevant authorities and interested stakeholders—the results of one study that showed a significant impact on juvenile male fish, even at low concentrations.

Stakeholder Engagement

Where engagement with stakeholders is viewed as important, it receives management focus, planning, and discipline (Figure 9.10)

Novo's business web analysis includes the socioeconomic impacts of its production and consumption activities. The company charts a "distribution of created wealth" that maps where cash comes from (100 percent from customers, i.e., people with health care needs and health care providers) and where it ends up (in 2002, 55 percent to suppliers, 34 percent to employees, 6 percent to investors and lenders, and 9 percent to the public sector via taxes, with 4 percent taken from cash reserves for future growth). The way Novo frames this analysis

Outcomes	Strategies
B-web and a-web engagement and competitive performance	Model, measure, and manage value exchanges and relationship development.
Results-effective prioritization of stakeholder programs and initiatives	Engage in direct, personal dialogue supplemented by reporting and technology.
	Seek optimal outcomes for all stakeholders.
Best-in-class employees and partners	Apply corporate values in stakeholder engagement processes.
	Enhance partnering capabilities.

Figure 9.10 Stakeholder Engagement

illuminates the depth of its stakeholder thinking. It refers to suppliers as "external economic stakeholders" and employee income as "a measure of the market value of people's productive capabilities."

Impressive too is the extent to which Novo depends on the allotment of corporate personnel to ensure the personal touch:

- Meetings with neighbors to reduce environmental impacts at production sites

- Evaluating suppliers' social and environmental performance

- Personal meetings between employees and patients

- Partnerships with NGOs on animal welfare

- Memberships of business organizations to promote sustainable development

- Raising public debate on stem cell research and the need for revised legislation

- Putting diabetes on the agenda of the European Parliament

- Building national health care capacity with local authorities in developing countries

- Funding international research partnerships

- Supporting educational programs for engineers from ethnic minority backgrounds

- Public awareness and fund-raising activities on World Diabetes Day

- Timely and proactive media relations on suspension of clinical trials

Products and Services

Transforming your core offerings to adapt to a stakeholder/sustainability agenda can be daunting (Figure 9.11). Tobacco companies are in the tobacco business whether they like it or not. They can sell out and use the money to try something else, but such action does not solve the fundamental problem. Other industries, like health care, are intrinsically "good." So when a Novo invents new technologies (e.g., to simplify patient self-administration of insulin injections) or broadens out to research and tackle the psychological and social aspects of the disease (as it has recently done), cynics can argue that such actions are calculated business innovations sugarcoated with virtue.

Many industries are somewhere in between; they offer some degrees of freedom to firms that see competitive advantage in sustainable products and services.

- Ikea responded to critics and adopted new principles for furniture materials and design; these resulted in new product ideas and a stronger brand.

- Whole Foods Market is a darling of Wall Street, distinguished in the grocery business by being "the world's largest retailer of natural and organic foods . . . highly selective about what we sell, dedicated to stringent Quality Goals, and committed to sustainable agriculture."

- Hewlett-Packard reinforces its image as a caring, ethical company when it rewards consumers who recycle inkjet packaging (though we wonder about the future of this materials-intensive product).

Operations

Operational matters—how the firm does what it does—arise both inside and outside the firm (Figure 9.12). This is the practical implementation of everything we've been talking about, be it sharing

Outcomes	Strategies
Competitive advantage	Revisit offerings in light of stakeholder interests, economic/social/environmental criteria.
Sustained value innovation	
	Use competitive differentiators.
Maximized economic, social, environmental benefits	Identify and resolve trade-offs. Multiphase, parallel rollout.

Figure 9.11 Products and Services

information with employees, customers, shareholders, and other stakeholders or realizing social and environmental policies and goals in
everyday business processes and practices.

Every firm will have its priorities. One that many are now tackling
is eco-efficiency, the alignment of quality and cost-effective processes
and procedures with good environmental practices. Another is transparency itself, full and proper disclosure to employees, consumers, regulators, shareholders, and community representatives.

Nestlé, Nike, Home Depot, and De Beers illustrate how firms face
risks to reputation and performance from issues that arise outside
their own firm's boundaries. In a world of business webs, stakeholders
increasingly hold firms accountable for the actions of their suppliers
and other business partners. In addition, business webs are easier to
build, more efficient and manageable, when information sharing, trust,
and social capital are high.

Novo Nordisk seeks alignment between these two factors—social
responsibility and trust-based partnership—in the way that it now
works with its business web. The company believes that setting high
standards of the environmental management and human (i.e.,
employee) rights, communicating these standards to suppliers through

Outcomes	Strategies
Industrywide responsible performance	Manage against new classes of risk (integrity, stakeholder, social,
No free riders	environmental).
	Integrate social and environmental
Risk reduction, license to operate	factors in quality, cost and process management.
Lower transaction costs	Cultivate trust and information sharing in business web.
Process and eco-efficiencies	Support supplier assessment, education, and audits.
Quality	Raise voluntary industry standards, seek regulation where necessary or mature.
Appropriate and efficient regulation	

Figure 9.12 Operations

dialogue, and monitoring compliance, ultimately increases the trust that contributes to operational efficiency.

With several years' experience in managing supply chain standards on environmental issues, Novo launched its human rights program with a series of supplier workshops in Europe, Mexico, India, and Japan. The objective was to consult key suppliers and external experts on how to assess social performance in the supply chain. The company also trained 100 employees, mainly in purchasing, on the issues and dilemmas of social responsibility. Novo says this training effort, which had strong management support, greatly fueled the success of the overall program.

In its 2002 launch year the program achieved several targets.

- Ninety percent of key raw materials suppliers and a range of key service and engineering suppliers completed an environmental and social questionnaire—300 in total.

- The vast majority of suppliers responded "very positively" to the initiative and delivered "satisfactory" information on environmental management and their positions on labor and human rights.

- All new supplier contracts include a clause stating mutual commitment to the UN Universal Declaration of Human Rights, the International Labor Organization conventions, and the International Chamber of Commerce's Business Charter for Sustainable Development. Suppliers agree to "promptly report inconsistencies with these principles to Novo Nordisk."

The company declares that it aims to "eliminate the risk" of having suppliers "that do not live up to basic human rights." It formed a cross-functional committee supported by external experts mandated to take action on violators if need be.

In 2003, Novo did an overall assessment of results and extended the program to other areas, including China, South Africa, and Brazil. Equally important from a program design perspective, the company began a move beyond supplier self-assessment to incorporate supplier environmental and social metrics into its formal audit systems.

Information and Communications Technology

As we described at the start of this book, information technology (Figure 9.13) may well be the most powerful single force for transparency in our time. Firms routinely use IT to communicate their agendas, notably by publishing their sustainability reports on the Web. Yet rarely do they fully capitalize on the power of IT to drive, enable, enhance—and embed—their stakeholder/sustainability agenda in the everyday life of the firm and its stakeholder interactions.

Most companies already use technology in all sorts of ways to enhance transparency and meet the needs and desires of stakeholders. And they also have many systems in place which, with minor changes, could meet such needs even better. Firms need to develop consistent messages and engagement models for their portfolio of what we call "stakeholder relationship management" applications. These encompass today's customer- and employee-relationship management tools, emerging partner relationship management tools, and future tools for managing relationships with shareholders and communities. Furthermore, a financial business case can be made for various new applications that, for example, use information to make business processes more "eco-efficient" or wrap information value around existing products and services.

Outcomes	Strategies
More efficient and effective delivery of stakeholder/sustainability strategies and objectives	Define and resource stakeholder/sustainability ICT vision, objectives, plans, and metrics
Early warnings of risks and threats to firm or stakeholders	Embed stakeholder/sustainability requirements in existing ICT services
Easy, usable stakeholder access to information	Create new user-friendly applications to advance specific stakeholder/sustainability strategies
Improved engagement, collaboration, process management with stakeholders	Leverage new and emerging technologies

Figure 9.13 Information and Communications Technology

Every transparency and stakeholder mandate should include an IT mandate. And every IT function should be mandated to rethink its applications solutions to embrace the firm's new integrity strategy. For example, today some companies have "partner relationship management" software that tracks the financial, delivery, and product performance metrics of suppliers. IT managers should think about how to enhance such applications to also provide reporting on environmental, working conditions, and other stakeholder/ sustainability metrics. In the absence of such initiatives, opportunities will be missed, costs will be higher, and some risks will not be mitigated.

One not so small example: A key issue in this entire area is compliance. How does a company ensure that its 150,000 employees on all continents "do the right thing" in accordance with its values and policies, stakeholder commitments, and the law? Kate Kozlowski, the lawyer responsible for compliance programs across Ford, describes how the company uses its employee portal to enhance engagement and support around the world:

Fordlaw is our legal access Web site. Everything is online. Anyone who needs to find a trademark lawyer or agreement can find it. If someone has a legal question or issue, they can access Fordlaw and search for legal forms, memoranda, or frequently asked questions; find a lawyer; send feedback; or seek advice on compliance or an ethical issue. We get 15,000 intranet hits a week and thirty to fifty email messages each day. We tried for years to increase awareness about compliance. This finally did it. And we also get advice to people quickly when they need it.

A second piece is Lawpac, our law and policy awareness center. It has over 100 training modules—on ethics, export rules, safety and so on, translated into several languages. There are 20-minute tutorials, handbooks, names of expert contacts in the legal department, and so on.

Thanks to the intranet, employees feel a much greater sense of ownership in the company. Before, senior managers got a daily news clip sheet, physically in paper form. It only went to senior managers, and they never passed it on to their staff. Now, on the intranet, everyone checks the clip sheet—unedited news about Ford, good and bad. Everyone, whether a clerk or a vice president, finds out. We all know if the company lost a lawsuit in California. We get thousands and thousands of hits on the clip sheet every morning.

A systematic strategy for IT-enabled transparency, stakeholder engagement, and sustainability means a variety of possible investments. You can't do them all at once, so prioritize them and roll them out over time.

- Information access tools will provide the right information to the right people at the right time, in accessible formats. It may be as simple as an annual report downloadable from an enterprise portal or a Web site. Or, it may be a daily summary, as we've suggested above, of corporate risks across the spectrum of issues—supplemented by real-time alerts when needed. Such daily summaries might depend on "rolling up" outputs from a variety of incompatible applications across the enterprise. Here advanced technologies like Web services may deliver key information to business analytics and reporting tools.

- Event monitoring technologies typically provide real-time information about happenings in the physical world. They can warn about the occurrence or impending occurrence of workplace or environmental disasters. Such technologies are becoming ever smaller, faster, cheaper, and sophisticated.

- Process-enabling applications include customer relationship management, supply-chain management, and the like. Firms can improve stakeholder trust, reduce inefficiencies, or enhance effectiveness through the use of timely and accurate information in their business processes. These in turn lead to reduced transaction costs, stakeholder loyalty, and faster/better/cheaper outputs. Many process tools are specific to an industry or activity. For example, trucking fleets use computerized maps to help drivers choose efficient routes. Now, a new generation of such maps also provides information about traffic jams and road hazards and how to find preferred gas stations. Such applications are truly eco-efficient: they save money and reduce consumption of carbon fuels.

If all that we've described in this chapter seems complicated . . . well, it certainly is not simple. And of course, we've barely covered the highlights. Like anything that is worth doing, transparency and the new integrity require a lot of disciplined work.

CHAPTER 10

BREACHING THE CRISIS OF LEADERSHIP

The new transparency has revealed a crisis of leadership in business today.

Transparency demands new thinking about the nature of the corporation, its relationship with other institutions and people, and even its role in society. When a change of this magnitude occurs, vested interests fight it. Niccolò Machiavelli wrote, "There is nothing more difficult to execute, nor more dubious of success, nor more dangerous to administer, than to introduce a new order of things; for he who introduces it has all those who profit from the old order as his enemies, and he has only lukewarm allies in all those who might profit from the new." Today, those vested in the past, from CEOs to corporate lawyers to PR departments, are resisting. Many firms claim to be open and have strong ethical values, but few truly operate with candor and integrity.

Some leadership initiatives already stand out. In 2002, investor Warren Buffett called on firms to expense stock options and make their real costs visible to investors. Within a year, more than 100 companies had announced plans to do so. Buffett's challenge made a difference.

Buffett also encouraged companies to stop "giving guidance," instead to take a page from Dragnet and give investors "the facts, ma'am, just the facts." Corporate leaders like U.K.-based Co-operative Bank pioneered a warts-and-all approach to reporting social and environmental performance. A growing list of firms in various sectors is finding the leadership capacity to "do the right thing" every day.

But others struggle to find leadership for change. Rather than actively harness the power of the new business integrity, they wait for transparency to be forced on them. Rather than address the need for integrity in everything they do, they spin their worthiness and good deeds. Many managers treat transparency as minimal compliance with the law. They see business integrity and stakeholder engagement as burdensome costs. They may think of corporate responsibility as someone else's job, perhaps the philanthropy department. Many are skeptical, even cynical about the claims, touchy-feely language, and perceived anticorporate motives of those who argue for openness and sustainability. Executives are so busy fighting fires in a brutal business environment that they can barely find the time, let alone the will, resources, knowledge, and skills to lead a transition to a new model of the firm. With the shakeups in accounting, consulting, and banking, traditional advisers seem ill-equipped to help.

How will your company muster the capacity to lead this transformation? What are the leadership opportunities for each of us in each of our many stakeholder roles? Who will lead? Who will open the door?

THE CEO: KEEPER OF THE KEY

For the last decade there has been considerable discussion regarding the genesis and nature of organizational leadership. Peter Senge, who coined the concept of organizational learning, argued that the person at the top, regardless of IQ, can't learn for the organization as a whole.[1] The Lee Iacocca–type leader who creates a vision and sells it down into the organization is being replaced by the model of the leader who draws on the collective brainpower of employees and other stakeholders and motivates them to collaborate for success.

There is a corollary to this new model: In the hundreds of firms we've studied, leadership can start anywhere—marketing directors, IT executives, public affairs managers, CFOs, business unit leaders, plant supervisors, and even corporate lawyers.

However, though change may begin anywhere in the firm, it must be driven from the top.

The CEO defines core values, norms, and culture. No matter how inspired, well meaning, or determined others may be, no one else can change the firm's fundamentals. A bank teller may develop an important new process; a salesperson may devise a more open approach to working with customers; an engineer may develop a new product that is more eco-efficient; a regional manager may develop a strategic service that transforms a company's offerings. But the CEO sets the corporate character. Some firms are fortunate to have been founded by CEOs who established a culture of integrity from the start. The Johnson & Johnson Credo came from the company's CEO and sole shareholder. Over the years that value system was propagated by successive leaders, chosen partly for their values. Recently retired J&J CEO Ralph Larsen was said to have never made a speech where he didn't talk about corporate values. "We're not perfect," he would say. "We're just trying to do the right thing." Similarly, the HP Way originated with Bill Hewlett and Dave Packard. The corporate character of these firms is rooted in the resilience and depth of these values in their culture.

CEOs lead by example whether they intend to or not. They determine the quality of conversations within a firm—combative or collaborative? Judgmental or open? Are controversial matters taboo? Do all interested parties participate in discussions of matters that concern them, or do secret cabals make decisions behind closed doors? When someone raises a new idea, is the reaction to explore it or to debunk and defeat it? Do people exaggerate or are they truthful and frank? Do managers keep their cards close to their chests or do they speak with candor? Do people hoard knowledge or share it? Is the workplace infested with corporate politics or enriched with trust? In a touchy situation involving values do managers ask "What is the right thing to do?" or "How do we get out of this mess?"

It all starts with the CEO.

A World of Dilemmas

CEOs face a complex challenge. Though transparency and related values drive business success, we live in a complex world filled with competing interests. Leaders constantly face dilemmas and hard choices. Doing the right thing can entail tough trade-offs. The 2001 Novo Nordisk report on its environmental and social performance is aptly titled *Dealing with Dilemmas*. The report states: "We do not pretend to have all the answers. Rather we believe in the value of openly and honestly presenting the facts as well as the issues that confront us. Indeed there is rarely an easy answer. . . . We often find ourselves on the horns of a dilemma. Our activities are in areas where values and ethics are put to the test on a daily basis."

With striking candor the report elaborates dilemmas in the pharmaceutical business and the company's struggles to resolve them.

- How do we improve access to health care and make our products affordable and yet continue to operate a profitable business?

- How can we continue to increase production and our use of resources and yet contribute to sustainable development?

- How do we protect our intellectual property rights and yet help share knowledge that can save lives and generate income for others?

- How do we stimulate diversity and equal opportunities and yet maintain a culture of shared values?

- How can we pay due respect to animal welfare and yet continue to use animals for testing in order to meet the safety requirements for pharmaceutical products?

- How can we use biotechnology to create significant advances for humankind and yet respect the public's anxieties about genetic engineering?

- How do we do business consistently in an unjust, unequal world and yet respect the diversity within that world?

Resolving Dilemmas

CEOs set the tone and the agenda. But most today are still locked into the old view. Even when the spirit is willing to provide effective leadership for the new thinking, there are still many dilemmas and tough choices. We shall now take a look at some of those dilemmas.

With candor comes vulnerability

Procter & Gamble CEO Alan Lafley says, "I want P&G to be the most transparent company in the world, so I have to set the example by being candid in my dealings with all stakeholders." But openness requires a willingness to be vulnerable—a trait that is not high on the personality profile of most CEOs. When stakeholders lack transparency sophistication, opening the kimono, especially when you're not superbly buff, presents risks.

When Lafley became CEO in 2000, the company was not performing well. Between January 2000, when the stock peaked at $116, and March 7, P&G stock fell 52 percent—a loss of $85 billion in market capitalization. On the June 2000 day Lafley was named as the new chief executive, P&G's stock fell another $4. After 15 days on the job, the stock fell another $3.85, as Lafley describes it "an early personal confidence builder!" He remembers, "The business media were not kind. Reporters and commentators had a right to express their views and they exercised that right with enthusiasm." From the *Cincinnati Enquirer*, March 9: "P&G Investor Confidence Shot"; from *Time* magazine, March 20: "Trouble in Brand City. We Love their Products. But in a Tech Crazed Market We Hate Their Stocks"; and from the Dow-Jones wire, April 27: "Analysts Unsure When Tide Will Turn for P&G." For Lafley the lowest point was a September 2000 front-page headline in *Ad Age*: "Does P&G Matter?"

Lafley says he dreaded media and analyst interviews. But he decided that rather than hide, he would "reframe the media encounter." In each discussion he shared at least one of his biggest problems and asked for advice. In early interviews he asked most of the questions, seeking insights on how to overcome dilemmas. Rather than in a P&G office, interviews took place in a retail store or consumer's home. "The goal was to engage the writer in thinking about the company through our eyes," he said. "Sure there are vulnerabilities that come with being open, but candor pays off."

Seagate CEO Bill Watkins says that when dealing with customers, "you've got to openly communicate your problems and even product weaknesses to your customers, and that's not easy." He says, "The normal tendency for most companies is to take data and put a spin on it— 'Let's not let too many people know about that.' Wrong. Let people know you have a problem. Tell your customers the truth. You get great accountability when you are open and you build trust."

He explains that "some customers overreact to bad news. But for most, they develop a closer relationship with you." As for making yourself vulnerable, "I've had very few problems telling people the truth. The problems always happen when I've tried to spin something. It always falls apart on you. Customers will find out about problems so you might as well tell them the truth. You're way more vulnerable if you hide stuff. Spin or concealment is like cheating on your wife. You get caught and you wonder 'what was I thinking?' "

Watkins describes how he had a big problem with one of his customers that could have been swept under the rug. Watkins opened up, explaining to the customer that the problem was actually worse than he thought and then committing to fix it. "The customer believed me and decided to stick it out, because he knows I don't BS him. When we fixed the problem our relationship was strengthened. If I'd tried to hide it I might have gotten away with it but I would have missed the opportunity to strengthen trust and our relationship." Says Watkins, "We strive to epitomize the open enterprise. These days it's hard to be too open."

What do you do if you're in an industry where competitors externalize costs and where acting with integrity could destroy your firm?

A central task of leadership is to define and redefine your organization's frame of reference. What seems a scary threat in one frame becomes a compelling opportunity in another.

Consider Patagonia. Outdoor enthusiasts live the irony that their activities degrade the very forests, lakes, and mountains that they cherish. True, there is a world of difference between dune buggy riders who plow up virgin wilderness and meticulous hikers who never leave behind an ounce of debris. But no matter how careful you are, it's nearly impossible to pass through the backwoods without a trace.

Most makers of outdoor sports equipment and clothing ignore the continuing contribution of their products to environmental pollution and degradation. Yvon Chouinard, founder and major shareholder of privately held Patagonia, chose a different path right from the founding days of the company in the early 1970s. He invented "clean" climbing tools and levied an "earth tax," 1 percent of all sales, for environmental causes, from 1985 on. The company did well in the

1980s, but then expanded too fast and faced an expense and cash crunch in 1991 when sales contracted. Bankers demanded reorganization, and the company laid off 20 percent of its employees, a painful experience for a firm that takes pride in its supportive workplace.

Chouinard responded not by giving up on his principles and making clothes on the cheap but by transparently redoubling them to reframe the company's future at, arguably, even greater risk. In Patagonia's 1991 product catalogue he wrote:

> Last fall we underwent an environmental audit to investigate the impact of the clothing we make. . . . To no one's surprise, the news is bad. Everything we make pollutes. Polyester, because it is made from petroleum, is an obvious villain, but cotton and wool are not any better. To kill the boll weevil, cotton is sprayed with pesticides so poisonous they generally render cotton fields barren; cotton fabric is often treated with formaldehyde. . . . We need to use fewer materials. Period. . . . We are limiting Patagonia's growth. . . . Last fall you had a choice of five ski pants, now you may choose between two. . . . We have never wanted to be the largest outdoor clothing store in the world, only the best.

Three years later, Chouinard led his company into its boldest move ever: it announced that henceforth it would only use organic cotton in its clothing. This entailed several risks, any one of which could have put the company under:

- At the time, the pool of organic cotton farmers was tiny. If demand for its products jumped unexpectedly, the company could be caught unable to serve its customers.

- Organic growing, absent pesticides, is risky and yields only one crop per season.

- Patagonia had to reorganize its outsourced supply chain in new ways, which might not have worked out.

- Organic cotton was 25 percent more costly than conventionally grown cotton, and, though the company absorbed part of the additional cost, it still had to ask consumers to pay more for the natural product.

The industry establishment responded with prophecies of doom, and its own spin. "[Conventionally grown cotton] doesn't use more pesticides than any other commodity," said David Guthrie, manager of cotton agronomy and physiology at the National Cotton Council. "Historically, cotton used chemicals damaging to the environment, but they have long since been removed from the arsenal. . . . Studies have shown that consumers aren't willing to pay more than 10 per cent more for organic cotton. It's limited to a small niche in the upscale market where price is not a consideration."[2]

Chouinard became an advocate for organic cotton across the industry and began to educate his competitors. Several times a year, Patagonia hosted companies like Lands' End, Levi Strauss, L.L. Bean, Eddie Bauer, Gap, Nike, REI, and (Canadian) Mountain Equipment Co-op on organic cotton field trips.

Its typical tour presented a scary enough picture of conventional cotton farming. The land is first sterilized to kill weeds. Young cotton plants are fed with chemical fertilizers and sprayed with insecticides and pesticides. In California alone, says the company, 57 million pounds of pesticides are applied to cotton each year. Five ounces of chemicals go into the cotton for every T-shirt. Harvesting uses hormones and defoliants. Not only does residue leach into the soil and groundwater, some of it goes directly into the human food chain. Pesticide-covered cotton seeds are fed to cows and so ultimately pesticides make their way onto your dinner table in beef, while cottonseed oil goes into snack foods. Meanwhile, at processing plants, employees who sweep excess cotton from the floors routinely lose toenails and suffer rashes from the waist down.[3]

Patagonia initially experienced a drop in cotton clothing sales due to its price hikes, but soon its "niche" of consumers roared back. Thanks to diligent effort, the price of organic cotton came down somewhat, while production systems improved. The company flourished right through the 2001–03 recession. Now, some of the competitors it has trained, including Nike, Norm Thomson Outfitters, REI, and Mountain Equipment Co-op, have begun the switch to organic cotton.

Chouinard has made a significant contribution. But in late 2002, an active semiretired 64 year old, he remained a man with no illusions, even a bit despairing. "There's no such thing as sustainable development. There's no such thing as making sustainable clothing, any of that stuff. We're causing a lot of pollution and a lot of waste. That's just the way it is and we recognize that and that's why we kind of do our penance."[4]

Stakeholder interests may not align with yours. How, for example, can you be open and engage NGOs if they have no interest in your success?

Where stakeholders and the firm share similar interests, engagement and resolution of differences is achievable. But some groups in your stakeholder web may want your company to fail or may make impossible demands—such as that McDonald's stop killing cows or that Shell stop selling oil. Effectively orchestrated engagement can change the values and motivation of all parties.

In 1990 Novo Nordisk began to develop its first proactive environmental strategy—the basis of today's "triple bottom line" thinking. It invited a stakeholder group, including some NGOs from around the world, to a two-day dialogue session. The guests toured the firm's plants and laboratories to see, for example, how animals were used in experimentation and how the company approached thorny issues like genetic engineering.

According to Lise Kingo, both the NGOs and Novo changed their thinking through the process. "We learned not only about their concerns but got important insights about what we could do differently. They learned about what a biotech company is and what dilemmas we confront." Whereas the NGOs may have initially been skeptical or hostile, they internalized the challenges facing Novo. They recommended a communications strategy where Novo would openly discuss its dilemmas.

"The key was being open," she says. "We decided in any interaction with stakeholders that we would be open and honest—explaining the things we were doing well and also where we have problems. If you try and paint a glossy picture you'll fail to engage. By being transparent we initiated a dialogue and gained trust. They learned as well. This is a two-way process."

This is not to suggest that firms should carelessly invite enemies into the corporate tent. Rather it illustrates that openness and engagement are so powerful that they can cause fundamental changes in the behavior of firms and their stakeholders—to the benefit of both.

How do you resolve conflicts between your personal economic interests and those of shareholders and other stakeholders?

When it comes to the central issue of compensation, CEOs face a dilemma. Due to the separation of ownership from control, many have the power to determine or unduly influence their own compensation. They have big leverage over board compensation committees. Shareholder resolutions are expensive to mount and have no binding power. Many boards still view their CEO as indispensable and buy outdated myths about the competitive CEO market. Close to retirement, many CEOs are willing to take some flack to sock away their nest eggs. They can usually find peer data to justify their expectations. And after all, their compensation is a pittance compared with the vast resources they command and critical decisions they make—isn't it?

But today the whole world is watching. Because of transparency, the cutting edge of leadership for CEOs is their own compensation. A CEO's compensation plan is a litmus test of personal and corporate integrity. When earnings are in the tank, employees laid off, and shareholders suffering, CEOs must do the right thing. And greed is not a good example to set, even when the company is doing well. The first step toward fixing executive compensation is to take control away from executives.

CEOs that we interviewed tackled the dilemma by first ensuring that their compensation is determined by an independent board committee, sometimes with help from independent external advisers or the firm's own human resources leadership. They worked with the committee to redefine the rules of executive compensation. These CEOs put honesty, accountability, consideration, and transparency into practice even if it hurt them personally.

Novo Nordisk says the driving principle for CEO compensation is competitiveness with similar international pharmaceutical companies and other major Danish companies. But Novo seems to weight its averages low. In 2002, CEO Lars Rebien Sørensen received remuneration of $740,000 (including a bonus of up to four months' salary) but no stock options (presumably because of the company's 2002 performance problems). This was a 3 percent increase in remuneration over the company's better-performing 2001 year, when he also received a reward of options worth $100,000. The value of all company options he accumulated over his career was $800,000, and his shares were worth $375,000.

CEOs like Sørensen are a minority. Many others still set the wrong example. In April 2003 *The Economist* said, "An analysis by the Investor Responsibility Research Centre of the 2002 packages of 180 [U.S.] chief executives (none of them new recruits) from the 1,500 largest S&P companies finds that the median salary rose by 9%, the median cash bonus by 24% and the median value of awards of restricted stock by almost 20% over 2001 levels. The median number of share options granted rose by 7.5%, and both the value of options held and the median value of options exercised held steady."[5]

An extreme example is the gain of $570 million realized in 1997 by Disney chairman and CEO Michael Eisner. From 1996 through August 2003, Eisner's cumulative pay was more than $700 million. During that same six-year period, Disney's share price fell 23 percent. Eisner, it seems, has been spending time in Fantasyland—to the detriment of Disney's real-world stakeholders.

BMO Financial Group CEO Tony Comper displays a different value system. In 2002, Comper reworked executive compensation with a board compensation committee and the bank's human resources executive. The new mix balances short-, mid-, and long-term incentives on the basis of the individual executive's ability to get results. The change reduced the use of stock options by more than two-thirds. More important, it tied options very tightly to demanding performance objectives, aligned with shareholder interests. BMO's stock options vest at the rate of 25 percent a year, over a period of four years—a practice that is common. However, the bank has added a performance feature that only allows executives to exercise options once a share price hurdle has been met. Most senior executives can only exercise a portion—33 percent of their options once the share price has risen 50 percent, and another portion (34 percent) once the share price has increased by 100 percent.

Says Rose Patten, the bank's EVP of human resources and head of its office of strategic management, "In setting these high hurdles, we are encouraging executives to hold options for the long haul and to realize gains only when other shareholders have also realized equally substantial gains." Few companies so closely align executive rewards with sustained shareholder returns.

How do you foster openness when your own management, especially your lawyers, fight you?

CEOs can find themselves at odds with the corporate culture. As described earlier, Seagate's Bill Watkins wants no secrets. He wants his customers to know everything, good and bad, about the company's products and strategy. But he faces opposition—his own lawyers.

"Our lawyers are just scared to death of transparency," he says. "They're hassling me all the time saying I can't do this or I can't say that." Watkins is not being critical of his legal team: "That's their job. They think the less you say the less there is for people to use against you. And I suppose they have a point. But I have a business to run too—and I view transparency as central to my strategy."

The same thing happens with some marketing staff, who like to downplay product weaknesses and exaggerate strengths—as the song goes "accentuate the positive and eliminate the negative." Watkins's view. "Every company has problems—quality, technical, features—we all have them. And if everyone is hiding them they don't get resolved as fast as if you were open. I've made more mistakes than anyone in the history of storage systems. Because I openly admit that I can create a culture where mistakes get fixed faster, everyone—customers, marketing and product people feel comfortable bringing their problems forward. We just don't have time to be closed."

In a world where you're as good as your last quarterly report and your job may hinge on your next one, how do you defend the strategic thinking and long-term perspective required to build an open enterprise?

CEOs have always confronted the dilemma between long-term strategy and short-term action. However, as transparency grows, business integrity cannot be relegated to the back burner. CEOs need to make choices that ensure the sustainability of their firm.

P&G's Lafley faced crisis when he took over the company in June of 2000. But the only solution was to get some fundamentals in order. "It's my job to build a sustainable firm and the first order of business is to ensure that the company and everyone in it behaves with integrity. I'm very forgiving on business failures. I'm unforgiving on integrity failures—the policy is no tolerance."

For him this is a very practical matter. Integrity is required for everything—short, medium, and long term. He took over a firm that needed to change and he understood that change is scary. "If the organization fears change, this kind of [new] thinking won't get the oxygen it needs to breathe. Core purpose and values help people overcome the fear of change because they clarify what will *not* change."

He also needed to ensure "trust and mutual interdependence" in the company. "It's imperative that people see their own success linked with that of others, inside and outside the organization. And that they trust one another to do the right thing to fulfill that mutual responsibility."

The third challenge was to "unleash and inspire" P&G people. "Command and control is long dead," he says. "I'm a believer that the role of top management is to make a few strategic choices that inspire, and then unleash the organization to deliver."

Integrity is the precondition to any short-term success. For Lafley, "Every one of our hundred-thousand employees is an ambassador for the company and our values." This is particularly important given that he views P&G brands as trust marks. "Our brands stand for election every day—a flaw in our integrity would instantly destroy trust and the brand. You find the time to be a good company." In 2002 P&G scored number 5 on *Business Ethics*'s 100 Best Corporate Citizens list. These firms illustrate model business strategies in how they handle challenges from layoffs and sweatshops to predatory lending and the environment. They show there are better ways to handle these issues than the ruthless practices that are too often the norm. According to researchers at De Paul University, these firms have significantly better financial performance than others in the S&P 500.[6]

Integrity is something firms need now. Just do it.

THE NEW INNOVATORS

Leadership must come from the top for a firm to harness the power of transparency. But leadership can also start from anywhere. It can start somewhere in the lower ranks or even through an external party. In open enterprises leadership can simply mean carrying the mantle of business integrity in everything you do.

On a cold morning in January 2003 we traveled to New Brunswick, New Jersey, to the headquarters of Johnson & Johnson to spend a day interviewing corporate executives. As we entered the main lobby we saw a 10-foot high stone tablet displaying the J&J "Credo"—the company's 65-year-old statement of corporate values. Receptionist Pat Doherty said, "Please hang your coats behind our Credo." We decided to get a jump on the day's interviews by asking her, "So what is this Credo anyway?" She became decidedly reverent, describing how "our Credo" was the foundation of the company, how everyone in the company worked and lived by "our Credo," how each year she completed a survey on how well she thought the company and her boss were behaving according to the credo, and how as a receptionist she was the public face of the company and had decided it was her job to make sure guests understood the credo and its importance to the company.

Later in the afternoon we told company CEO Bill Weldon the story. "I'm not really surprised," he said. "You'll get that reaction from many people in the company." He described how every few days a tough problem will arise where he'll ask someone at J&J, "Is this a Credo issue?" Weldon says his first and foremost job as CEO is to protect and strengthen J&J's corporate character. From receptionist to CEO, people throughout the company champion business integrity as their personal responsibility.

The fight for candor and values can come from other surprising places. Johnson & Johnson general counsel Roger Fine is disarming. He doesn't sound like a corporate lawyer. Former J&J CEO Ralph Larsen describes Fine as a "compulsive truth teller." Fine believes that "unless corporations act out of a sense of responsibility to stakeholders including society, they will forfeit their freedom to operate." The forced transparency of Sarbanes-Oxley and other government initiatives are the logical result of firms acting irresponsibly. "It's like we're now spending 70 percent of our time dissipating heat rather than building the business. When trust is destroyed governments have to step in and create a surrogate—a process of forced transparency. This is unfortunate—a few murders have occurred and now everyone is being treated as a murderer."

Fine thinks corporate lawyers need to be the leaders, not the blockers, of transparency. Lawyers, almost by definition, seek control. But in J&J's decentralized culture, no one is "in command." Two hundred relatively autonomous companies, each with its own management and governance structures, work together. "No one is telling them how to succeed. So my job is to facilitate transparency, open communications, strong personal relationships and adherence to core values—rather than pulling structured levers, setting rules and doing the other things that corporate lawyers typically do."

In corporations around the world, people at various levels work hard to build open enterprises. Cisco VP of positioning Ron Ricci views transparency, values, and stakeholder engagement as central to the firm's reputation. "Trust and reputation flow from behavior. You need to show people what you are and what you've done. Customers say, 'Don't just tell me how to do it: tell me how you did it.' " He argues that a corporate value system "enables people to make decisions that are not in the guide book" and this is best done through "cultural stories." At Cisco a corporate value is frugality. Company founder John Morgridge rejected the expense report of CEO John Chambers when Chambers had upgraded an airline ticket to first class. Says Ricci, "That story keeps the value part of our DNA."

LIVING AND WORKING IN AN OPEN WORLD

The rise of transparency and the changing values of firms will lead each of us to rethink our relationships with corporations as well as our personal values, priorities, and actions.

Leadership and Work

If you're fortunate, you work for a firm that has adopted an open enterprise model dedicated to transparency, stakeholders, and sustainability. Your world is rich with opportunities to participate in its transformation and success.

If you work for a traditional opaque, short-term-oriented firm, you face a dilemma. You can tune out—go through the motions. You can look for another job. If you think your firm has little hope of changing and you have alternatives, it may make sense to abandon ship. Let's face it, open enterprises are better places to work. They are companies where people listen and where the quality of conversations is high. They have an interest in knowledge development of everyone and in the sharing of knowledge necessary for effective work.

Involvement with a company that lacks the new business integrity can be dangerous. Many corporate directors face personal legal action or even criminal charges and would like to turn back the clock. There may be conflicts of interest in your business that undermine your firm's integrity that can get you into trouble. Increasingly these firms will be vulnerable in the marketplace—undermining your job security. Like many hardworking and decent people at Enron, Andersen, Tyco, and WorldCom, the brush of irresponsibility can tarnish you and your career.

If you conclude your company has hope, there is much you can do to be a leader for change. The starting point is to be clear about your own values and to ensure that you conduct your working life accordingly.

Just as business integrity pays off in the age of transparency, so, obviously, does *personal* integrity. Yes, the ambitious, deceitful, game-playing back stabber who claws his way up the corporate ladder at the expense of others and the firm has always been with us. Perfidy has benefited many. But it is increasingly likely that bad behavior will be seen as a liability by boards of directors and top management. With trust so important to collaboration, those who undermine trust are harmful and will be isolated. Human nature is not somehow changing; people will still have ambition. However, personal integrity is fast becoming a critical asset for ambitious people and those who simply want to do their part.

This is not to suggest we each strip down completely. Personal information belongs to you, and you should tightly control its distribution. Corporations have the right to have secrets—called information security. As individuals we have a right to something different—privacy. This is a human right that does not apply to firms. You may provide companies with personal information but that information is still yours, to be used only for the purposes for which it was provided.

Measure, demonstrate, and popularize the impact of integrity on everything from employee loyalty to brand relationships and share price. Create an awakening in your firm and with its external stakeholders. Disarm people with your candor. In a transparent world, the honest broker has new power. Use it to shape the future of your company.

Leadership as a Consumer

You also have new power as a customer. When companies fail, don't let it stand. When companies are dishonest, punish them. When they make promises, hold them accountable.

The new transparency has revealed deep conflicts of interest in many industries: professions from investment bankers to accountants, physicians, and even journalists, need to get buff. As a consumer you have the power to identify such conflicts and demand integrity.

As the business environment opens up, expect a Pandora's box of conflicts to be revealed. As a customer, get active. Scrutiny pays.

Leadership as a Business Partner

You and your company have partners, as business webs replace vertically integrated firms. Sure, look for best price and quality. But also be sure your partners behave with integrity. Your company—whether you produce chocolates, running shoes, cosmetics, diamonds, or fence posts—will be held responsible for what happens in your supply chain, as Nestlé, Nike, P&G, De Beers, and Home Depot learned. Stand up to coercion in the supply chain by the 800-pound gorillas at the top. Organize for fair supply-chain practices. Abide by your commitments—pay your suppliers on time and deliver what you promised. Be open as transparency builds trust, drops transaction costs, and improves metabolism. These words ring true for the business web: "Excellence is the result of habitual integrity."

Leadership as a Shareholder

As an investor you own the economy through stocks and mutual funds. Your fiduciaries have the tools to be active investors. And you have access to the information required to hold them accountable. Firms with the new business integrity perform better. Demand that your fiduciaries get wise and invest accordingly. Don't passively accept proxy-voting statements if you aren't happy with management's choices. It is far easier to find other investors and organize protests than ever before.

Leadership as a Citizen

How do the firms in your community give back, in exchange for their license to operate? Many old style corporations have manipulated our world, in everything from electric power markets and cozy government contracts to government elections and policies—typically to our detriment.

What our communities and the world needs now are corporations who understand the link between business integrity and success. In our communities we need to move beyond philanthropy. We need firms that understand how externalizing costs hurts not just society but themselves, that see the link between integrity and their own viability and sustainability, that understand the deadly liabilities of the corporation as a fortress, and that know that firms cannot succeed in a failed world.

Forging the Twenty-First-Century Corporation

Each of us has an opportunity to ensure that our personal values are not only appropriate for ourselves but are consistent with the firms we work for or lead, the companies we buy from, the stocks we purchase, the business partners we select, and the corporations that we as citizens license to exist. Transparency brings clarity to the stakeholders of the firm. It's as if we're all emerging from a dark age; increasingly we can see clearly and take action. We can discern right from wrong, worthy from unworthy.

There has probably never been a more exciting time to be in business, nor a more dangerous one. The transparency genie has escaped from the bottle, wreaking havoc on some and bestowing sustainability and long-term success on others who embrace it. The genie demands that the corporation change, from paternalistic, inward-looking, and self-indulgent to engaged, stakeholder focused, responsive, and responsible. It also calls forth a new kind of leader—the executive who has integrity in his or her bones; who leads with intent and by example; who, rather than hunker down in the face of transparency's power, galvanizes the firm to harness it; and who has the courage to do the right thing and the vision to build a corporate character to withstand the vicissitudes of a volatile new century.

Transparency calls on yesterday's managers to be tomorrow's leaders. As we enter the age of transparency, the future won't just happen. It will be created. If we all get involved, our values, aspirations, and blossoming expectations can transform the corporation—and the world—for the better.

NOTES

Acknowledgments

1. We divested our interests in Digital 4Sight in 2002. Paul Woolner was also a cofounder.
2. Don Tapscott, David Ticoll, and Alex Lowy, *Digital Capital: Harnessing the Power of Business Webs* (Boston: Harvard Business School Press, 2000).

Introduction

1. More than a third of the public (35 percent) say they have no confidence in corporations to fulfill their responsibilities. Pew Charitable Trust CEO Rebecca Rimel in a speech to The Conference Board's 2003 Leadership Conference on Global Corporate Citizenship, New York, February 10, 2003.

Chapter 1. The Naked Corporation

1. "Our shareholders hire us to manage their money, and we can do the best job of that without public disclosure of our proxy votes," said David Weinstein, chief of administration at Fidelity. He added that the "only interest we consider when we vote our proxies is the economic interest of our mutual-fund shareholders." "Fidelity Faces Rally by AFL-CIO," *Wall Street Journal*, July 31, 2002.
2. "Take Action! Tell Fidelity to Disclose Its Shareholder Votes," www.unionvoice.org/campaign/fidelity.
3. Under public and media pressure, Stanley Works backed off its decision to move in August 2002.
4. Fidelity spokesperson Vincent Loporchio, "SEC to Consider Rules on Voting by Mutual Funds," *Wall Street Journal*, September 16, 2002.
5. "No Disclosure: The Feeling Is Mutual," *Wall Street Journal*, January 14, 2003.
6. Watson Wyatt Worldwide, *WorkUSA 2002—Weathering the Storm: A Study of Employee Attitudes and Opinions* (Washington, 2002).
7. Don Tapscott, David Ticoll, and Alex Lowy, *Digital Capital: Harnessing the Power of Business Webs* (Boston: Harvard Business School Press, 2000), 4.

8. Jim Ericsson, "Supply Chains: Where Next?" Line56.com, October 31, 2002.
9. Jeffrey N. Gordon, "What Enron Means for the Management and Control of the Modern Business Corporation: Some Initial Reflections," *Columbia Law Review*, Summer 2002, 6.
10. 57 percent strongly agree and 31 percent agree. *Consumerism: A Special Report* (Toronto: Environics International, 2001).
11. *2003 Corporate Social Responsibility Monitor* (Toronto: Environics International, 2003).
12. Edmunds.com.
13. "Upstart Web Sites Help Keep Hotel Sector in Low-Rate Mode," *Wall Street Journal*, August 9, 2002.
14. Noreena Hertz, *The Silent Takeover: Global Capitalism and the Death of Democracy* (New York: Free Press, 2002), 116–117.
15. United Nations Environment Program, World Business Council for Sustainable Development, and World Resources Institute, *Tomorrow's Markets: Global Trends and Their Implications for Business, 2002*, 3.
16. Example provided by Simon Zadek, chief executive, AccountAbility.
17. The researchers corroborated this data by measuring the number of purposely lost wallets that people returned in various countries. Paul J. Zak and Stephen Knack, "Trust and Growth," *Economic Journal*, 111: 295–321, 2001.
18. Stefano Baldi, "The Internet for International, Political, and Social Protest: The Case of Seattle," research paper no. 3, Policy Planning Unit of the Ministry of Foreign Affairs of Italy, Rome, 2000, hostings.diplomacy.edu/baldi/articles/protest.htm.
19. Don Tapscott, *Growing Up Digital: The Rise of the Net Generation* (New York: McGraw-Hill, 1998), 20.
20. Roger L. Martin, "The Virtue Matrix: Calculating the Return on Corporate Responsibility," *Harvard Business Review*, March 2002.

Chapter 2. Transparency Versus Opacity: The Battle

1. "A Survey of the Global Environment," *The Economist*, July 6, 2002, 6.
2. Ann Cavoukian and Tyler Hamilton, *The Privacy Payoff: How Successful Businesses Build Customer Trust* (New York: McGraw-Hill, 2002).
3. Ned Desmond, "Repeal the Sarbanes-Oxley Tax Now!" *Business 2.0*, December 2002.
4. AccountAbility, *AA1000 Assurance Standard, Guiding Principles*, consultation document, June 2002.
5. "They Know You Like a Book: Amazon.com Lets Users See What Their Neighbors Are Reading," *Morning Call*, February 17, 2000.
6. "Seizing the Initiative on Privacy: On-Line Industry Presses Its Case for Self-Regulation," *New York Times*, October 11, 1999.
7. Lawrence Lessig, *The Future of Ideas: The Fate of the Commons in a Connected World* (New York: Random House, 2001), xxi–xxii.

8. Reporters Committee for Freedom of the Press, "Homeland Security Act Criminalizes Leaks of Business Information," www.rcfp.org/index.html.
9. Joseph E. Stiglitz, *Globalization and Its Discontents* (New York: Norton, 2002).
10. Mario I. Blejer (International Monetary Fund), "Asian Crisis Four Years Later and Its Implications for Emerging Market Economies" (address to Leon Komisky Academy of Entrepreneurship and Management, June 12, 2001).
11. Transparency International, *Global Corruption Report 2001*, 229.
12. "Cooking the Books: The Cost to the Economy," Brookings Institution Policy Brief No. 106, August 2002.
13. Amy Cortese, "Network Armies," *Chief Executive Magazine*, June 2003. Sustain-Ability, a consulting firm, described the concept of a "stakeholder web" in *Virtual Sustainability: Using the Internet to Implement the Triple Bottom Line* (London: SustainAbility, 2001). In our book *Digital Caital*, (with Alex Lowy, 2001) we describe the rise of business webs—networks of companies and stakeholders that conduct business using the Internet as a primary basis for communications and transactions. Stakeholder webs are a form of business web—specifically a self-organizing alliance. In *Ethical Corporation Online* (April 2, 2002) Anthony Williams and Phil Dwyer explain the concept of the "Transparency Network" as "a collection of individuals and organizations that monitor and scrutinise the behaviour of firms and try to hold them accountable." Simon Zadek, John Sabapathy, Helle Dossing, and Tracey Swift have described "Corporate Responsibility Clusters." These clusters link the business community, labor organizations as well as wider civil society, and the public sector together with the goal of improving corporate responsibility. The authors argue that clusters can lead to competitive advantage. *Responsible Competitiveness: Corporate Responsibility Clusters in Action* (Copenhagen and London: The Copenhagen Centre, and AccountAbility, 2003.) See also Susanne Holmstrom, "The Reflective Paradigm," Roskilde University, November 2002. In *World Without Secrets* (John Wiley and Sons, 2002) Richard Hunter describes "network armies"—collections of individuals with differing agendas who come together over a common cause. "Smart mobs" is the term proposed by Howard Rheingold in *Smart Mobs: The Next Social Revolution*, Perseus Publishing, 2002.
14. Malcolm Gladwell, *The Tipping Point: How Little Things Can Make a Big Difference* (New York: Little, Brown, 2000), 34.
15. Ibid., 9.
16. Williams, "Transparency in the Networked Economy." Describes the Vortex State as "event-driven accelerations of activity and information flow."

Chapter 3. The Open Enterprise

1. Stephen J. Arnold, Robert V. Kozinets, and Jay M. Handelman, "Hometown Ideology and Retailer Legitimation: The Institutional Semiotics of Wal-Mart Flyers: Company Profile," *Journal of Retailing*, 77, June 22, 2001.

2. "Mr. Sam: The Folksy Tycoon with a Killer Instinct," *Times* (London) June 10, 2001.

3. Sam Walton, *Sam Walton: Made in America, My Story* (New York: Doubleday, 1992), 110, as quoted in Naomi Klein, *No Logo: Taking Aim at Brand Bullies* (Toronto: Knopf Canada, 1999).

4. In our discussions with Young, a software executive and social critic, he used Wal-Mart to illustrate the concept that in a free market democracy the consumer and the citizen are the same person. He argues that it was the customer demand for better and less expensive software that made the success of Red Hat inevitable. This was in response to a question he frequently fielded from audiences about "what role government regulation should play in curtailing the Microsoft monopoly and helping with the introduction of Linux."

5. Marina Whitman, *New World, New Rules: The Changing Role of the American Corporation* (Boston: Harvard Business School Press, 1999), 115.

6. These are commonly used formulations.

7. John Cavanagh et al., *Alternatives to Economic Globalization: A Better World Is Possible* (San Francisco: Berrett-Koehler Publishers, 2002), 134.

8. Ibid., 135.

9. Ibid., 145–146.

10. Ibid., 148.

11. Jonathan Rowe, "Supreme Court Defined Corporations," in "Reinventing the Corporation," *Washington Monthly*, April 1996.

12. Cited in Jack Beatty, ed., *Colossus: How the Corporation Changed America* (New York: Broadway Books, 2001), xvii.

13. Cited in Robert B. Reich, *The Future of Success: Working and Living in the New Economy* (New York: Knopf, 2001), 72.

14. Milton Friedman, "The Social Responsibility of Business to Increase Profits," *New York Times Magazine*, September 30, 1970.

15. Sophia A. Muirhead, Charles J. Bennett, Ronald E. Berenbeim, Amy Kao, and David Vidal, *Corporate Citizenship in the New Century: Accountability, Transparency and Global Stakeholder Engagement*, R-1314-02-RR (New York: Conference Board, 2002).

16. The term has been used by many, most notably George Soros in *Open Society: Reforming Global Capitalism* (New York: Public Affairs Publishing, 2000) and Joseph Stiglitz in *Globalization and Its Discontents* (New York: Norton, 2000)

17. We first introduced this term over a decade ago as we believed it summed up how open systems standards, networking, and business relationships would change the firm. The idea never caught on. But to elaborate on Victor Hugo's famous statement: There's nothing so powerful as an idea whose time has come, again. See Don Tapscott and David Ticoll, "Open Systems" (Toronto: DMR, 1988) and Don Tapscott and Art Caston, *Paradigm Shift: The New Promise of Information Technology* (New York: McGraw-Hill, 1993).

18. Of course, third parties can also verify truthfulness. Auditors, in theory at least, certify financial statements and add credibility. The American Medical

NOTES

321

NOTES

321

Association certifies that someone has the credentials to be a physician, enhancing that person's believability with regard to assertions on medical information but not with regard to automotive information.

19. Francis Fukuyama defines trust as "the expectation that arises within a community of regular, honest, and cooperative behavior, based on commonly shared norms, on the part of other members of that community." Francis Fukuyama, *Trust: The Social Virtues and the Creation of Prosperity* (New York: Free Press, 1995), 26.

20. Discussed in Chapter 4.

21. Rosabeth Moss Kanter, "Rising to Rising Expectations," *Worldlink*, January 2002. Harvard's Kanter recently called this idea a "new law of physics for the Internet Age."

22. Discussed in Tapscott, Ticoll, and Lowy, *Digital Capital*.

23. Charles O. Holliday, Jr., Stephan Schmidheiny, and Philip Watts, *Walking the Talk: The Business Case for Sustainable Development* (San Francisco: Berrett-Koehler, 2002), 23.

24. BT, *Delivering Enlightened Shareholder Value*, slide presentation, 2002.

25. Innovest, *Carbon Finance and the Global Equity Markets*, February 2003, 10–12.

Chapter 4. Whistleblowers and Other Employees

1. www.historymatters.gmu.edu/d/5138/bill.

2. Art Preis, *Labor's Giant Step: Twenty Years of the CIO* (New York: Pathfinder, 1982), 265.

3. Peter M. Senge, *The Fifth Discipline: The Art and Practice of the Learning Organization* (New York: Doubleday, 1990), 274.

4. www.greatplacetowork.com.

5. H9382-83, *Cong. Rec.* 132, October 7, 1986.

6. C. Fred Alford, *Whistleblowers: Broken Lives and Organizational Power* (Ithaca, N.Y.: Cornell University Press, 2001).

7. "You Know How to Whistle, Don't You?" *Dallas Morning News*, February 27, 2002.

8. Marion Exall, *Employee Feedback: The Cornerstone of Corporate Compliance* (The Network, 2002), 8.

9. Francis Fukuyama, *Trust: The Social Virtues and the Creation of Prosperity* (New York: Free Press, 1995), 28–32.

10. See Tapscott and Caston, *Paradigm Shift*; Don Tapscott, *Digital Economy: Promise and Peril in the Age of Networked Economy* (New York: McGraw-Hill, 1996); and Tapscott, Ticoll, and Lowy, *Digital Capital*.

11. Fukuyama, *Trust*.

12. There has been recent research that U.S. social stratification is based more strongly on traditional characteristics, primarily birthright.

13. www.mwr.org.uk

Chapter 5. Transparency Among Business Partners

1. Eric Schlosser, *Fast Food Nation: The Dark Side of the All-American Meal* (New York: Houghton Mifflin, 2001), 204.
2. This is particularly true when you subtract the value of the cartridge from the price of a cheap printer. These vendors are "giving away the razor [the printer] so they can sell the blades [replacement cartridges]."
3. Mark Roberti, "RFID: From Just-in-Time to Real Time," *CIO Insight*, April 12, 2002.
4. IBM study cited in "The Best Thing Since the Bar-Code," *The Economist*, February 6, 2003.
5. "Gillette to Purchase 500 Million EPC Tags," *RFID Journal*, November 15, 2002.
6. Accenture, *Seize the Day: The Silent Commerce Imperative*, 2002, 18.
7. Ibid., 13.
8. Mark Roberti, "Wal-Mart, Early Adopter," *Business 2.0*, May 2002.
9. C. Manley Molpus, "A Message to the Australian Food and Grocery Council," *GMA News*, May 14, 2002.
10. Robert Sobel, *IBM: Colossus in Transition* (New York: Times Books, 1981), 78.
11. Ronald Coase, "The Nature of the Firm" in *The Firm, the Market, and the Law* (Chicago: University of Chicago Press, 1998), 44.
12. Tapscott, Ticoll, and Lowy, *Digital Capital*, 26–27.
13. Robert J. Samuelson, "Economic Darwinism," *Washington Post*, March 19, 2003.
14. Stanley E. Fawcett and Gregory M. Magnan, *Achieving World-Class Supply Chain Alignment: Benefits, Barriers, and Bridges* (Arizona State University Research Park: Center for Advanced Purchasing Studies, 2001).
15. Voluntary Interindustry Commerce Standards Association, "Nine-Step Process Model."
16. Interview with Robert Parker, AMR Research.
17. Yochai Benkler, "Coase's Penguin, or, Linux and *The Nature of the Firm*," *Yale Law Journal* 112 (Winter 2002–03), 2.
18. We use the terms *peer production* and *alliance* interchangeably in this section.
19. Benkler, 56.
20. Lawrence Lessig, *The Future of Ideas: The Fate of the Commons in a Connected World* (New York: Random House, 2001), 12, 19.
21. For example, Michelle R. Henry, Mildred K. Cho, Meredith Weaver, and Jon F. Merz, "DNA Patenting and Licensing," *Science*, August 23, 2003.
22. David Blumenthal et al., "Withholding Research Results in Academic Life Science: Evidence from a National Survey of Faculty," *Journal of the American Medical Association* 277, April 16, 1997, 1224–28.

Chapter 6. Customers in a Transparent World

1. Environics International, *Consumerism Survey, 2001* (Toronto, 2001). Almost eight in ten indicate that they gather information online about products before they make an important purchase.
2. Environics International, *2002 Corporate Responsibility Monitor* (Toronto, 2002).
3. As discussed in Tapscott, Ticoll, and Lowy, *Digital Capital,* 189–99.
4. "Bargain Hunters Beware: Comparison Shopping Sites Can Be Helpful—Or Misleading," *San Francisco Chronicle,* November 25, 2002.
5. As discussed in Tapscott, Ticoll, and Lowy, *Digital Capital,* 39–58.
6. Charles Smith, author of *Auctions: The Social Construction of Value,* says, "The transaction is the means to the price rather than the price a means to the transaction." Ibid., 40.
7. www.globalwitness.org.
8. De Beers press release, June 14, 2000, bridge.netnation.com/~debeersc/conflict/nfogm.html.
9. De Beers press release, July 17, 2000, bridge.netnation.com/~debeersc/conflict/release-1.html.
10. Environics International, *Corporate Social Responsibility Monitor* (Toronto, 2002).
11. Deborah Doane, "Taking Flight: The Rapid Growth of Ethical Consumerism" (London: New Economics Foundation, 2001).
12. www.ran.org.
13. Ibid.
14. "Home Depot Retooling Timber Policy, But Criticism Persists," *Associated Press,* January 2, 2003.
15. Ibid.
16. "Taking Aim at the Mod Squads," *Business 2.0,* October 14, 2002.
17. www.cokewatch.org.
18. www.bt.com.
19. "No Logo, Pro Logo, or Yo Logo?" *Research International Observer Report 2002,* www.riusa.com.
20. Ann Cavoukian and Don Tapscott, *Who Knows: Safeguarding Your Privacy in a Networked World* (Toronto: Random House, 1995).
21. "Insurer Is Fined by State," *San Jose Mercury News,* January 17, 2003.
22. Ibid.

Chapter 7. Communities

1. "Are Transnationals Bigger Than Countries?" UN Conference on Trade and Development (UNCTAD) press release (August 12, 2002). Using total sales, others have cited an even higher number of multinationals (51) in the Top

100 economies. UNCTAD comments, "Using sales to compare firms with the GDP of countries is conceptually flawed, as GDP is a value-added measure and sales are not. A truly comparable yardstick requires that sales be recalculated as value added. For firms, value added can be estimated as the sum of salaries and benefits, depreciation and amortization, and pre-tax income."

2. "Government by Computer—India," *The Economist*, March 20, 2003.

3. Environics International, *2003 Global Issues Monitor* (Toronto, 2003).

4. Robert D. Putnam, *Bowling Alone: The Collapse and Revival of American Community* (New York: Simon & Schuster, 2000), 183.

5. Pippa Norris, *Democratic Phoenix: Reinventing Political Activism* (Cambridge: Cambridge University Press, 2002), 189.

6. UN Environment Program, World Business Council for Sustainable Development, and World Resources Institute, *Tomorrow's Markets: Global Trends and Their Implications for Business* (Washington: 2002), 52.

7. The term *banana republic* originated in O. Henry's 1904 novel, *Cabbages and Kings*. An American on the lam explains his fictional destination for a tropical hideout: "At that time we had a treaty with about every foreign country except Belgium and that banana republic, Anchuria."

8. "Chiquita, Yes We Have No Profits: The Rise and Fall of Chiquita Banana: How a Great American Brand Lost Its Way," *Fortune*, November 14, 2001.

9. "How to Become a Top Banana," *Time*, February 7, 2000.

10. "Chiquita Secrets Revealed," *Cincinnati Enquirer*, May 3, 1998. Sourced from third-party Web sites.

11. International Union of Food, Agricultural, Hotel, Restaurant, Catering, Tobacco, and Allied Workers' Associations (IUF), press releases.

12. Chiquita Brands International, *2001 Corporate Responsibility Report*, 36.

13. "Scandal-Filled Year Takes Toll on Firms' Good Names," *Wall Street Journal*, February 12, 2003. Based on a survey by Harris Interactive.

14. California Global Accountability Project, *Beyond Good Deeds*, July 2002, xv.

15. "Luxury Tanks Rolling Off Showroom Floors," *Philadelphia Inquirer*, January 28, 2003.

16. "Fossilized Thinking Has Detroit Driving in Reverse," *Los Angeles Times*, February 23, 2003.

17. Ibid.

18. Jason Mark, *Automaker Rankings: The Environmental Performance of Car Companies* (Cambridge, Mass.: Union of Concerned Scientists, September 2002), 1.

19. "Interview with Cho Fujio, President of Toyota Motor Corporation," *Journal of Japanese Trade and Industry*, July/August 2002.

Chapter 8. The Owners of the Firm

1. Charles R. Geisst, *Wall Street: A History* (New York: Oxford University Press, 1997), 131.
2. Ibid., 228.
3. Adolf A. Berle and Gardiner C. Means, *The Modern Corporation and Private Property* (New York: Macmillan, 1933)
4. Ibid., 114.
5. Peter F. Drucker, *Management: Tasks, Responsibilities, Practices* (New York, Harper & Row, 1973), 628.
6. Ibid., 629.
7. Michael C. Jensen, *A Theory of the Firm: Governance, Residual Claims, and Organizational Forms* (Boston: Harvard University Press, 2001), 21.
8. "Unsettling," *The Economist*, May 3, 2003.
9. *McKinsey Quarterly*, 1999–4, 75.
10. *Institutional Investment Report: Financial Assets and Equity Holdings*, vol. 5, no. 1 (New York: Conference Board, 2003).
11. Institutional assets have also shifted toward equity at the expense of debt (excepting 2000–03 when investors sought haven in bonds rather than volatile stocks). In 1980, equity represented 21.4 percent of institutional assets, whereas bonds were 35.8 percent. By 2001, even with the flight from stocks of the postboom period, equity represented 44.7 percent of total institutional investments and debt 33.7 percent.
12. Intersec Research, www.intsec.com/Research%20and%20Consulting.htm.
13. From calculations conducted by Robert A. G. Monks, *The New Global Investors: How Shareholders Can Unlock Sustainable Prosperity Worldwide* (Oxford: Capstone Publishing, 2001), 93.
14. Asset size as of 1999, *Pension and Investments/Intersec World 300 Pension Funds*, www.intsec.com.
15. The Conference Board, 35.
16. According to a study that drew controversial conclusions, shareholding increased dramatically from 1989 to 1995 among every age group, income bracket, racial cohort, and occupational category for which statistics are available. The rate of increase was particularly steep among laborers and farmers (106 percent), householders 34 years old or younger (64 percent), and families with incomes under $25,000 (80.4 percent). Richard Nadler, "The Rise of Worker Capitalism," CATO Institute Policy Analysis, November 1, 1999.
17. And a whopping 93 percent of U.S. families own some financial asset including savings accounts, bonds, and other managed assets.
18. Total pension fund value in 2001 was $7.87 trillion divided by 104 million households. The Federal Reserve System, 2003.
19. Peter F. Drucker, "Reckoning with the Pension Fund Revolution," *Harvard Business Review*, March 1, 1991, 316–18.

20. Nadler, "The Rise of Worker Capitalism."
21. There is a gray area between the two types of plans, as pointed out by Robert A. G. Monks, 96–98. Nevertheless, the trend toward employees' benefiting or suffering as their pension portfolios grow or shrink is a real one.
22. Edward N. Wolff, Twentieth Century Fund Report, "Top Heavy: A Study of the Increasing Inequality of Wealth in America." Wealth is calculated by adding together the current value of all assets a household owns—financial wealth like bank accounts, stocks and bonds, life insurance savings, and mutual funds; houses and unincorporated businesses; cars and major appliances; and the value of pension rights—and subtracting from that mortgage balances and other outstanding debt.
23. Thomas Piketty and Emmanuel Saez, "Income Inequality in the United States, 1913–1988," National Bureau of Economic Research, no. w 8467, working paper, Washington, 2001.
24. Paul Krugman, "For Richer," New York Times, October 6, 2002.
25. James Felton and Jonchai Kim, "Warnings from the Enron Message Board," Journal of Investing 2, no. 3, fall 2002, 29–52.
26. Shelley Taylor & Associates, "Full Disclosure 2002," Palo Alto, Calif. 2002.
27. Meg Voorhes (director, Social Issues Service, Investor Responsibility Research Center) speech notes to The Role of Governments in Promoting Corporate Citizenship Conference, June 11–12, 2001, Washington, D.C.
28. Ibid.
29. Adolf A. Berle, Jr., The Twentieth Century Capitalist Revolution (Orlando: Harcourt, 1954).
30. Investor Responsibility Research Center, www.irrc.org.
31. Jim Surowiecki, "Rogue Missives: Challenging the Rules," Motley Fool, July 25, 1997.
32. The company had adopted a policy banning workers "whose sexual preferences fail to demonstrate normal heterosexual values which have been the foundation of families in our society." The move was legal in the states in which the company operated. Cracker Barrel's shareholders included the New York City Employees Retirement System (NYCERS). In 1992 NYCERS filed a shareholder proposal directing the company to adopt a sexual orientation nondiscrimination policy. Cracker Barrel argued that the issue fell under the "ordinary business" provisions and refused to include it in its shareholder proxy resolutions. NYCERS argued that, for ethical and financial reasons, discrimination was not "ordinary business." The SEC sided with the company and announced that henceforth all employment-related issues fell under the "ordinary business" exclusion. All NYCERS efforts to have the decision overturned in the courts failed. Opponents of Cracker Barrel today rely on an old standby of the social activist; they ask customers to boycott the restaurant until it changes its policy. "A Brief History of Gay and Lesbian Shareholder Activism," www.planetout.com.

33. "SEC Looking to Stop Businesses Quashing Shareholder Activism," *Financial Times* (London), September 24, 2002.

34. Beverly Goodman, "SEC Proposes to Force Fund Firms to Disclose Proxy Votes," *TheStreet.com*, September 19, 2002.

35. "SEC Wants Funds to Disclose Votes: Rules Proposed on Proxy Records," *Washington Post*, September 20, 2002.

36. "Pay Gap Between CEOs, Workers Now a Chasm," *Albany Times Union*, December 15, 2002.

37. Jonathan Charkham and Anne Simpson, *Fair Shares: The Future of Shareholder Power and Responsibility* (Oxford: Oxford University Press, 1999), 224, as quoted in Robert A. G. Monks, *The New Global Investors: How Shareholders Can Unlock Sustainable Prosperity Worldwide* (Oxford, UK: Capstone Publishing, 2001), 120.

38. www.socialinvest.org.

39. Moses Pava and Joshua Krausz, *Corporate Responsibility and Financial Performance: The Paradox of Social Cost* (Westport, CT: Greenwood Publishing Group, 1995).

40. Joshua Daniel Margolis and James Patrick Walsh, *People and Profits? The Search for a Link Between a Company's Social and Financial Performance* (Mahwah, NJ: Lawrence Erlbaum Associates, 2001).

41. "Socially Responsible Funds Earning Top Marks Edged Even Higher in 2002," news release, Social Investment Forum, January 29, 2003.

42. "Shares of Corporate Nice Guys Can Finish First," *New York Times*, April 27, 2003.

43. Sandra Waddock and Sam Graves, "Finding the Link Between Stakeholder Relations and Quality of Management," *Journal of Investing*, 1997.

44. Margolis and Walsh, *People and Profits*, 10–11.

45. Waddock and Graves, 1997, and Sam Graves and Sandra Waddock, "Beyond *Built to Last*: Stakeholder Relations in the 'Built-to-Last' Companies," *Business and Society Review*, 1999.

46. After adjusting for everything imaginable, companies with better environmental records appear to have better than average returns on assets. Michael V. Russo and Paul A. Fouts, "A Resource-Based Perspective on Corporate Environmental Performance and Profitability," *Academy of Management Journal*, 1998.

47. Robert Repetto and Duncan Austin, *Pure Profit: The Financial Implications of Environmental Performance* (Washington: World Resources Institute, 2000).

48. Graves and Waddock, "Beyond *Built to Last*."

49. Glen Dowell, Stuart Hart, and Bernard Yeung, "Do Corporate Global Environmental Standards Create or Destroy Market Value?" *Management Science*, 2000.

50. Graves and Waddock, "Finding the Link Between Stakeholder Relations and Quality of Management."

51. James Hawley and Andrew Williams, "Can Universal Owners Be Socially Responsible Owners?" in Peter Camejo, ed., *The SRI Advantage: Why Socially Responsible Investing Has Outperformed Financially* (Gabriola Island, BC: New Society Publishers, 2002).

52. "Investor Coalition Finds U.S. Corporations Face Multi-Billion Dollar Risk from Climate Change," CERES News Release, Boston, April 18, 2002.

53. Ibid.

54. Roger L. Martin, dean, J. L. Rotman School of Management, University of Toronto.

55. Jeffrey A. Sonnenfeld, "What Makes Great Boards Great," *Harvard Business Review*, no. 2365, December 1, 2002.

56. Lewis Braham, "Bring Democracy to Boardroom Elections," *Business Week*, October 21, 2002.

57. "Will SEC Allow Shareholder Democracy?" *New York Times*, April 4, 2003.

58. Ibid.

59. McKinsey & Company, *Investor Opinion Survey*, 2002.

60. "For the purpose of the surveys, a well governed company is defined as having a majority of outside directors on the board with no management ties; holding formal evaluations of directors; and being responsible to investor requests for information on governance issues. In addition, directors hold significant stockholdings in the company and a large proportion of directors' pay is in the form of stock options." McKinsey & Company, *Investor Opinion Survey*.

Chapter 9. Harnessing the Power

1. As quoted by Chris Anderson, "Organizational Alignment in the Age of Information and Global Capitalism," International Masters in Practicing Management thesis, McGill University, Montreal, March 2002.

2. "Gaps in Sea Laws Shield Pollution by Cruise Lines," *New York Times*, January 3, 1999.

3. David Wheeler, Barry Colbert, and R. Edward Freeman, "Focusing on Value: Reconciling Corporate Social Responsibility, Sustainability and a Stakeholder Approach in a Network World," paper presented at the Academy of Management, Denver, Colorado, 2002.

4. Wheeler, Colbert, and Freeman, "Focusing on Value."

5. Novo Nordisk, *Sustainability Report 2002*, 8.

6. Novo Nordisk, *Reporting on the Triple Bottom Line: Dealing with Dilemmas*, 2001, 28.

7. Ibid., 28.

8. Ibid., 2–3.

9. Novo Nordisk, *Sustainability Report 2002*, 36.

10. Global Reporting Initiative, *2002 Sustainability Reporting Guidelines* (Boston: GRI, 2002).

11. A. J. Vogl, "Does It Pay to Be Good?" *Across the Board*, January 1, 2003.
12. GRI, *2002 Sustainability Reporting Guidelines*, 51.
13. AccountAbility's full name is Institute for Social and Ethical Accountability.
14. Institute of Social and Ethical Accountability, *AAA Assurance Standard* (London: ISEA, 2003).
15. BearingPoint, *KPMG International Survey of Corporate Sustainability Reporting 2002* (Amsterdam: KPMG, 2002), 14.
16. Novo Nordisk, *2002 Sustainability Report*, 8.
17. Novo Nordisk, *Reporting on the Triple Bottom Line*, 31.
18. Nancy Bouchard, "Pleading the Cause," *Sporting Goods Business*, June 1, 2002.
19. Bjørn Lomborg, *The Skeptical Environmentalist: Measuring the Real State of the World* (Oxford: Cambridge University Press, 2001), 4.
20. John Rennie, "Misleading Math About the Earth," *Scientific American*, January 2, 2002.
21. Novo Nordisk, *2002 Sustainability Report*, 47.
22. Ibid.

Chapter 10. Breaching the Crisis of Leadership

1. Peter M. Senge, *The Fifth Discipline: The Art and Practice of the Learning Organization* (New York: Doubleday, 1990).
2. Joyce Barrett, "Patagonia: Only Organic Cotton from Now On," *Women's' Wear Daily*, August 14, 1995.
3. Katharine Bowers, "Taking the Organic Route," *Women's Wear Daily*, November 20, 2000.
4. "Profile: Patagonia Clothing Company and Founder Yvon Chouinard," *National Public Radio: Morning Edition*, November 12, 2002.
5. "Corporate Governance Mom," *The Economist*, April 11, 2003.
6. www.business-ethics.com.

INDEX

Abbey National, 91
academia: industrialization of, 150–51
Accenture, 5, 8, 128, 132
accountability, 9–10, 60, 119, 139,
   190; and Chiquita, 197, 198, 200,
   201, 202; and communities, 186,
   203, 206; and corporate responsibility, 67, 72; and customers, 152,
   171; and leadership, 301, 306,
   313; and minimal versus maximal
   transparency, 258; and open
   enterprises, 73, 74, 75–76, 78, 84,
   87–88, 92, 93, 267, 291; and
   shareholders, 212–13, 214, 220,
   221, 222, 223, 225, 230, 232, 239,
   240, 246, 247, 249, 267, 313; of
   suppliers, 171; and sustainability
   paradox, 206
AccountAbility, 271, 272, 273
accounting, 50–51, 214, 231, 298
ActionAid, 192
Adams, Guy, 247
Adelphia, 16
AFL-CIO, 4–5, 8, 9, 55
Africa, 35, 59–60, 185, 274
Agilent, 107–8
agoras, 160–64
Albertson's, 13
Alcan, 40
Alford, C. Fred, 111–12, 113
Alien Technology, 128
alliance production, 144–45, 146
Allianz Insurance, 91
Allied Signal, 137
Allstate Insurance Company, 180–81

Altria Group, 282
Amazon, 13, 18, 40–41, 137, 145
American Federation of State, County
   and Municipal Employees
   (AFSCME), 248
American Medical Association, 80
American Steamship, 130
Amoco, 43–44
AMR, 243
analysts, 16, 215, 301
Anderson, Harry W., 97
Angola, 80, 164–65, 228
annual reports. *See* reporting
Anova Holding, 89
AOL Time Warner, 15
Apple Computer, 163, 284
Aristotle, 77–78
Arthur Andersen, 3, 15, 52, 103, 110,
   215, 312
Asia, 25, 35, 47–49, 51
Association of Chartered Certified
   Accountants, 271
AT&T, 69, 160, 217, 269
auctions, 140, 161
Austin, Duncan, 239–40
Australia, 35, 50, 91, 113, 189
Auto-ID technologies, 125–27, 128,
   129, 143, 145
auto industry, 12, 82–83, 100, 132,
   207–9. *See also* automobiles;
   specific maker
automobiles, 169–70, 207–8

b-webs. *See* business webs
Baker, Malcolm, 175–76

Internet (*cont.*)
  and forced transparency, 6–7;
  inaccurate information on, 43; and
  obstacles to transparency, 42,
  43–45; and open enterprises, 83,
  294–95; and privacy, 179; and
  product cocreation, 168–69; and
  shareholders, 214, 221; and social
  capital, 188, 189; and stakeholder
  webs, 54, 60, 61; as tool for
  dialogue, 179
inventory, 128, 136, 138, 139, 240
Investment Company Institute,
  230
Investor Responsibility Research
  Center (Harvard University), 228,
  231, 307
investors. *See* shareholders; *type of
  investor*
ISO, 198
Israel, Eric, 269
Ivory Coast, 59–60, 194
Iwata, John, 119–20, 285–86

J. P. Morgan Chase, 3
Japan, 209, 273, 292; auto industry in,
  208–9; competition from, 213;
  and corporate character, 115; and
  costs of opacity, 50, 51; and
  customers, 155–56; and open
  enterprises, 93; trust in, 114
Jarvis, Ron, 167
Johnson, Robert Wood, 116–17, 204,
  249
Johnson & Johnson: business partners
  of, 128, 132, 140; CEO at, 299;
  and communities, 10, 204;
  corporate character at, 114; Credo
  of, 10, 58, 116–17; customers of,
  10, 204, 249; employees of, 10,
  58, 102, 117, 204, 249; leadership
  at, 310–11; and open enterprises,
  269; reputation of, 204; shareholders of, 10, 204, 249; and social
  responsibility, 117, 204; and
  Tylenol case, 117
Johnson, Edward III, 5–6
judicial environment, 50–51
Justice Department, U.S., 110

K-Mart, 14
Kasky, Marc, 42
Kellogg Company, 22, 23–24, 38, 45
Kelly, Geraldine, 109
Kennard, Joyce, 42
Kerr, Steve, 101
Kim, Jongchai, 221–22
Kingo, Lise, 259, 266, 276–77, 278,
  279, 305
Klein, Naomi, 175
knowledge, 123, 180; and business
  partners, 133, 135, 145; and
  drivers of transparency, 27–28;
  liberation of, 101; limits to,
  37–38; and obstacles to trans-
  parency, 37–38; and open
  enterprises, 86, 312; of share-
  holders, 221–25; sharing of, 300,
  312
knowledge work/workers, 26–28, 73,
  82, 97–101, 102, 103, 108,
  114–15
Kozlowski, Kate, 281–82, 294–95
KPMG, 271
Krausz, Joshua, 236
Kroger, 114
Krugman, Paul, 220
Kurtzman, Joel, 224
Kyoto Accord (1992), 70, 190, 203

Labor Department, U.S., 235
Lafley, Alan, 300–301, 309
Lander, Eric, 146
Lands' End, 304
Larsen, Ralph, 116, 117, 299,
  310–11
lawsuits, 41–42, 93, 215, 240
lawyers/legal environment, 50–51, 85,
  224, 308, 310–11
Lay, Kenneth, 109, 112
layoffs, 108, 303, 309
leadership: and business partners,
  139–41, 313, 314; for change,
  312–15; and communities, 314;
  crisis of, 297–315; and customers,
  301–2, 304, 308, 311, 313; and
  integrity, 256, 297, 298, 299,
  302–5, 308, 309, 310, 313,
  314–15; and new innovators,

and costs of opacity, 47–53;
definition of, 22–25; as double-
edged sword, 118; drivers of,
25–36; fatigue and paralysis,
42–43; forced, 6, 22, 23, 298, 310,
311; geopolitical context of,
45–47; importance of, 25–26; as
information, 22; internal, 98; and
knowledge work, 98–101; law of
diminishing returns in, 135; levels
of, 257–58; limits to, 61; literacy,
40–41; minimal versus maximal,
257–58; obstacles to, 37–45;
questions about, 9; reverse, 25;
and trust, 77, 92, 127
transparency crisis, 51–53
transparency industry, 49
Transparency International (TI), 20,
49–50, 286
Trevino, Mike, 181
trust: blind, 82; and business webs,
134–41; and Chiquita, 199, 202;
and corporate character, 114–16,
117; and corporate responsibility,
71, 72; and costs of opacity, 51,
52; and drivers of transparency,
26, 27–28, 33; and globalization,
205; importance of, 3, 25–26; and
integrity, 171–72, 256; and
leadership, 301, 302, 309, 311,
312, 313; and naked corporation,
10, 13; and obstacles to transparency, 39; and open enterprises,
72, 73, 74, 75, 76, 77–82, 86, 87,
88–89, 92, 265, 285, 286, 291,
295; and peer production, 144,
145; and privacy, 180, 182; and
social capital, 190; and
stakeholder webs, 58, 59–60, 61;
and transparency, 77, 92, 127;
validation of, 82; and whistleblowers, 114; within firm, 102–8.
See also trust crisis; type of
stakeholder
trust crisis, 58, 59–60, 65, 90, 115,
116, 123, 171–72, 221
Turner, Kevin, 129
Twain, Shania, 32
Tyco International, 3, 71, 110, 312

uBid.com, 161
UBS Warburg, 88, 91
Uniform Code Council, 143
Union Carbide, 20, 43–44
Union of Concerned Scientists, 209
Union of International Organizations,
190
unions, labor, 115, 120, 194, 196–97,
198, 199–200, 201
United Auto Workers (UAW), 97
United Food and Commercial Workers,
11
United Fruit Company, 192, 202
United Kingdom, 24–25, 33, 35, 50,
51, 93, 175, 177, 190, 273
United Nations, 21, 37, 49, 267, 271
United Nations Environmental
Program, 39–40
United Nations Global Compact,
266–67
United Nations Universal Declaration
of Human Rights, 175, 202, 280,
292
United States: and battle between
opacity and transparency, 61; and
Chiquita, 195, 201–2; and costs of
opacity, 50, 51; crisis of inequality
in, 220; environmental reporting
in, 273; and social capital, 189;
trust in, 114
United States Underwriters Laboratories, 141–42
United Steelworkers of America, 170
"universal owners," 242
Unix, 131
UPS, 132
U.S. Labor in the Americas Project,
200
U.S. Patent and Trademark Office, 143,
148, 149

validation, 78, 80–81, 82
value: creation of, 84–85, 85, 101, 108;
and customers, 156–58, 164–67,
175, 178; and drivers of transparency, 32; and employees, 101,
106, 108; and open enterprises,
84–92
value-based investing, 233–35

ABOUT THE AUTHORS

DON TAPSCOTT is one of the most sought after speakers for business audiences on the continent. Known for his extensive research into the nature of the firm and the impact of technology on business and society, he has written or coauthored a number of bestselling books, several with longtime collaborator DAVID TICOLL. They are the authors of *Digital Capital* and *Blueprint to the Digital Economy*. Tapscott is also the author of *The Digital Economy* and *Growing Up Digital*. Separately and together they have written for publications such as *The Wall Street Journal*, *The Financial Times*, and *Forbes*. Both live in Toronto, Canada.